cook
LIKE A **PRO**

FROM THE EDITORS OF WILLIAMS-SONOMA

FOREWORD BY **THOMAS KELLER**

PHOTOGRAPHY **TUCKER** + **HOSSLER**

weldon**owen**

Contents

TOOLS

1 Bakeware

5 Bakeware Materials

6 Baking Tools

8 Cook's Tools

16 Cookware

18 Cookware Materials

19 Cutlery & Accessories

23 Knife Construction

25 Electrics

27 Grilling Tools

29 Measuring Tools & Timers

32 Pasta & Bread Equipment

TECHNIQUES

34	Baking & Pastry Basics
59	Breads & Batters
71	Cakes
85	Cookies & Bars
96	Cooking Basics
112	Egg Cookery
120	Fish
135	Fruit
151	Grains & Legumes
161	Grilling Basics
172	Herbs & Spices
185	Knife Skills
191	Meat
219	Pasta
235	Pies & Tarts
248	Poultry
268	Sauces
286	Shellfish
294	Stocks
302	Vegetables

347	Cooking Charts
348	General Index
349	Recipe Index
350	Tool Index

RECIPES

BAKING & PASTRY BASICS

41 Citrus Curd

44 Pastry Cream with flavoring options

45 Choux Pastry

52 Chocolate Ganache

53 Classic Puff Pastry

54 Quick Puff Pastry

BREADS & BATTERS

65 Pizza Dough

66 Baking-Powder Biscuits

67 Currant-Cream Scones with variations

68 Buttermilk Pancakes with variations

69 Classic Waffles with pancake or waffle toppings

70 Sweet Crêpes

CAKES

80 Buttercream with assorted flavors

EGG COOKERY

117 Classic Omelet with a selection of fillings

118 Vegetable Frittata with flavoring options

119 Quiche Lorraine with variations

FISH

129 Fish Steamed in Parchment

130 Poached Salmon

131 Deep-fried Fish Fillets

GRAINS & LEGUMES

160 Basic Risotto with variations

PASTA

223 Fresh Egg Pasta Dough (food processor) with variations

224 Fresh Egg Pasta Dough (by hand)

229 Semolina Pasta Dough

234 Potato Gnocchi

PIES & TARTS

237 Sweet Tart Dough with flavoring options

240 Flaky Pie Dough (food processor) with variations

241 Flaky Pie Dough (by hand) with fruit pie fillings

POULTRY

263 Buttermilk-fried Chicken

264 Basic Roast Chicken with variations

265 Classic Roast Turkey with flavor embellishments

SAUCES

275 All-Purpose Pan Sauce

276 All-Purpose Pan Gravy

277 Bechamel Sauce with flavor embellishments

278 Beurre Blanc with variations

279 Hollandaise Sauce with variations

282 Mayonnaise with flavoring options

283 Basic Vinaigrette with variations

284 Basil Pesto with variations

285 All-Purpose Tomato Sauce

SHELLFISH

291 Boiled Fresh Crab

STOCKS

294 Vegetable Stock

295 Fish Stock

296 Fish Fumet

297 Shellfish Stock

298 Chicken Stock

299 Brown Chicken Stock with variations

300 Beef Stock

301 Brown Beef Stock with variations

VEGETABLES

326 Classic Mashed Potatoes with flavoring options

343 Steamed Vegetables with variations

344 Sautéed Vegetables with variations

345 Roasted Vegetables with variations

346 Braised Vegetables with variations

Chuck Williams, along with Julia Child and Robert Mondavi, has transformed the culinary landscape of our country by raising the caliber and sophistication of home cooks. I fondly call them the holy trinity of American gastronomy. Millions of us benefited when Julia Child began teaching us how to cook on her television show, Robert Mondavi started making world-class wines for our budding palates; and Chuck Williams began providing the necessary tools to bring all these components together. They made our tables complete.

More than a half-century ago, Chuck had the foresight to start a business in Sonoma, California, selling what he felt American home cooks would want and need in their kitchens. Although Chuck started small, he sold only the highest-quality products and introduced many restaurant-grade tools to the general public. He knew deep inside that his clients would appreciate these items and easily integrate them into their kitchens.

I remember the first time I walked into the Williams-Sonoma store and how it inspired me. I felt like a kid again. I bought a palette knife—the first and one of many purchases that I use to this day.

In certain ways, Chuck and I are kindred spirits, bound by our desire to give only the best to our customers and by our passion to excel. While his stores have grown in number, his vision remains clear. The Williams-Sonoma brand continues to be synonymous with quality, longevity, and usefulness. His philosophy permeates each and every store, and I feel this energy every time I visit one.

I met my mentor, Roland Henin, when I was twenty-one years old. He made me realize the emotional connection to cooking, and helped feed my desire to become a professional chef. I realized that to be at the level to which I aspired, I had to establish the proper foundation, so I set out to train under some of the top chefs in France. Just as I learned from the best, I know that Chuck's latest book, Williams-Sonoma *Tools & Techniques,* will provide you with that solid base and help you become more accomplished in the kitchen. It proudly carries on his tradition of excellence and is very much in keeping with the Williams-Sonoma spirit. Carefully written and mindful of various skill levels, this cookbook is comprehensive and challenging at the same time. It provides valuable information and sound techniques for everyone who wants to make memorable meals at home.

Running a household and running a restaurant share many similarities. Planning, budgeting, and, of course, cooking are just three parallels. However, it is the passion to learn something new and the desire to complete a task to the best of one's abilities that define the difference between mediocrity and success. And as you sample your way through the recipes of Williams-Sonoma *Tools & Techniques,* don't despair if you don't get it right the first time. There is always something new to learn. Some of my greatest eureka moments have been a direct result of failure.

This book is a tremendous tool. With it, you are more than halfway through your culinary journey to preparing countless amazing meals for your hungry audience.

THOMAS KELLER
THE FRENCH LAUNDRY

how to use this book

Consider this book a bible of essential kitchen tools and fundamental cooking techniques. The first section is a comprehensive guide to basic tools and equipment for the home kitchen. There, you'll find special features explaining the uses for bakeware and cookware, and a primer on cutlery styles and uses. The second section is filled with more than 250 cooking techniques that will help you accomplish—and understand—some tricky cooking tasks, like carving a roast, shucking oysters, or whipping egg whites to form soft peaks. More than 50 staple recipes, such as Basil Pesto, Mashed Potatoes, or Roast Turkey—crucial to any cook's repertoire—are peppered throughout. Even if you're using a recipe from another cookbook, you can use this book as a guide for such things as julienning carrots, creating crosshatch grill marks, or making a lattice-topped pie.

The book is divided into two sections, one covering tools and equipment and the other cooking techniques and recipes, both organized alphabetically by subject. Instead of page numbers, numbered tabs mark each tool category and technique. You can also use the comprehensive indices in the back of the book to find a specific cooking tool or task or consult the charts in the back of the book for measurement equivalents, doneness temperatures, and ingredient substitutions.

Whether you're a novice in the kitchen or an accomplished home cook, this book will be a primary source of kitchen wisdom for many years to come.

tools

A kitchen stocked with the basics—a variety of carefully chosen pots and pans, a good selection of sharp knives, and durable bakeware—is the starting point for great cooking and baking. Begin by purchasing the best-quality tools and equipment that you can afford, and you'll be rewarded with evenly cooked meats and silky-smooth soups for years to come. In the next 50 pages, you'll find a comprehensive visual guide to basic cooking tools and equipment along with information on sizes, materials, and uses to help you outfit your home kitchen.

1

a

b

2

a

c

d

b

e

BAKEWARE

Bakeware

When choosing bakeware, remember the old adage: "You get what you pay for." Poorly constructed pans and dishes made from inferior materials will warp or crack with use, resulting in poor heat conduction and unevenly baked foods. By contrast, good-quality bakeware that is cared for properly can last a lifetime.

Baking sheets

a RIMMED BAKING SHEETS
Made of aluminum or aluminum-coated steel, these durable pans are used for baking everything from pastries to roasts. Placed under small pans and baking dishes, rimmed baking sheets help retain and conduct heat and catch drips.
Half-sheet pan (bottom) Half the size of commercial sheet pans, a half-sheet pan measures 18 by 13 inches (45 by 33 cm) with a 1-inch (2.5-cm) rim.
Quarter-sheet pan (middle) Measuring 12 by 9 inches (30 by 23 cm) with a 1-inch (2.5-cm) rim, this pan is the smallest standard baking sheet.

Jelly-roll pan (top) This pan measures 15 by 10 inches (38 by 25 cm) and has a ½- or 1-inch (12-mm or 2.5-cm) rim. Traditionally, it is used to make jelly rolls, thin sponge cakes that are spread with jelly and then rolled up. It can also be used for baking small items.

b COOKIE SHEETS
Standard cookie sheet (bottom) A flat metal pan, the cookie sheet is designed to allow maximum heat circulation around cookies and to make it easy to slide them onto a cooling rack. Most cookie sheets have a low, sloping rim on one or two ends to provide stability. They generally measure 15 by 12 inches or 16 by 14 inches (38 by 30 cm or 40 by 35 cm). Those with nonstick surfaces work well and are easy to clean (see entry 5), but you can also prevent sticking by lining a cookie sheet with parchment (baking) paper or a silicone baking mat (see entry 4g). Avoid cookie sheets with dark surfaces, which can cause overheating.
Insulated cookie sheet (top) Insulated cookie sheets are made of two layers of metal with a cushion of air between them. This design helps prevent scorching and promotes even browning.

Pie & tart pans

a PIE PANS
Regular (bottom and middle) Round aluminum pie pans are generally found in 9- to 10-inch (23- to 25-cm) diameters with sloping 1½-inch (4-cm) sides. The pans are available in light and dark finishes, the latter producing more darkly browned crusts, as well as nonstick finishes (see entry 5). Double-crust fruit pies, as well as prebaked crusts for cream-filled pies, bake especially well in aluminum pans because the metal absorbs heat well, helping the pastry turn brown and crisp. Choose pans with wide rims for attractive fluted crusts.
Deep dish (top) Perfect for abundantly filled top-crust-only fruit pies, cobblers, and savory pot pies, deep-dish pie pans look like regular pie pans but are 2–3 inches (5–7.5 cm) deep.

b PIE DISHES
Ceramic (top) These dishes go from oven to table with style. Deeper and wider than standard 9-inch (23-cm) pie pans, with depths from 2–3 inches (5–7.5 cm), they can hold up to twice as much filling as a conventional pie recipe, so they work best for deep-dish fruit pies and pot pies, as well as for crisps, cobblers, and crumbles. Ceramic and porcelain pie dishes conduct heat less effectively than metal, making them good choices for pies without bottom crusts since they will help prevent fillings from scorching.
Glass (bottom) Made from heat-resistant Pyrex, glass pie dishes, also called pie plates, are a popular and attractive choice. The primary advantage of glass is that it lets you see how the crust is actually browning. However, because tempered glass does not conduct heat as well as metal, bottom crusts may take 10 to 15 minutes longer to bake.

c QUICHE DISH
Made from porcelain, this decorative, fluted, shallow baking dish is perfect for baking and serving quiche. You can also use it to bake a variety of savory custards or fruit- or custard-based desserts, with or without crusts. Quiche dishes are typically 10 or 11 inches (25 or 28 cm) in diameter. Quiches can also be made in metal tart pans (see below).

d TART PANS
Metal tart pans have shallow, usually fluted sides and are available in regular or nonstick surfaces (see entry 5). Some tart pans are sold with stationary bottoms and can come in a variety of shapes such as squares and rectangles for making specialty tarts. However, the most versatile choice is a round tart pan 10 or 11 inches (25 or 28 cm) in diameter with a removable bottom, which makes it easier to unmold the tart.

e TARTLET PANS
Small metal pans are used to make individual tarts, cakes, and other sweet and savory baked goods. Like tart pans, these are available with both stationary and removable bottoms and regular and nonstick finishes. You'll find tartlet pans in a wide variety of shapes and sizes, both plain and fluted, deep and shallow.

Cake pans

a ROUND PANS

Choose good-quality, seamless, heavy metal pans; aluminum or aluminum-coated steel are best, although stainless steel and black steel are also available. If you make layer cakes often, buy at least two round cake pans in the sizes you are likely to use. The most popular are 8 or 9 inches (20 or 23 cm) in diameter and 1½–2 inches (4–5 cm) deep.

b SQUARE PANS

Available in the same materials as round cake pans (and also in Pyrex) and usually made from one-piece construction, these pans are ideal for brownies, bar cookies, and cakes without fillings. The standard sizes are 8 or 9 inches (20 or 23 cm) with 2-inch (5-cm) sides.

c RECTANGULAR PANS

Use these pans, which typically measure 13 by 9 inches (33 by 23 cm) with sides 2–2½ inches (5–6 cm) high, for baking sheet cakes, brownies, corn bread and coffee cakes. You can also use these pans for making casseroles.

d SPRINGFORM PANS

These deep metal cake pans have sides secured by a clamp that, when closed, forms a tight seal with the bottom. When the clamp is released, the sides expand and lift off, making the cake easy to remove. Springform pans are commonly used for cakes that are otherwise difficult to unmold, such as cheesecakes and mousse cakes. Although they come in a range of sizes, a 9-inch (23-cm) diameter round pan is the most common. Look for pans made of heavy-gauge steel. Some are also coated with a nonstick surface (see entry 5). You can sometimes find these sold as nesting sets of three pans.

e TUBE PAN

Any pan with a central tube, a feature that helps a tall, airy cake rise and bake evenly from both the middle as well as the outside, is called a tube pan. An angel food cake pan (shown), is the most common type of tube pan and usually has an uncoated surface, which helps the cake rise. It also has a removable bottom, so the cake is easier to unmold, and small "feet" that extend above the rim, which permit the inverted pan to stand clear of the counter during cooling so no moisture is trapped. For most uses, buy one 10-inch (25-cm) tube pan, which holds 3 quarts (3 litres) of batter. You can use a tube pan to make other cakes, but you'll need to coat it well with butter and/or flour before use.

f BUNDT PAN

Usually made of heavy cast aluminum, with or without a nonstick coating, this specialized, one-piece tube pan, which is German and Austrian in origin, has deeply fluted sides that distinguish the dense cakes baked in them. Thanks to the hole in the center, the finished, unmolded Bundt cake is easier to slice than a traditional round cake.

Other bakeware

a SOUFFLÉ DISH

Designed with tall sides so that airy soufflés can rise straight and high, these baking dishes are commonly circular and fluted, range in size from ½ cup (4 fl oz/ 125 ml) or less to 2 quarts (2 litres), and are made of porcelain. They can also be used as molds for a variety of hot and cold and sweet or savory dishes.

b RAMEKINS

These small, round porcelain baking dishes, usually 3–4 inches (7.5–10 cm) in diameter, are used for cooking or serving individual portions of sweet or savory foods.

c BAKING DISHES

Used for baking savory main courses, casseroles, or side dishes, these deep, ovenproof glass, porcelain, or ceramic dishes come in a variety of shapes. Many have handles or lips to make them easy to hold. The most popular sizes range from 2½–5 quarts (2.5–5 litres).

d LOAF PANS

Standard loaf pans measure 8–12 inches (20–30 cm) long, 4–5 inches (10–13 cm) wide, and 3–4 inches (7.5–10 cm) deep, and are made of aluminum, tinned steel, or aluminum-coated steel, as well as heat-resistant glass. Use them to bake sweet or savory yeast breads, quick breads, pound cakes, meat loaves, or layered terrines.

e MUFFIN PANS

Standard muffin pans have 6 or 12 cups that each hold about 6 tablespoons (3 fl oz/90 ml) of batter. Also available are pans with jumbo cups or miniature cups, sometimes called "gem" cups. These pans are often made of aluminum or steel and nonstick coatings (see entry 5) are popular features.

f POPOVER PAN

Resembling a muffin pan, this pan is used for baking egg-rich popover batter. The deep, narrow cups and the construction—whether old-fashioned solid cast iron, or newer black steel with metal strips connecting the cups—promote puffing.

g SILICONE BAKING MATS

These flexible, nonstick, heat-resistant mats are used to line baking sheets. They alleviate the need to grease the pan and are especially handy for delicate cookies.

h COOLING RACKS

These wire racks have feet, which raises them above the counter, allows air to circulate, and prevents moisture from being trapped under baked foods. Cooling racks come in a range of sizes; use square or rectangular shapes for cookies and round shapes for cakes or pies. Choose racks made of heavy-duty metal.

BAKEWARE

Bakeware materials

The greatest advancement in bakeware over the past half century has been the development, and continued improvement, of materials that help keep food from sticking to the pan during baking. Three materials in particular represent the current state of this culinary revolution.

a TRADITIONAL NONSTICK

Many brands of traditional nonstick bakeware ensure the easy release of baked goods and quick cleanup. Most coatings consist of the synthetic chemical compound polytetrafluoroethylene (PTFE), which is so smooth and slick that food seldom sticks to it. PTFE coatings for cookware became increasingly popular in the 1950s following the 1949 introduction of the Teflon brand. (That name is often wrongly applied to all nonstick cookware; but while all Teflon-coated cookware is based on PTFE technology, not all PTFE cookware is sold under the Teflon brand.) When buying nonstick bakeware or cookware, choose products made with two coats of the nonstick finish to ensure top performance and durability.

When baking or cooking with nonstick pans, avoid using metal utensils, which could scratch the surface. A number of kitchen tools are available that have been designed specifically for use with nonstick bakeware and cookware (see entry 151). For the same reason, do not put nonstick bakeware in the dishwasher; instead, clean it with warm soapy water and a soft sponge and resist using harsh scrubbers or abrasive cleaning powders. Recently, concern has been raised about the possible health risks of perfluorooctanoic acid (PFOA), a chemical used in the manufacture of PTFE, especially when cooking at high temperatures. Experts claim that PFOA is eliminated during the manufacturing process of nonstick coatings, and government agencies have found no substantial risks in the use of PTFE-coated bakeware or cookware.

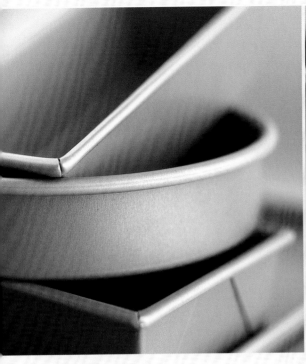

b GOLDTOUCH NONSTICK

A prime example of the advances being made in nonstick surfaces, Goldtouch nonstick bakeware features two layers of a high-performance ceramic-reinforced nonstick coating that is ten times as resistant to scratching as traditional nonstick products and will not chip or peel. To withstand frequent use, the special nonstick layers, made from a process developed in Switzerland, are bonded to commercial-gauge, aluminum-coated steel, the same construction used by professional kitchens. This metal alloy distributes heat quickly and evenly and resists rust and corrosion, producing consistent baking results. A thick band within each pan's lip prevents warping or flexing. The pans are distinguishable from traditional nonstick bakeware by their handsome matte gold color. Another plus to this bakeware is that, unlike traditional nonstick pans, Goldtouch bakeware is dishwasher safe. Goldtouch bakeware can be found in a variety of shapes and sizes, such as muffin pans, loaf pans, round and square cake pans, and sheet pans.

c MOLDED SILICONE

Another recent development in stick-resistant bakeware is molded silicone. Based on the chemical element silicon, found in sand, this rubberlike compound is formed into molds for baking muffins, cakes, loaves, and other items, as well as pressed into textured sheets to make nonstick baking mats (see entry 4g). Silicone's extremely slick surface, flexibility, and durability allows foods baked in it to virtually pop out—or for the mold to be peeled away—even with intricately shaped items such as madeleines. But the material does not conduct heat as well as metal, so it's a good idea to support silicone baking pans with a metal baking sheet. You may also need to adjust baking times or temperatures to promote browning. Molded silicone is made in a variety of bright colors and whimsical shapes, so it has great appeal to kids. It can also help save money and limit waste, as items such as silicone muffin liners or baking mats can be reused to replace paper muffin cups or parchment (baking) paper. Silicone bakeware is safe for use in the microwave and can be cleaned in the dishwasher.

BAKING TOOLS

Baking tools

Having the right tool for the job makes baking easier and more enjoyable. While you can roll out pastry dough with a wine bottle, or cut biscuits with an inverted water glass, these tasks go more smoothly with a rolling pin or a biscuit cutter. If you buy good, sturdy tools, they will last for years and serve you well.

Pie & pastry tools

a PASTRY BLENDER

Look for a pastry blender, also known as a pastry cutter or dough blender, with a sturdy wooden or metal handle securely anchored to rows of parallel U-shaped steel wires or blades. Pressed down repeatedly into cubes of chilled butter or other fat in a mixing bowl with flour, the wires or blades act as cutters to reduce the fat to small flour-coated pieces, which bake into flaky pastry.

b PASTRY BOARD

Rolling out pastry dough calls for a smooth, hard surface—preferably one that is cool to keep the fat in the dough from melting. Marble is the ideal choice, but you can also find pastry boards made of hardwood and plastic. Resist any temptation to use a marble pastry board as a cutting board, which will scratch its surface—not to mention dull your knives. Chill marble pastry boards in the refrigerator before use on warm days to help keep your pastry as cool as possible, which is important for a flaky crust.

c ROLLING PINS

Rolling pins are available in different sizes, shapes, and materials, but hardwood pins are the most common choice. In general, the type you choose is a matter of personal taste, although sturdy, heavy, well-made pins will always do the best job. To avoid warping, never submerge wooden pins in water; simply wipe them clean with a damp cloth, then rub dry with a kitchen towel.

Traditional pin (left) Straight hardwood rolling pins with offset handles are great for rolling out pie crusts and other doughs. One of the most efficient types of these is known as a baker's rolling pin; it has a steel rod running from handle to handle through the heavy wooden pin, which rolls smoothly on ball bearings inside. For fine pastry work, look for marble or stainless-steel pins, which stay cool for a long period of time.

Straight pin (middle) This French-style pin, usually made of hardwood, is a level, heavy dowel that is rolled back and forth across the dough by placing your outstretched hands over both ends. Some bakers say a straight pin allows them to get a better feel for the dough than a traditional pin with its offset handles.

Tapered pin (right) A lightweight, hardwood rolling pin, this style is favored by some bakers because the thicker central portion and narrow ends enable them to pivot and rotate the pin during use, making it easier to roll out dough in a neat circle of uniform thickness.

d COOKIE CUTTERS

Cookie cutters come in different shapes and sizes, from basic rounds to whimsical figures, holiday icons, to seasonal themes. Large round cookie cutters can also be used for cutting biscuits and scones. Although some are plastic, the best cookie cutters are still made of metal, which retains a sharp cutting edge.

e PASTRY CUTTERS

Similar to cookie cutters, these sets of heavy tinned steel tools—in a range of three to ten graduated sizes—are used to cut cookies as well as pastry dough for recipes that range from hors d'oeuvres to desserts. The cutters can be round, oval, boat-shaped, or square, with either straight or fluted edges.

f COOKIE PRESS

Sometimes called a cookie gun because of its shape, this tool consists of a sturdy metal tube that is filled with soft cookie dough. A squeeze of the handle at one end forces the dough through one of up to two dozen different decorative plates that can be secured to the other end, forming fanciful shapes when pressed onto the cookie sheet.

g PASTRY WHEEL

Consisting of a circular straight or fluted rolling blade, or wheel, attached to the end of a sturdy wooden or metal handle, this tool is used to cut out or trim rolled-out pastry dough and pasta, particularly ravioli. Fluted wheels are sometimes referred to as "jaggers" because of the jagged edge they produce. Some wheels come with a straight edge at one end of the handle and a fluted edge at the other.

h PIE WEIGHTS

Also known as pastry weights, these small aluminum or ceramic pellets are used to weigh down pie dough when it is blind baked—that is, prebaked without a filling (see entry 247). A sheet of aluminum foil is fitted into the pastry-lined pan and then the weights are spread over the bottom to hold the pastry in place as it bakes, preventing it from buckling and ensuring that the bottom crust stays neat and level.

i PASTRY BRUSHES

Use these tools to brush water, egg wash, melted butter, or glaze on pastry. The brushes come in a variety of widths, but be sure that they have fine bristles that are firmly attached to the handle and are made especially for kitchen use. Wash pastry brushes in hot, soapy water, and to avoid imparting unwanted flavors to your foods, keep them separate from brushes that you use for savory foods.

Cake-baking tools

a SIFTERS

Flour sifter (left) This metal or plastic canister is fitted with two or three overlapping wire-mesh screens and a handle that, when squeezed or turned, rotates an inside blade that moves flour, cocoa powder, or other dry ingredients through the screens to sift and aerate them. A 2- or 3-cup (16– or 24–fl oz/ 500- or 750-ml) capacity is fine for most home baking.

Mesh sieve (right) A mesh sieve, suspended over a bowl, does a fine job of sifting dry ingredients. Pour the item into the sieve, and lightly tap the edge to encourage it to fall through into the bowl.

Decorating tool alternatives

If you only bake and decorate cakes occasionally, you do not need to purchase a lot of specialty tools. You will need to purchase some decorating tips (see entry 7f). However, if you don't have a cake decorating stand (see entry 7c), you can cover the outside of a cake pan with plastic wrap, turn it so the bottom faces up, and build and frost cake layers on this plastic-covered surface; you can manually rotate the pan to help you smooth the frosting. A gallon-sized resealable plastic bag can be substituted for a pastry bag: Cut a small hole in one corner of the bag, secure a pastry tip in the hole, and fill the bag with frosting, pressing it down towards the tip. Squeeze the air out of the bag and seal it well before piping.

b SCRAPERS

Bench scraper (top) Professional bakers often refer to their work surface as "the bench," which is where this handy tool gets its name. It consists of a broad, straight-edged metal blade attached to a sturdy handle made of wood, rolled metal, or plastic. You can use a bench scraper for scraping sticky dough from work surfaces, cutting dough into portions as called for in a recipe, or transferring chopped ingredients from the cutting board to a bowl or pan.

Bowl scraper (bottom) Bowl scrapers are about the same size as bench scrapers (above), but they are made entirely of flexible plastic. The rounded edge is the perfect shape to follow the contours of a mixing bowl. This handy tool helps you get every last bit of cake batter into a pan, and efficiently scrape down the sides of mixing bowls when beating cookie dough.

c CAKE DECORATING STAND

Professional bakers use small, round turntables (shown) to ensure precision when frosting, filling, or piping cakes. This tool is equally convenient for home bakers: Set your cake on the rotating aluminum top, then turn it as needed to frost or decorate the cake. You can also use a pedestal-style round cake stand made of porcelain, glass, stainless steel, or another attractive material. Like a turntable, cake stands elevate a cake for ease in icing, but they are harder to turn. That said, you can, after cleaning up any drips, serve the cake on the same cake stand as it was iced.

d ICING SPATULAS

Also called frosting spatulas or pastry spatulas, these long, flat metal utensils have slender, 6- to 12-inch (15- to 30-cm) blades that resemble round-tipped knives. They are very flexible to facilitate the smooth spreading of icing or frosting onto cakes, pastries, and other baked items, particularly on rounded surfaces. Offset spatulas have handles that angle slightly off the blade, a feature some cake decorators feel makes the spreading more efficient. Icing spatulas come in a range of widths: a wide spatula is useful when covering a large area, such as frosting a sheet cake; a thin spatula is helpful when doing precise work on small pastries or cakes.

e PASTRY BAG

Also known as decorating bags or piping bags, funnel-shaped pastry bags are made of plastic-lined canvas, plain canvas, polyester, nylon, or disposable plastic. The most useful bags are 8 to 12 inches (20 to 30 cm) long and have a wide opening for filling them at one end and a narrow opening at the other. Fitted with any of a variety of tips inserted into the narrow opening inside the bag, they are used for neatly and decoratively forming doughs, icings, mousses, and other soft, spreadable ingredients into a wide range of shapes. If you plan to do much piping with pastry bags, it is a good idea to have at least two, so you can switch quickly back and forth between different colors of frosting without having to wash the bag. Wash pastry bags with warm, soapy water, then turn them inside out to dry. Be sure to keep bags used for savory preparations separate from those used for desserts.

f PASTRY TIPS

Designed to fit snugly into the narrow ends of pastry bags (above), this array of conical tips—usually made of tinned or chromed steel—make it possible to achieve a wide variety of decorative effects when piping frosting or icing, or shaping soft pastry or cookie dough. Popular tips include small circular openings for writing messages; larger circular openings for rounded strips of icing or dough, small to wide slits to shape ribbons, and star shapes to pipe ridged bands or rosettes. Try to buy a set with a coupler and screw-on tips so you can change tips easily without emptying the frosting out of the bag.

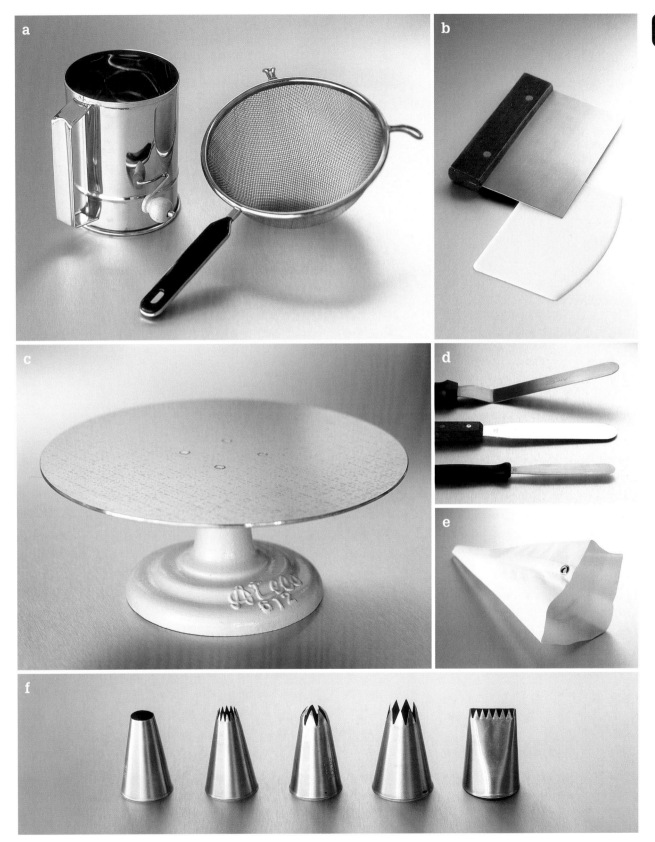

BAKING TOOLS

COOK'S TOOLS

Cook's tools

Stocking a kitchen with a range of useful cooking tools is a lifelong process. Some tools designed for very specific, seldom-performed tasks may quickly begin to feel like kitchen clutter, while others may wear out, get lost, or break. However, efficient, high-quality, everyday tools will likely last for decades.

General tools

a SPOONS

Slotted spoon (left) Slotted spoons are essential for lifting solids from liquids. Choose spoons made from stainless steel, which are durable and don't absorb flavors or contribute a metallic flavor.
Solid spoon (middle) Sturdy stainless-steel spoons are good for stirring large quantities of thick preparations or for transferring food from one container to another. You can also use them for skimming the fat from stocks or sauces.
Wooden spoon (right) Indispensable in the kitchen, wooden spoons are sturdy, do not scratch bowls or pans, and stay cool. The longest-lasting spoons are made of hard, fine-grained woods.

b LADLES

With their deep bowls angled off of long handles, ladles are essential for serving soups and sauces. The bowl should be made of stainless steel or heat-resistant plastic, and the handle should be long enough to dip conveniently and safely into your deepest pots. Smaller ladles are useful for saucing foods and transferring stocks to containers for freezing.

c METAL SPATULAS

Solid spatula (top) A spatula is perfect for turning a variety of foods when sautéing, grilling, or baking. Select stainless steel for durability or heat-resistant plastic for use with nonstick cookware (see entry 15 l). The edges should be thin or tapered to help slip under food, and the handles should be wood or another material that stays cool.
Fish spatula (middle) Some spatulas are made specifically for lifting and turning delicate fish, with wider or longer, thinner, and more flexible blades to slip easily beneath and fit the dimensions of fillets.

Slotted spatula (bottom) Used mainly in frying, the slots in the blade let grease drip through, helping to prevent splatters.

d SILICONE SPATULAS

Flexible silicone spatulas are excellent for blending or folding ingredients together and for scraping mixing bowls. Their tapered blades vary in size to suit tasks both large and small. Since they are made of heat-resistant silicone, these spatulas are perfect for stirring and blending during cooking.

e TONGS

These hinged tools with blunt ends are useful for picking up pieces of food without piercing them, tossing salads, and many other jobs. Some have a spring in the hinge and may include a locking device that keeps them closed for storage. Look for durable stainless-steel tongs with tips that meet precisely.

f WHISKS

With heads of looped metal wires attached to sturdy metal or wood handles, whisks are used to beat foods rapidly and to blend them thoroughly. Also called whips, they come in a variety of sizes.
Straight-sided whisk (left) This whisk features wires formed into fairly straight, narrow loops. Use it to mix ingredients thoroughly without adding excess air.
Balloon whisk (middle) Balloon whisks have pronounced, rounded loops. Too flexible for regular stirring, their spherical shape facilitates incorporating the maximum amount of air while beating egg whites or cream.
Flat whisk (right) Also called a roux whisk, a flat whisk is used to stir sauces as they thicken, while pressing out and smoothing lumps on the bottom of a pan.

g SALT & PEPPER MILLS

Look for a well-made wood or lacquer pepper mill with a hardened-steel grinder that lets you adjust the coarseness of the grind. Salt mills with noncorroding ceramic, hard plastic, or stainless-steel grinding mechanisms help you derive maximum flavor from large salt crystals.

h GARLIC PRESS

This hinged tool includes a perforated hopper into which one or more garlic cloves are placed, and a flat-sided plunger that pushes the garlic through the perforations forming tiny pieces.

i PEELERS

Traditional (top) This peeler has a fixed, slotted, stainless-steel blade extending from the handle. The best models come with blades that swivel, to adjust to the contours of whatever you're peeling.
Y-shaped (bottom) This style of peeler features a broad handle with two prongs extending in a Y shape, between which a swiveling blade is secured. The unique shape makes it possible to peel foods easily with a gentle swipe of the wrist.

j POT HOLDERS

Critical for lifting or holding hot pots, pans, or utensils safely, these cloth squares are thickly insulated, padded, and generously sized. Some include pockets that let you slip your hand inside.

k OVEN MITTS

For handling large items, as well as for adjusting hot oven shelves, choose cloth oven mitts that are thickly insulated and padded. The gloves should be large enough to provide maximum coverage, yet close-fitting and flexible enough to allow you to maintain a secure grip.

Bowls

a GLASS NESTING BOWLS

Glass bowls, in sets of as many as ten graduated sizes ranging from 1¼ fl oz (40 ml) up to 4½ quarts (4.5 litres) or more, are indispensable for tasks as varied as holding small measured amounts of recipe ingredients (a cook's *mise en place)* to mixing cake batters. Glass has the advantages of not reacting with acidic ingredients, being easy to clean, and letting you see how well ingredients have blended. The nesting style also saves storage space in the kitchen. Choose bowls made of tempered glass, which can stand up to the microwave oven, freezer, or dishwasher.

b CERAMIC MIXING BOWLS

Sturdy ceramic bowls have been kitchen standards for centuries for mixing cake and cookie batters and other cooking tasks. Part of their appeal could be that they are found in a multitude of colors that will match any kitchen decor. Ceramic bowls change temperature slowly, keeping hot contents warm and cold ingredients cool. Make sure the ceramic bowls you buy have glazes that are food-safe, and avoid unglazed bowls that can absorb flavors.

c MELAMINE BOWLS

Heat-resistant melamine or plastic bowls, sold individually or nested in graduated sizes, are desirable because they're lightweight, don't react with acidic ingredients, and are easy to clean. They're also available in a wide array of cheery colors, even in kid-friendly sizes for aspiring young cooks. Look for bowls with rubber-ring bases that prevent skidding on counters, as well as for those with handles at one end and lips at the other to facilitate pouring batters, marinades, and other fluid mixtures.

d STAINLESS-STEEL BOWLS

Every kitchen needs at least one stainless-steel bowl, if not a nesting set of various sizes. Stainless steel won't react with food, like copper or aluminum will, and it is lighter and more durable than ceramic or glass. You can also find some with lips for easy pouring (shown).

e COPPER BOWL

Devoted bakers swear by unlined copper bowls for use in beating egg whites. A harmless chemical reaction between copper and the albumen in the whites gives greater stability to the air bubbles as they are beaten into the whites, yielding fluffier, more stable results. Although they can be found in a range of sizes, those 10 or 12 inches (25 or 30 cm) in diameter are the most versatile for the home kitchen.

f WOODEN BOWL

Solid hardwood bowls, especially those made of maple, are prized by some cooks for their rustic good looks and durability. Favored as salad bowls, they can also be used for chopping ingredients with the crescent-shaped chopping blade known as a mezzaluna (see entry 24f). If you use a wooden bowl for chopping, do not use it for serving to avoid contamination. Wash out wooden bowls by hand with warm, soapy water and dry immediately; do not put them in the dishwasher or leave liquids standing in them.

Graters & shredders

a BOX GRATER-SHREDDER

Made of stainless steel, this old-fashioned kitchen standby presents you with a choice of different cutting surfaces, typically four, one on each side of its boxlike shape. Some manufacturers are now making grater-shredders with up to six cutting surfaces, providing an even larger array of options. On the grating side, a profusion of small, pointed rasps produce fine particles when a piece of food—such as hard cheese, stale bread, or chocolate—is moved up and down across the surface. At least two shredding sides are covered, respectively, in medium- and large-sized holes with sharp raised edges, which cut foods such as root vegetables or medium-soft to firm cheeses into shreds as they are moved over the holes. Finally, the remaining side typically features one diagonal, raised, sharp-edged slit for cutting shavings or broad ribbons of ingredients. Look for a box shredder-grater of heavy-duty construction, with a firmly attached and comfortable handle at the top. Some grater-shredders feature a plastic or metal end cap that conveniently keeps the food inside the grater until you are ready to use it.

b RASP GRATERS

Originally developed as woodworking tools, rasp graters were introduced nearly a decade ago and have been gaining popularity in restaurants and in home kitchens ever since. Made under the brand name Microplane, rasp graters now set the standard for easy and precise grating of foods. Handheld rasp graters can be found in two shapes: a long, thin shape that resembles a ruler, with or without a plastic handle; and a shape that resembles a wide, flat paddle. Choose handheld graters with ergonomic, soft rubber handles, large grating surfaces, and that are dishwasher safe. Some rasp graters are sold with a protective plastic sheath that protects the sharp blades when the graters are not in use. You can now find rasp graters in a box grater style, featuring multiple cutting blades and a sliding attachment that protects your fingers.

Fine grater (left and middle right) The fine grater zests citrus fruits and purées garlic, peppers, ginger, and onion.

Ribbon grater (middle left) The ribbon grater grates soft cheeses and chocolate, and shreds cabbage and potatoes.

Coarse grater (right) The coarse grater is ideal for grating chocolate and hard cheeses or for shredding coconut.

COOK'S TOOLS

Strainers

a COLANDERS

A workhorse among strainers, free-standing colanders can be used for rinsing produce or draining cooked pasta or vegetables. They feature a bowl that is perforated with holes for drainage, a pair of handles that make it easy to transfer from place to place, and a low pedestal base or feet that holds it steady in the sink or on the counter. Choose one that feels sturdy and durable, whether it's made of stainless steel, aluminum, or heavy-duty molded resin or plastic. You can also now find colanders and other cook's tools made from silicone, which is extremely durable and can withstand high temperatures. Consider purchasing two colanders, one for large quantities, such as pasta or blanched vegetables, and one for small items, such as boiled eggs or individual portions of cooked vegetables.

b HANDHELD STRAINERS

Made of wire mesh, these strainers can be found with either fine or coarse mesh. They also come in a range of sizes, from very small to very large, all are useful for particular purposes: a small strainer can be used to sift small amounts of confectioners' (icing) sugar or cocoa powder over desserts; a large strainer for a multitude of kitchen tasks. Long handles make strainers easy to hold with one hand while pouring from a measuring cup, bowl, or saucepan with the other.

Some also have metal hooks that help steady them on the rim of a bowl or pot. Coarse-meshed strainers come in handy for blanching vegetables, transferring them quickly from boiling water into an ice bath. Fine-meshed strainers remove lumps and provide a smooth consistency for delicate sauces or purées. Sturdy models can even be used to purée soft foods, which are pushed through the strainer with the back of a large spoon.

c CONICAL STRAINER

These strainers are made of stainless steel, tin-plated steel, or aluminum, perforated with tiny holes. They are used not only for straining solids from liquids but also, more particularly, for puréeing soft-cooked vegetables or fruits with the aid of a large spoon or wooden plunger in a fashion similar to a chinois (see below).

d CHINOIS

Taking its fanciful French name from a resemblance to an old-fashioned Chinese hat, this type of conical strainer is typically made of very fine stainless-steel mesh. A wire stand usually holds the chinois steady inside a large mixing bowl while a slender, pointed wooden pestle—sold with the strainer—is rapidly rotated around the inside to force the food through the holes. Use a chinois to make ultrasmooth soups and sauces, and to clarify stocks.

e SKIMMER

Think of a skimmer as a cross between a metal spoon and a colander or strainer. At the end of a long handle is a shallow metal bowl perforated with small holes. You can use a skimmer as you would a slotted spoon, to lift solids out of hot liquids; or, as its name suggests, to remove foamy impurities, fat, and other surface residue from stocks and soups while they simmer.

f SPIDER

Sometimes referred to as a wire skimmer, this professional-style, handheld device gets its name because of its resemblance to a spider's web. At one end of a long handle is a broad, circular, shallow bowl of loosely spaced but sturdy wire mesh, which enables the cook to use the spider to scoop up and strain a wide range of ingredients, such as vegetables or pasta simmering in water or broth, boiled dumplings, like potato gnocchi, or anything deep-fried or stir-fried.

g CHEESECLOTH

Traditionally used in cheesemaking, cheesecloth (muslin) is lightweight, cotton gauze that is free of dyes and finishes. It is primarily used for fine straining and filtering. Use it to hold together the herb bundles known as bouquets garnis, or to line strainers or colanders when straining stocks and sauces.

Fish & shellfish tools

a FISH TWEEZERS

Fish tweezers are invaluable if you like to cook fish fillets frequently, especially fish like salmon or trout. These types of fish often contain residual fine bones, called pin bones, which the fishmonger may not remove as part of the cleaning process. Surgical-quality, stainless-steel fish tweezers allow you to get a strong, secure grip on the ends of even the most slippery bones to pull them out easily. (If you don't have fish tweezers, clean needle-nose pliers will do the same job.)

b SHELLFISH KNIVES

Clam and oyster knives each have a short stainless-steel blade attached to a sturdy wooden handle. The designs differ, tailored to the particular shellfish they are made for. They are not interchangeable. **Oyster knife (left)** The pointed tip of this knife is made to slip between the shell halves of an oyster and pry them apart. **Clam knife (right)** The rounded blade of a clam knife has one slightly sharpened edge made to slide between the shells and cut the clam meat free.

c LOBSTER CRACKER

A cast-metal lobster cracker resembles a heavy-duty nutcracker with extra serrations and curves to help split the shells of cooked lobsters or crabs. One lobster cracker will do if you're just extracting the meat in the kitchen, but if you plan to serve whole lobsters or crabs to your guests, you'll need one for each person. Lobster crackers are often sold with thin metal picks to help extract the lobster meat from the cracked shells and the narrow openings of the legs.

Meat & poultry tools

a BUTCHER'S TWINE
Also called kitchen string, butcher's twine is commonly used to truss whole chickens or turkeys and to tie up rolled roasts, a preparatory step that ensures these items will cook evenly in the oven and come out neat and attractive. The twine can also be used for other tasks like securing a bouquet garni. Choose strong, natural, uncolored linen string, which won't char or impart flavor or color.

b BULB BASTER
Resembling a giant eyedropper, this tool consists of a large metal, heatproof glass, or plastic tube with a narrow opening at one end and, at the other, a squeezable rubber or silicone bulb. The baster extracts hot juices from the bottom of a roasting pan, or a flavorful marinade or glaze mixture from a cup, and then disperses it over the surface of a turkey, chicken, or meat roast. Metal basters are the most versatile, as they won't break, melt, or warp.

c POULTRY LIFTERS
This pair of large, metal, fork-shaped implements helps you reach underneath both sides of a large bird in its roasting pan and lift it easily—either to turn it for even browning or to transfer it to a carving board or serving platter.

d BASTING BRUSHES
Basting brushes generally have long handles and broad bristles that make it easy to soak up pan juices, marinades, or glazes and apply them across the surface of a roast, steak, or chop as it cooks. **Natural bristle (top)** The best natural-bristle basting brushes are made from sterilized boar bristles, which withstand high temperatures, and are anchored in a sleeve at the end of a hardwood handle. Avoid those made from synthetic materials, which can melt if exposed to high temperatures.
Silicone bristle (bottom) Specially made bristles of silicone facilitate applying a basting liquid or glaze when working with high oven or grill temperatures. Brushes with detachable bristle heads make them easy to clean.

e FAT SEPARATOR
Also called a gravy separator, this clear heatproof glass or plastic container resembles a measuring cup with a long spout rising from its bottom. Pour pan juices into the vessel (some have a strainer insert to remove browned bits) and let the liquid stand for a few minutes. The liquid fat will rise to the surface, making it possible to pour out the juices from the bottom to make a sauce.

f MEAT POUNDER
This tool consists of a flat, heavy metal disk or square with a sturdy handle rising from its center. Pick it up by the handle and pound down on a boneless piece of meat or poultry to flatten it to a uniform thickness. Some meat pounders have a toothed surface on one side of the head for tenderizing tough meat cuts.

Fruit & vegetable tools

a CITRUS REAMER
This wood or metal tool is designed to squeeze juice from citrus halves using a ridged, mound-shaped surface against which the fruit is pressed and twisted. Its ingenious design, made in England, allows you to add citrus juice to a dish just a drop or two at a time.

b CITRUS PRESSES
These cast-metal devices extract juice from citrus halves by means of a lever action. You can find different-sized presses that are used to extract the juice from limes, lemons, or oranges.

c MANUAL CITRUS JUICER
The manual juicer positions a reamer on a circular, bowl-shaped base that collects the juice as the citrus half is pressed down and twisted. Some juicer models include strainer inserts to separate the pulp from the juice.

d FOOD MILL
A food mill looks like a stainless-steel or plastic saucepan with a perforated bottom and an interior crank-shaped handle. It may also have arms that extend out so you can fit it securely over a bowl or pan. At the bottom of the mill is a circular, paddle-shaped blade that rotates against a disk perforated with small holes. As you turn the handle, the blade forces food through the holes and into a bowl or pan, while any seeds, peels, or fibers are trapped. Some mills feature interchangeable disks to make purées of various consistencies. Food mills treat food more gently than food processors and yield more even-textured purées.

e POTATO MASHER
With a heavy wire grid or perforated metal disk attached to a sturdy handle, the potato masher makes quick work of puréeing boiled potatoes or other items.

f RICER
This device is prized for making smooth purées from boiled potatoes and other vegetables. A plunger attached to a lever pushes cooked food through a hopper, to which a perforated disk is attached, reducing the food to a fine consistency.

g SALAD SPINNER
A salad spinner quickly dries rinsed salad greens or other leafy vegetables by rapidly rotating them in a perforated basket that spins inside a slightly larger bowl. Excess water is spun off by centrifugal force and collects in the bowl.

h STEAMER BASKET
This collapsible tool is made of perforated metal with hinged, fanned sides that enable it to adjust to fit different-sized pans. It sits on small feet to hold the food being cooked above the boiling or simmering liquid.

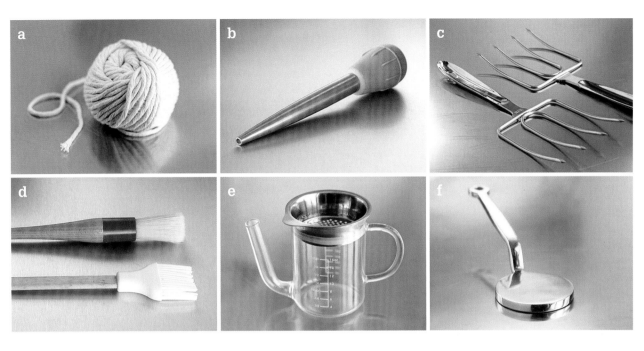

COOK'S TOOLS

COOK'S TOOLS

Specialty tools

a APPLE CORER

This device removes the core and seeds from whole apples. It consists of a handle attached to a sharp-edged stainless-steel tube. The tube is long enough to push all the way through the center of the apple, from top to bottom, and wide enough to cut out all the seeds. When you pull the tool out of the fruit, the core stays inside the tube.

b LEMON STRIPPER

This tool's sharp, V-shaped tip easily cuts decorative, narrow channels in the surfaces of fruits and vegetables. Bartenders use this tool to add a "twist" of citrus to a cocktail.

c CITRUS ZESTER

The zester's stainless-steel blade, at the end of a short handle, is fitted with a row of four to six sharp-edged small holes that, when drawn across the surface of a citrus fruit, removes thin strips of the colorful and flavorful outermost part of the peel—the zest—while leaving behind the bitter white pith.

d MELON BALLER

This standard-sized tool has a small, sharp-edged hemispherical metal bowl about 1 inch (2.5 cm) in diameter at one end. With a twist of your wrist, the scoop easily cuts decorative balls from melons or other semi-firm foods. It is also useful for coring pears and other soft fruits and vegetables, or for scooping out their centers for stuffing. Some models feature a slightly smaller scoop at the opposite end. It is also available in smaller sizes.

e CHERRY/OLIVE PITTER

This tool speeds the process of removing the pits from whole cherries or olives. The pitter has a hollowed-out cradle in which a single fruit is placed. With a squeeze of the tool, a punch pushes through the fruit, ejecting the pit out while leaving a whole cherry or olive behind. It's a good idea to have a couple of prep bowls on hand to collect the pits and the fruit.

f GRAPEFRUIT KNIFE

This knife has a small, angled, flexible metal blade with serrated edges. The knife is designed to cut neatly around grapefruit segments and their tough membranes while following the fruit's natural contours.

g CULINARY TORCH

The most common use for this handheld device is making crème brûlée. Fueled by a canister of butane gas that is inserted into the handle, the miniature nozzle produces a small but intense flame, like a miniature blowtorch, that quickly and precisely caramelizes a sugar topping to form a glossy golden crust.

h ICE CREAM SCOOPS

Besides their obvious use to scoop ice cream into serving portions, ice cream scoops are versatile kitchen tools. The half-sphere model has a deep bowl and a trigger-operated metal band that swings through the interior to release the scoop. Available in a variety of sizes, you can use ice cream scoops to make evenly sized cookies or to portion out uniform amounts of meat mixture for meatballs.

i MANDOLINE

This flat, rectangular tool usually comes with an assortment of both smooth and serrated blades, enabling you to slice, julienne, or waffle-cut a wide variety of firm ingredients. The advantages of using a mandoline are the precision and regularity it offers, plus its surprising speed when compared to a knife. A mandoline is best used for large quantities; so the minutes you save in cutting may not make up for the time spent assembling and washing it. Mandolines are available in a variety of designs. Some must be steadied by hand, while more sophisticated versions have foldaway legs that hold them up at an ergonomic angle. Be sure to look for a mandoline that includes a hand guard to keep your fingers safely clear of the sharp cutting edge as you work.

j MORTAR & PESTLE

Before electricity and food processors revolutionized kitchen work, a cook needed a mortar and pestle to grind, purée, and blend. Some cooks still prefer the rustic, handmade texture imparted by the mortar and pestle for recipes like pesto, mole, or curry. This timeless tool uses a bowl-shaped mortar to hold the ingredients and a club-shaped pestle to crush and grind them. Mortars vary in size and material, from palm-sized porcelain bowls to substantial marble or wooden vessels to huge stone blocks that serve as permanent fixtures in many Indian homes. Although a pestle is often made of the same material as the mortar, it can also be carved from hardwood. Either the mortar or pestle must have an abrasive surface for the tool to work effectively.

k PIZZA CUTTER

Also called a pizza wheel, this tool features a rolling blade at the end of an angled handle. It efficiently cuts a hot pizza into neat pieces, hence its name. But a pizza cutter can also be used for a variety of tasks, such as cutting strips of dough to make a lattice-topped fruit pie. The sharp-edged wheel measures 2–4 inches (5–10 cm) in diameter. Some models feature a finger guard to protect your fingers as you cut. Buy the sturdiest pizza cutter you can find and make sure it has a strong handle.

l NONSTICK COOKING TOOLS

If you own any nonstick bakeware or cookware (see entries 5 and 18d), you should consider investing in a set of tools specially designed not to scratch their surfaces. Many manufacturers are now making tools from hard, heatproof rubber, silicone, and nylon (or coated with those materials) specifically designed to be safe for use on nonstick surfaces. Spoons, ladles, spatulas, whisks, and tongs are all good choices. You can also use wooden tools or silicone rubber spatulas, which are heatproof, soft, and nonabrasive.

Cookware

Along with your stove top and oven, good cookware is one of the most important long-term investments you can make as a cook. Many people stocking new kitchens want to buy complete matching sets, but you can also select a few pieces at a time, slowly building your collection as you learn more about how you like to cook.

Basic cookware

a FRYING PANS
Also called skillets, these broad pans have sides that flare outward, making them useful for cooking foods that must be stirred often or slid from the pan. To suit recipes of various sizes it's a good idea to have both a smaller frying pan measuring 9–10 inches (23–25 cm) in diameter, and a larger pan 12–14 inches (30–35 cm) in diameter. If you only buy two pans, make one of them nonstick. For more about cookware materials, turn to entry 18.

Cookware in history

The first cookware brought to the U.S. from Europe was most likely made of cast iron. But it was the discovery of aluminum that revolutionized modern-day cooking, as it is lightweight, fairly strong, and an excellent conductor of heat. But aluminum also has distinct disadvantages, including reacting with acidic ingredients and heating unevenly, causing hot spots in a pan. Today's manufacturers have overcome the metal's drawbacks by alloying it with other metals, changing its chemical structure through anodizing, and coating pots and pans with nonreactive coatings. For more on cookware materials, turn to entry 18.

b SAUTÉ PAN
Sauté pans have high, angled handles and relatively high sides to help prevent food from bouncing out of the pan when it is being stirred, turned, or flipped. The sides can range from 2½–4 inches (6–10 cm) high, with 3 inches (7.5 cm) being the most popular. Sauté pans can measure from 6–14¼ inches (15–36 cm) in diameter, and volume capacities generally range from 1–7 quarts (1–7 litres), with 2½–4 quarts (2.5–4 litres) being the most useful for home cooks. Sauté pans often come with lids, which are useful for containing evaporation in recipes that call for long, gentle simmering. For this reason, sauté pans are also nicely suited to braises or any stove top recipes that call for large amounts of liquid.

c SAUCEPAN
This simple round pan has either straight or slightly sloping sides and generally ranges in size from 1–5 quarts (1–5 litres). If you are buying only one, consider a 2-quart (2-litre) saucepan, which is most versatile. The pans are designed to facilitate rapid evaporation so that a sauce thickens and cooks efficiently. Straight-sided pans with high sides are ideal for longer cooking, since the liquid will not evaporate as quickly. For more information on slant-sided saucepans, see entry 17d.

d DUTCH OVEN
Large, round or oval pots with tight-fitting lids and two loop handles, Dutch ovens are used for slow cooking methods like simmering and braising on top of the stove or in the oven. Dutch ovens range from 4–12 quarts (4–12 litres), but an 8- or 9-quart (8- or 9-litre) size is recommended for most home kitchens.

e STOCKPOT
Sometimes called a soup pot, a stockpot is a high, narrow pot designed for minimal evaporation during the long, slow cooking of stocks, soups, and stews. For the most efficient cooking, the pots should be made of heavy-gauge metal with a good heft. The smallest stockpots have an 8-quart (8 litre) capacity, although most home cooks find stockpots with 10- to 12-quart (10- to 12-litre) capacities to be the most useful. Stockpots can also be used to boil large quantities of water needed for cooking pasta, lobster, or corn on the cob.

f ROASTING PAN
This large, rectangular pan has low sides to allow the oven's heat to reach as much of the food as possible during roasting. For roasts and whole birds, choose a heavy-duty roasting pan to help keep the bottom of the food and the pan juices from burning. Although roasting pans with nonstick surfaces make cleanup easy, a regular cooking surface allows more brown bits to stick to the pan during roasting, which will yield a darker and more flavorful pan sauce or gravy.

g ROASTING RACKS
Placed inside a roasting pan to support a large piece of meat or a whole bird, a metal roasting rack keeps the bottom of the food from stewing in the pan drippings and allows more of the food to brown without the need for turning. It also encourages the formation of clearer pan drippings, which contributes to a flavorful pan sauce or gravy. A V-shaped roasting rack is useful for whole birds. An adjustable flat rack can be used for roasts or smaller items. Racks featuring nonstick coatings make cleanup easier.

COOKWARE

Specialty cookware

a BRAISER

Resembling a Dutch oven, a braiser is, as its name suggests, ideally suited to braising, or gently cooking smaller pieces of meat, poultry, or other ingredients in a relatively small amount of liquid. The gently sloping sides neatly confine the food being cooked in just the right amount of liquid, and the dome-shaped, tight-fitting lid accommodates a tall roast and encourages the steam that is generated inside the pan to slide down the lid and back into the pot, keeping the environment moist. Usually made of heavy metal, which retains heat, braisers are designed for effective browning on the stove top before the liquid is added, at which time the pan can be moved to the oven for gentle covered cooking.

b CRÊPE PAN

This shallow pan with gently flared sides and a long, flat handle enables you to cook thin crêpe batter quickly and evenly. Crêpe pans come in a variety of sizes, but a pan about 10 inches (25 cm) in diameter is the most popular and versatile. The flat handle is shaped so that you can rotate the pan easily during cooking, first to spread the melted butter over its surface, and then the batter. The shape also makes it easy to flip the crêpe during cooking.

c DOUBLE BOILER

A double boiler is a set of two pans, one nested atop the other, with a lid that fits both pans. Water is brought to a simmer in the lower pan, and delicate foods such as chocolate, custards, and cream sauces are cooked in the upper pan. Double boilers are also good for keeping foods warm without cooking them further—or at least not too quickly. A tight fit between the pans ensures that no water or steam mixes with the ingredients, which can cause melting chocolate to seize. In many double boiler sets, the lower pan can also be used on its own as a saucepan. If you don't have a double boiler, you can easily create one by placing a heat-resistant mixing bowl or slightly smaller saucepan over a larger saucepan, although it may not be as steady or the fit as tight.

d SAUCIER

This variation on a saucepan (see entry 16c) has short, outwardly sloping sides that promote rapid evaporation, making this pan perfect for making sauces, particularly reduction sauces. Some models also feature rounded edges to ensure that a roux does not get trapped in the pan's corners, where it can burn.

e GRIDDLE PAN

A flat pan made of cast iron or cast aluminum, often with a nonstick finish, a griddle pan sits flat on the stove top over one or two burners, depending on the size. Use it to cook pancakes, eggs, bacon, thin steaks, sandwiches, and other recipes that call for a broad, smooth surface and intense, even heat. Some griddle pans have depressions running around their rims to catch grease.

f GRILL PAN

A grill pan is a cast-iron or anodized aluminum skillet or griddle with ridges across its bottom, which deliver nicely browned marks resembling those from the cooking grid of an outdoor grill. Although the actual results are closer to pan-frying than grilling, grill pans have the advantage of draining off some of the fat from food, while also providing an attractive appearance. Some grill pans are designed for use in the broiler; others go on top of the stove, fitting over one or two burners, depending on their size.

g MULTIPURPOSE POT

This tall pot with a tight-fitting lid is outfitted with a perforated insert that holds up to 2 pounds (1 kg) of pasta, which can be lifted from the pot for easy draining. It also features a steamer insert for steaming large quantities of vegetables. Multipurpose pots usually have 6- or 8-quart (6- or 8-litre) capacities, making them smaller than stockpots (see entry 16e)—although they can be used for small batches of stock, soup, and stew as well. They are also excellent pots for blanching vegetables.

h PAELLA PAN

This large, round, shallow pan with two handles usually ranges from 13–14 inches (33–35 cm) in diameter. The size and shape, as well as the heavy metal from which it is traditionally made, make it ideal for cooking the eponymous rice dish from Spain's Valencia region, delivering results that are concentrated in flavor, with grains of rice that are tender yet chewy, featuring an appealing crust on the bottom of the pan.

i TAGINE

Bearing the same name as the traditional Moroccan stew cooked in it, this cooking vessel consists of a shallow circular pan and a conical lid that fits over the pan, designed to trap moisture and allow it to drip back onto the slowly cooking food. A small hole in the top of the pan allows some of the steam to escape without dripping onto the food. Tagines are traditionally made of glazed earthenware or other ceramics.

j WOK

This versatile Chinese pan is ideal for stir-frying, deep-frying, and steaming. Traditionally made of plain carbon steel, the wok has a rounded bottom that allows small pieces of food to be rapidly tossed and stirred. It also has high, gradually sloping sides to help keep food circulating inside the pan during stir-frying. In Western kitchens, round-bottomed woks are held in place over gas burners by a metal ring that allows the flames to rise and distribute heat around the pan. Woks with flat bottoms have also been developed to sit securely and distribute heat more efficiently on electric burners. Woks can have one long and one short handle, or two short handles, depending on the manufacturer. They are sometimes sold with a lid for steaming.

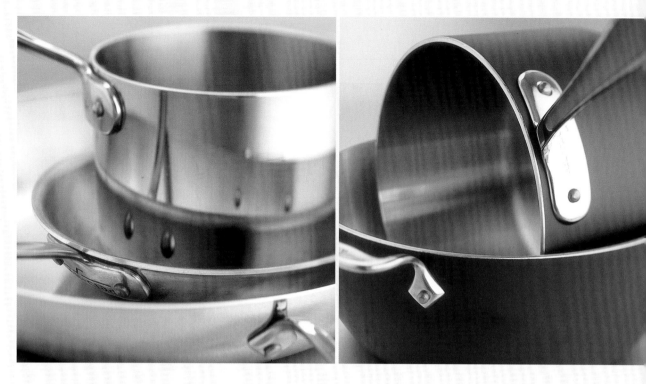

Cookware materials

Today's cookware comes in an array of materials far beyond the cast-iron and thin aluminum pans of the past. When outfitting your kitchen with pots and pans, keep in mind your cooking style and tolerance for cleaning in order to choose what will work best for your household.

a STAINLESS STEEL

Stainless steel is a favored material for cookware because of its extreme durability, beauty, and the fact that it is dishwasher safe. In addition, stainless steel does not corrode or react with acidic ingredients, and it is relatively resistant to sticking. That said, on its own, stainless steel can be a relatively poor conductor of heat, is prone to hot spots, and, over time, tends to warp. Cookware manufacturers have overcome the metal's drawbacks by bonding cores of aluminum to the bases of their pots and pans to achieve more rapid and uniform conduction of heat. Professional-grade stainless-steel cookware is durable, reliable, and can be less expensive than some other materials—perfect for cooks who are just beginning to stock their kitchen.

b ALUMINUM-CLAD STAINLESS STEEL

Aluminum is an excellent conductor of heat, but it reacts with acidic foods and tends to warp if used alone. By fusing a stainless-steel interior to a solid aluminum core, and finishing it with a hard anodized aluminum exterior, you get the best qualities of both metals in one pot. The stainless-steel interior won't corrode or react to acidic ingredients, while the double-layer of aluminum in the core and exterior helps distribute heat efficiently, making the pieces highly responsive to temperature changes. Aluminum-clad cookware does require a little more care than pure stainless steel pots and pans and hand washing is recommended. High-quality cookware should be relatively heavy, easy to lift, and have securely riveted, comfortable handles that are designed to stay cool.

c BONDED COPPER

This attractive cookware features multiple layers of metal that are bonded together for maximum efficiency. The interior layer of pure copper—a metal known for its rapid, even distribution of heat—is bonded between layers of stainless steel on both the cooking surface and the exterior of the pot. Copper can react to acidic substances, may cause some foods to stick, and takes a great deal of care to keep it gleaming. Sandwiching it between layers of stainless steel prevents these problems, as stainless steel is nonreactive, resists sticking, and gives the cookware a shiny finish without needing to polish it. Try to seek out a good-quality brand that continues the copper core all the way up the sides of the cookware, rather than just confining it to a disk in the bottom of the pot or pan. This feature ensures that the heat more fully surrounds the food, which is especially beneficial during moist-heat cooking, such as braising or stewing. Bonded copper pans, heavy by design to cook evenly and resist hot spots, require hand washing to keep them looking and performing at their best.

d NONSTICK COOKWARE

You'll find the same range of nonstick coating surfaces used for bakeware (see entry 5) on a wide array of cookware. Such surfaces are prized because they release foods cleanly and easily, which yields attractive results and quicker and easier cleanup. Since nonstick surfaces also require little if any fat, they are especially helpful in low-fat and nonfat cooking, perfect for a healthy lifestyle. In good-quality lines of nonstick cookware, alternating layers of aluminum and stainless steel regulate heat distribution, eliminating hot spots and ensuring precise temperature control, which is especially helpful when searing meat, poultry, or fish over high heat with little or no fat to create a well-browned crust. Many cookware manufacturers make pans with nonstick surfaces whose exteriors match those of their other cookware lines. This means you can assemble a set that looks the same, but has different attributes. It is important to have on hand tools specifically designed for use with nonstick cookware (see entry 15l) to ensure that you don't scratch their surfaces. Always wash nonstick cookware by hand with warm, soapy water and a nonabrasive sponge.

e COPPER

Copper is a highly sought after cookware material because it is an excellent conductor of heat, it warms up and cools down rapidly, and it distributes heat evenly, preventing hot spots. Because of copper's sensitivity to heat, it allows the cook maximum control over the final results of the cooked food, unlike with other cookware materials that retain heat and continue to cook the food, even when removed from the heat. Copper cookware must be lined to prevent the metal from reacting with acidic foods and to aid in stick resistance. In the past, tin was a traditional material for lining copper pans, but its low melting point and relative softness led to the modern practice of lining the pans with stainless steel. Despite all the cooking benefits and aesthetic appeal of copper cookware, it can be hard to care for because it scratches easily and needs to be polished to keep its luster. To clean copper cookware, use a soft cloth and a mild soap, then polish with a commercial copper cream. Heavy-duty, well-made copper pots and pans are expensive, but they will last through many generations if properly cared for.

f ANODIZED ALUMINUM

Cookware made of anodized aluminum (also called "hard-anodized aluminum") is known for its versatility: It is durable, heats evenly, resists sticking, and has excellent browning capabilities. The cookware is treated with an electrolytic process that makes the aluminum harder than stainless steel and denser than in its natural state. In addition, the anodizing process renders the aluminum nonreactive to acidic substances and the metal will not leach into cooking liquids. Anodized aluminum cookware, with its signature charcoal-gray color, is oven-safe, but it needs to be washed by hand; the detergents used in dishwashers can stain the surface of the pans, impact its luster and stick resistance, and affect the hardness of the surface. Prior to 1975, this type of cookware could only be found in restaurants and commercial kitchens. Today, anodized aluminum cookware is widely available and is a popular, and attractive choice in home kitchens. Recently, some manufacturers have introduced lines of anodized aluminum cookware with nonstick cooking surfaces, rendering them even more versatile.

g ENAMELED CAST IRON

Pots and pans made of enameled cast iron heat up slowly, but once hot, retain heat extremely well. Unlike traditional cast-iron pans (right), enameled cast-iron cookware does not require seasoning and it will not react with acidic foods or impart metallic flavors. The enamel-coated cooking surface is also stick resistant, so it is well suited for low-fat cooking. The brilliant exterior colors of the pans are usually bonded to a matte black enamel finish, which is then fused to the pan to provide better bonding of the surface enamel. This type of cookware can be used both on the stove top or in the oven, and is attractive enough to go from kitchen to table with style. Dutch ovens are perhaps the most popular choice in the enameled cast-iron format, but frying pans and casserole dishes are among other useful shapes available in this material. The enamel coating can scratch, so avoid using abrasive cleaning detergents and scouring pads. Light-colored cookware may darken with use, but with proper care, it should still perform well for many years.

h CAST IRON

Cast iron heats up slowly, but retains heat extremely well and distributes it uniformly, even at high temperatures. These properties make this cookware material an excellent choice for frying and searing foods. Some manufacturers suggest avoiding using acidic ingredients in cast-iron pans because they will react with the material, imparting an off flavor and color to foods. Cast iron pots and pans with the traditional, uncoated finish have been handed down in American families for generations, which attests to their durability. New pans require seasoning before use, a process in which they are heated several times while coated in cooking oil to help their cooking surfaces resist sticking. Some manufacturers also make a pre-seasoned line of cast iron cookware that has a ready-to-use stick-resistant finish. In addition to frying pans, you can also find ridged grill pans, griddles, Dutch ovens, and other pots and pans fashioned from cast iron. To prevent rusting and to maintain the pan's seasoning, dry the pans thoroughly right after washing, then rub a small amount of cooking oil all over the interior surface of the pan.

Cutlery & accessories

Knives are the most fundamental and versatile of cooking tools. With a well-made, keenly sharpened blade of the right size and shape, you can easily and efficiently complete almost any kitchen task. Start with a basic set of knives, then add more specialty knives as you determine your cutlery needs.

Basic knives

a PARING KNIFE

The small, evenly proportioned, tapered blade of this knife usually measures 3 or 4 inches (7.5 or 10 cm) in length. Use it for small-scale work such as peeling, coring, trimming, and slicing fruits and vegetables and for chopping small ingredients such as shallots. It is also useful to test cooking vegetables for doneness. The paring knife's pointed tip also makes it easy to do finely detailed work, such as trimming vegetables for garnishes. Because it is so easy to handle, many home cooks find paring knives among their favorite tools. The small size also means that some cooks use a paring knife in one hand while holding the ingredient being trimmed or peeled in the other, an approach that calls for extra caution.

b UTILITY KNIFE

Similar in appearance to a paring knife, this knife is slightly larger, with a blade measuring anywhere from 4½–8 inches (11.5–20 cm) long. As its name suggests, you can use a utility knife for a wider range of tasks than a paring knife, from peeling, slicing, mincing, and dicing to carving small cuts of meat or poultry and trimming them of fat. Some utility knives also include serrated edges, making them especially well suited for cutting through hard bread crusts, the tough skins of sausages, the dense interiors of cheeses, or delicately textured items like ripe tomatoes.

c BONING KNIFE

About the length of a utility knife, with a blade 5–7 inches (13–18 cm) long, this knife has a very narrow, curve-edged blade designed to maneuver easily around the bones, between the bone joints, and through the tendons and cartilage of raw poultry or meat. These features make a boning knife essential if you want to do this type of work at home, a more cost-effective approach to cooking than buying boneless cuts of meat or poultry. While you can use one boning knife for all these tasks, look for a stiffer blade if you tend to bone red meat more often, and a more flexible blade if you work more frequently with poultry. A boning knife, particularly one with a flexible blade, can stand in for a fillet knife (see entry 20c) in a pinch.

d CHEF'S KNIFE

Distinguished by a larger, evenly proportioned, tapered blade, also sometimes referred to as a cook's knife or a French knife, a chef's knife is used for a variety of kitchen tasks. The name underscores the fact that many professional chefs consider the chef's knife an indispensable tool, the one knife that every serious cook should have. Chef's knives range from 4–12 inches (10–30 cm) in length, with 8 inches (20 cm) being the most versatile. A slight curve on the cutting edge of the wide, rigid blade combined with the perfect weight balance between the handle and blade enables a rhythmic, highly efficient rocking motion on the work surface when slicing and chopping.

e SERRATED KNIFE

The sharp serrated edge of this long, straight blade, which can measure from 7½–12 inches (19–30 cm) long, cuts easily through both the tough crusts and tender interiors of bread loaves, yielding neat, clean, slices with a minimum of crumbs. Some cooks also like to use a serrated knife for such tasks as chopping chocolate or cutting tomatoes. The sharp serrated blade also makes it a breeze to cut through canned crushed tomatoes and citrus fruits.

f HONING STEEL

A honing steel is not actually a knife, but it is an important part of a basic knife set. Good cooks use it frequently to realign the sharp cutting edge and keep the knife working at its best. It is sometimes erroneously referred to as a "sharpening steel." For more on honing steels and sharpening and honing knives, turn to entries 185–187.

Caring for your knives

Fine cutlery should always be washed by hand, as a dishwasher will dull the knife blade and can cause the handle to deteriorate. After each use, carefully wash knives in warm, soapy water, then rinse and thoroughly dry them with a soft towel. Always store your knives in a knife storage block (see entry 24h) or in an in-drawer storage tray (see entry 24i). This will protect the blades and keep sharp edges safely covered. Wall-mounted racks, magnetic knife bars, or individual knife sheaths are other safe ways to store cutlery. Avoid storing your cutlery loose in a drawer or in containers with other utensils.

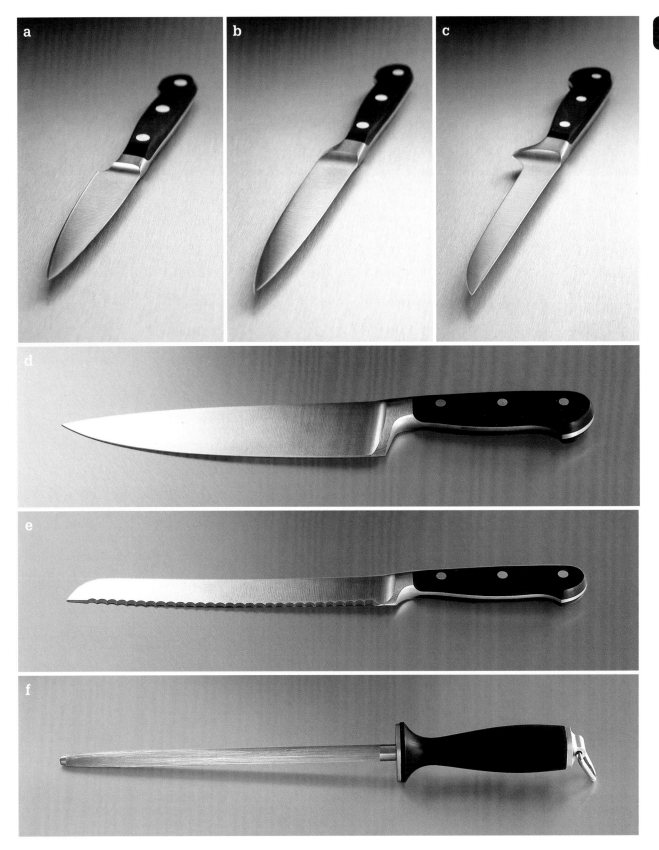

CUTLERY & ACCESSORIES

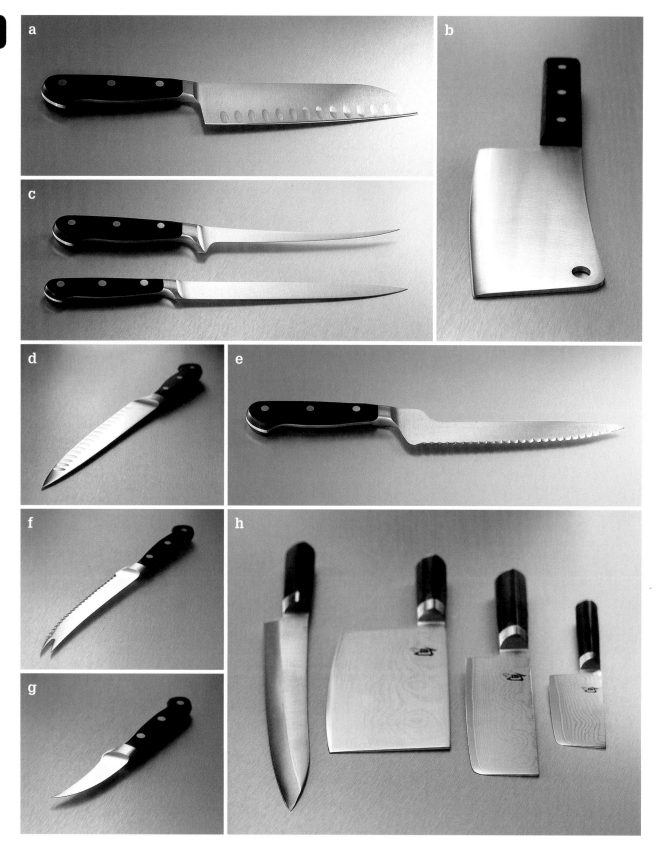

a

b

c

d

e

f

g

h

CUTLERY & ACCESSORIES

Specialty knives

a SANTOKU
The Japanese name of this increasingly popular kitchen knife means "three benefits," a reference to the fact that the multipurpose blade—which looks like a cross between a chef's knife and a cleaver—is equally adept at slicing, dicing, and mincing. Oval indentations on the blade reduce friction. For information on Japanese knives, see below and entry 23.

b CLEAVER
The large, heavy, rectangular blade of a cleaver is designed to make short work of splitting bones or chopping through cartilage when you're cutting up poultry, meats, or seafood. Some cooks like to use a cleaver when working with vegetables, particularly dense ones like carrots. Select a cleaver with a blade that feels heavier than you might first think is comfortable; the weight of the blade actually makes the task at hand easier, requiring less exertion. The broad surface of the blade also makes it convenient for scooping up generous quantities of the foods you just sliced or chopped to transfer to a bowl, pot, or pan.

c FILLET KNIVES
Resembling tapered boning knives, these knives are used for filleting raw fish. With their fine tips inserted between the bones and flesh, the very thin, highly flexible, well-honed blades are adept at following the contours of whole seafood. If you enjoy working with fish at home, consider purchasing a fillet knife with a highly pointed tip, which is also helpful for cleaning fish. Most fish filleting knives measure 6–8 inches (15–20 cm) long, with blades generally no wider than ½ inch (12 mm).

d SLICING KNIFE
This long, slender, fairly flexible blade is well adapted to carving small, tender main courses such as roast poultry and whole fish. It's also good for cutting neat slices of fruits and vegetables and for cutting bread and fillings for sandwiches.

The most useful, popular sizes have blades that measure 6–10 inches (15–25 cm) long. You'll find some slicing knives made with hollow-ground depressions on their cutting edges that help prevent sticking as the blade cuts through ingredients.

e OFFSET BREAD KNIFE
This knife has an extra-long serrated blade for slicing neatly through crusty country loaves. In contrast to a regular serrated knife, this model features an offset handle that provides extra knuckle clearance, while its scalloped edge allows you to slice cleanly through even the crustiest bread without tearing or squashing it.

f TOMATO KNIFE
With a razor-sharp, serrated blade 4½–5 inches (11.5–13 cm) long, a tomato knife cleanly cuts through the skin of even the ripest of tomatoes as well as through its flesh, yielding even slices, both thick or thin. Some tomato knives also have forked tips, making it easy to pick up and serve delicate tomato slices without having them fall apart.

g BIRD'S BEAK PARING KNIFE
In this specialized variation of the classic paring knife (see entry 19a), this short, 2–3 inch (5–7.5 cm) blade curves downward toward its tip, on both the cutting and top edges, in a way that resembles the elongated beak of a bird. In classical French cooking, this shape facilitates cutting and trimming vegetables into neat, uniform oblongs for garnishing, a shape referred to as *tournée*, or "turned." In today's kitchens, the knife's shape makes it convenient for peeling fruits and vegetables because it easily follows their curves.

h JAPANESE KNIVES
Master Japanese craftspeople have, over the centuries, developed knives that are particularly suited to the preparation of their country's cuisine. With the growing popularity of Japanese cooking abroad, home cooks everywhere have discovered the virtues of these knives, including their superbly sharp blades, as well as adaptability to a wide range of Western-style culinary tasks.

Yanigiba knife (left) Popular among Japanese sushi chefs, this knife's long, slender blade slices effortlessly. The cutting edge is beveled on one side for an incredibly sharp cutting surface, gliding through delicate raw fish without sticking or tearing.

Cleaver (middle) Asian cooks do everything with a cleaver, far beyond simply cutting meat and poultry. A lightweight cleaver, such as this one, is perfect for working with vegetables and fruits, particularly those with hard or tough shells or skins.

Nakiri knife (right and middle right) This all-purpose knife is shaped like a slender cleaver. It can be used for a wide variety of tasks, including chopping, slicing, and mincing fresh produce. The blade ranges from 4–8 inches (10–20 cm) long.

Choosing knives

Whether you choose Western- or Eastern-style knives (see entry 23), the knives should feel comfortable and relatively heavy in your hand. Before deciding which to purchase, hold a range of different knives to find those that feel balanced, and seem like an extension of your own hand. If you purchase the knives as a set, you may also want to buy some individual knives for specific tasks. Having more than one chef's knife is a good idea, too, so that friends or family can help with the prep work.

Cutting surfaces

Opinions diverge on whether wood or plastic cutting boards are superior, but steer clear of those made from marble or glass, which can dull your knives. For the most versatility, choose cutting boards that measure at least 12 by 18 inches (30 by 45 cm). To limit the transfer of food-borne bacteria to different foods, consider reserving one cutting board for meat, poultry, and seafood, and a second for vegetables, fruits, and other uses.

a WOODEN CUTTING BOARDS
The best wooden cutting boards are made of maple, oak, cherry, birch, and walnut—all hardwoods with a long life. Bamboo is also a beautiful—and increasingly popular—material for cutting boards. Carefully clean all cutting boards after each use and store them away from heat, which can cause even heavy wood to warp and split. Every month or two, sanitize wooden cutting boards with a mild solution of 4 cups (32 fl oz/1 litre) warm water mixed with 1 teaspoon bleach, rinse well, and let air dry.

b PLASTIC CUTTING BOARD
When looking for a plastic cutting board, seek out one made of polypropylene. This nonporous substance resists penetration of dirt or food juices that could lead to bacterial growth. In addition, polypropylene boards are dishwasher safe, so you can sanitize them after each use.

c CARVING BOARD
Carving boards are made from the same range of hardwoods as wooden cutting boards, but they have a groove around their perimeters to capture meat or poultry juices as they are being carved. Many also feature an indentation in one side that prevents a roast from slipping while you carve it.

Sharpeners & honing devices

a HONING STEEL
Also called a sharpening steel or a butcher's steel, this tool is an important part of a basic knife set, where it is used not to sharpen knives, but rather to maintain the edge of an already sharp knife between uses.

Caring for wooden boards

Before using a new wooden cutting board, rub it with food-grade mineral oil to season it. Use a paper towel to spread a thin layer of oil over the wood. Rub it with fine steel wool and then let it soak in for 5 or 10 minutes. Wipe the board dry with a soft cloth or paper towel. Repeat this seasoning process once a month for 10 to 12 months. After this time, oil the board periodically, especially if it appears dry. Never let a wooden board soak or put it in the dishwasher.

Metal (bottom) Resembling a short, heavy, rounded spear attached to a sturdy handle, with a metal hand guard in between, this device is made of extremely hard, magnetized steel. Its surface, which tapers to a rounded point, is covered in very fine grooves that perfectly align the cutting edge of a knife when the entire length of the blade is drawn from tip to handle. For information on honing a knife, turn to entry 187.

Ceramic (top) A ceramic steel is favored by many for honing Japanese knives and other delicate blades with its fine-grit honing surface.

b ELECTRIC SHARPENER
This machine consists of a series of precisely angled slots that, in turn, sharpen and hone a knife's cutting edge and then polish it to absolute smoothness. Some models are specially designed for sharpening Japanese knives and serrated knives.

c WHETSTONE
You can hone a knife's cutting edge to razor sharpness with one of these sharpening devices. Soak the ceramic block in water for about 15 minutes. Then, holding the knife's cutting edge at a constant 15- to 20-degree angle to the whetstone, draw the blade repeatedly back and forth across the stone, alternating sides. (You'll know you're maintaining the right angle if the sound produced by the blade as it moves across the stone remains unchanged.) Some models include a clip that fits on the back of the blade to ensure a consistent angle. The fine, wet powder that develops on the stone only adds to its sharpening power. When the edge is fine and smooth, wash the knife with hot water and dry it thoroughly. For more information on using a whetstone or oilstone, turn to entry 185.

d OILSTONE
Used precisely in the same way as a whetstone (above), this natural rectangular stone is lubricated with mineral oil instead of water, which activates the stone's surface. Be sure to wash and dry knives thoroughly after sharpening with an oilstone.

e HANDHELD SHARPENER
This manual device sharpens knives by pulling the blades at a fixed angle through two sets of grinding surfaces: a coarse set for creating a sharp edge on a dull blade and a fine set to hone and finish the edge. Some models can also be used to sharpen scissors. Look for a comfortable handle and nonslip rubber feet to ensure steadiness as you sharpen.

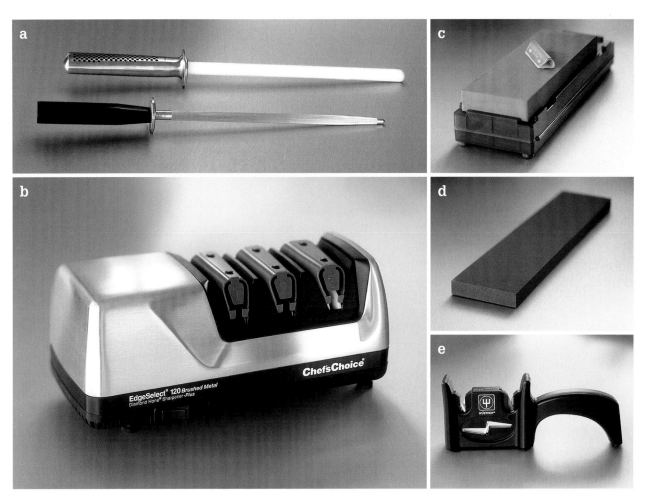

CUTLERY & ACCESSORIES

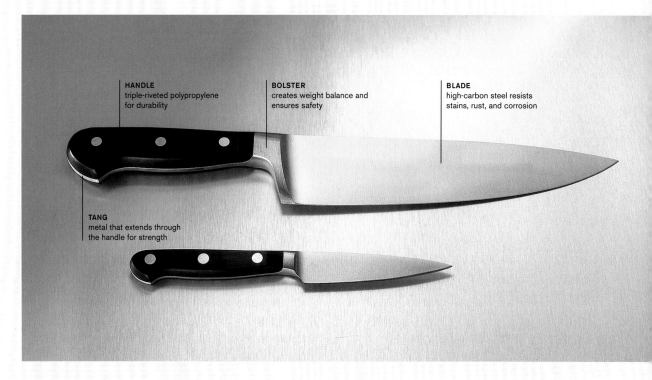

HANDLE
triple-riveted polypropylene
for durability

BOLSTER
creates weight balance and
ensures safety

BLADE
high-carbon steel resists
stains, rust, and corrosion

TANG
metal that extends through
the handle for strength

Knife construction
Germany and Japan represent two traditions of quality craftsmanship in cutlery. Western-style German knives are perhaps more familiar to the average home cook, but Eastern-style Japanese knives are becoming increasingly popular. Following is a primer on their respective traits.

a WESTERN-STYLE KNIVES

A Western-style knife has four main parts: the blade, the bolster, the handle, and the tang. Each is specially constructed for balance and precision.

A Western knife's blade has two edges: the sharp cutting edge and the spine on top. Most blades taper from the heel end, near the handle, to the pointed tip. The raised area between the handle and the blade is called the bolster, which provides a center of gravity for strength and balance. It also serves as a safety guard for fingers and makes the knife more comfortable to hold. The handle of the knife should fit securely and comfortably in your hand. The tang is the metal extension of the blade enclosed by the handle. Made from a single piece of steel, a full or partial tang provides strength and stability and balances the knife.

The process of making a good Western-style knife begins with a single piece of metal, which is forged, then shaped to taper evenly from the spine to the cutting edge and from the handle to the tip. The best knives, arguably, are made from high-carbon stain-resistant steel or steel alloy. These blades hold a keen edge, yet they are soft enough to be sharpened. Knives are said to have a "full tang" when the metal from which the knife is formed extends the entire length of the handle and follows its shape. Some manufacturers feel a three-quarter or rat-tail tang, a narrow shaft that runs the length of the handle, is adequate for balance and heft. The most durable handles on Western knives are made of polypropylene that is triple riveted through the tang, or permanently bonded around it. Fine cutlery should always be washed by hand.

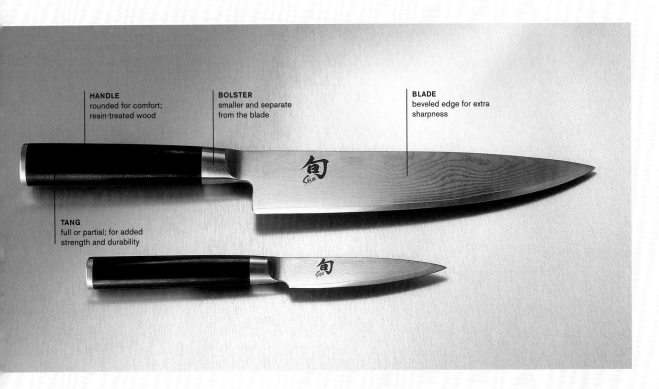

HANDLE
rounded for comfort;
resin-treated wood

BOLSTER
smaller and separate
from the blade

BLADE
beveled edge for extra
sharpness

TANG
full or partial; for added
strength and durability

b EASTERN-STYLE KNIVES

Like Western knives, Eastern-style knives consist of a blade, a bolster, a handle, and a tang, but the construction is noticeably different.

A Japanese knife blade often features a beveled edge, which makes it extraordinarily sharp. The blades on fish knives—fish is an important part of Japanese cuisine—tend to be very long, allowing you to use fluid slicing motions to take advantage of the blade's full length. The bolster is smaller on a Japanese knife and is separate from the blade, which enables you to sharpen the knife blade all the way to its heel. It is common for the handles of Japanese knives to be rounded in shape to fit comfortably in your hand. An end cap on some brands of knives assists the bolster in providing balance for the knife. The tang can be full or partial, depending on the manufacturer and style of knife.

Knife making in Japan is a legacy of the Samurai sword-making tradition, in which very hard, but flexible steel is forged and then hand ground to make ultrasharp blades. The handles are made either from a resin-treated wood that resists water, or simply an extension of the metal blade with a textured surface for an enhanced grip. Some Japanese knives are stamped pieces of metal mounted on wood handles. When they wear out, the blades can be replaced with new ones.

Because of the differences in construction, Asian knives should be sharpened with tools especially designed for them or sharpened by a professional. When using a honing steel on an Asian knife, it is recommended that you use an angle of 15 degrees in order to maintain the ideal edge.

In traditional Asian cultures, each knife shape is designed for a particular purpose (for more on Japanese knife shapes, turn to entries 20a and 20h). Today, Eastern knife manufacturers are also making knives in shapes that resemble traditional Western models. But no matter which knife style you choose, consider the following criteria to help in your decision: The knife should be made by a manufacturer with a reputation for quality; it should feel relatively heavy but balanced in your hand; it should be made of solid materials that resist rust and corrosion; and finally, the knife should hold a keen edge.

CUTLERY & ACCESSORIES

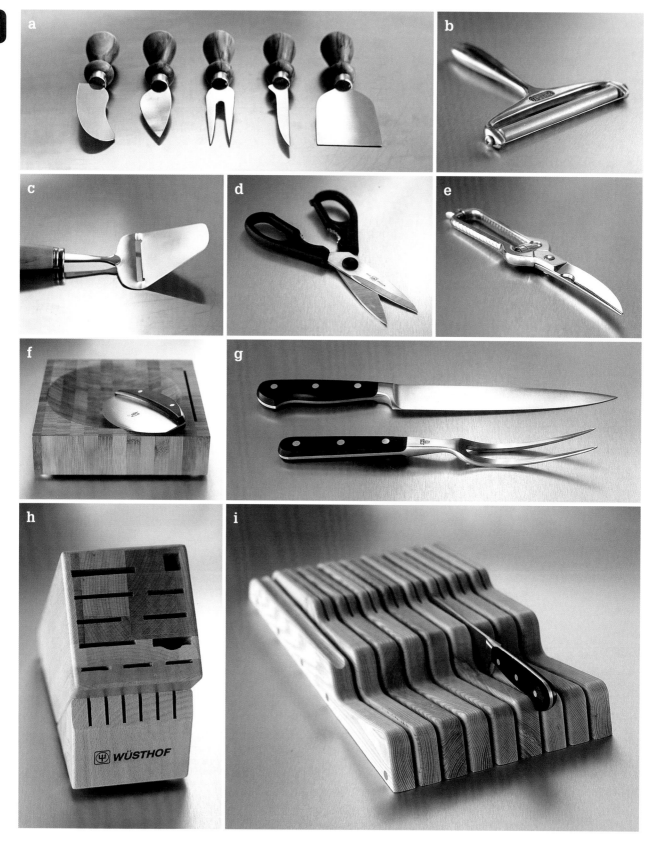

CUTLERY & ACCESSORIES

Other cutlery and accessories

a CHEESE KNIVES

If you enjoy serving cheese, either as an hors d'oeuvre or after dinner, consider investing in a set of specialized cheese knives. Each knife is constructed to ease the cutting of a specific type of cheese. **Spatula or spreading knife (far left)** The curve-tipped, wide blade of this knife is ideal for cutting and spreading soft cheeses such as Brie or Camembert. **Parmesan knife (middle left)** With its elongated heart shape, the short, sharp, sturdy blade of this knife cuts easily through hard cheeses, including classic Parmigiano-Reggiano. **Serving fork (middle)** This tool is used to steady blocks of hard cheese for cutting, as well as to transfer cheese pieces to individual serving plates. **Thin blade (middle right)** This low-profile blade is used for cutting portions of semi-soft or crumbly cheeses such as Gorgonzola or Roquefort. **Wide blade (far right)** Used with a downward motion like a chisel, the wide blade is best suited to cutting semihard cheeses such as Emmenthaler.

b WIRE CHEESE CUTTER

Try this device for cutting firm to semi-soft cheeses, such as Parmigiano-Reggiano or Monterey Jack. Its thin, Y-shaped handle is fitted with a taut wire that glides smoothly through the cheese.

c CHEESE PLANE

The rounded or triangular blade of a cheese plane has a slot near its handle with a sharp edge capable of shaving cheese as the plane is pulled across its surface. The device does a good job with semifirm cheeses such as Cheddar or Gruyère, but it will not work well on soft cheeses such as fresh mozzarella (for those, use a thin, sharp knife). Take care to buy a good-quality model with a blade that will not bend when you exert pressure while shaving slices. You can also use a cheese plane to effectively remove dry or moldy bits from pieces of cheese with little waste.

d KITCHEN SHEARS

Sometimes called kitchen scissors, these heavy-duty clippers come in handy for tasks as varied as cutting sheets of parchment (baking) paper, lengths of kitchen string, or pieces of cheesecloth (muslin), as well as for cutting up fresh herbs, pieces of fruit, or even flowers. Basic kitchen shears should have sturdy stainless-steel blades to help them cut more efficiently and cleanly through a wide variety of ingredients.

e POULTRY SHEARS

These specialized kitchen shears have heavier-duty, longer blades. The slightly curved points will help you reach into and cut through awkward poultry joints to create serving portions, a process that is much easier accomplished with shears than with a knife. Poultry shears also make quick work of cutting out the backbone of poultry, so the bird can be grilled flat, and for cutting up poultry carcasses to make stock. Many poultry shears also include a curved notch in one blade located close to the hinge. This notch enables the shears to get a better grip on poultry bones while allowing you optimum leverage to cut through the bones with minimal effort. Look for models with a strong spring mechanism and that lock closed for increased safety and easy storage.

f MEZZALUNA

Meaning "half-moon" in Italian, the mezzaluna features a curved, crescent-shaped blade that helps you chop herbs and small vegetables quickly, safely, and easily, especially when used in conjunction with a shallow wooden bowl or a board with a deep, rounded impression in the center. Some models have a wooden handle at each end, allowing you to grip them with both hands and cut in a rocking motion; others have a single handle bridging the two ends, which you can grip with one hand and rock or hold to chop up and down. Some models have a double set of blades.

g CARVING KNIFE & FORK

If you cook and serve whole roasts and birds on a regular basis, a carving knife and fork—sold as a set—are convenient tools to have on hand. While an all-purpose slicing knife may be used for carving any type of roast, different knives are better suited to some roasts than others; so look for a set with a blade that best suits your preferences. One with a long, flexible, but still sturdy blade is best for following the contours of a large turkey. A shorter, sturdier knife makes quick work of smaller chickens. Long, straight blades with scalloped edges cut more readily through red meats. Choose a set with a sturdy, two-pronged carving fork that will hold whatever you've cooked steady as you carve. The fork is also useful for picking up and serving the sliced meat or poultry.

h KNIFE STORAGE BLOCK

Knives should never be stored loose in kitchen drawers or in receptacles with other utensils. Such practices can result in both injuries to your hands and the dulling or nicking of your blades. Sturdy wooden knife blocks with slots for a variety of different-sized blades sit on a kitchen counter at an angle and hold your knives within easy reach. Look for blocks with horizontal slots, so that the blades will not slide and rest on their cutting edges, dulling them; or, if you've selected a block with vertical slots, slide in the knives with their cutting edges facing upward. Look for a block that includes a square slot into which a honing steel can fit.

i KNIFE STORAGE TRAY

If your kitchen counter space is at a premium, an in-drawer knife storage tray is an excellent alternative to a block. Designed to fit into most standard-sized kitchen drawers, its slots are designed to accommodate blades and handles in a wide range of sizes and shapes, keeping your knives conveniently and safely within reach just below the kitchen counter.

Electrics
From basic food-preparation tasks such as slicing, chopping, puréeing, and blending, to more specialized kitchen purposes such as making coffee, steaming rice, or slowly simmering a stew, a wide range of modern electric appliances offer unparalleled convenience and outstanding results.

Blenders, mixers & food processors

a FOOD PROCESSOR

Efficient, powerful, and capable of performing a wide variety of functions in the kitchen, the food processor has become so popular since its widespread introduction in the 1970s and 1980s that recipe writers today commonly assume that every kitchen has one. Most models consist of a vertical-sided circular work bowl that sits atop a motorized base. Various disks and blades fit into the center of the bowl, to be turned by a rapidly rotating shaft. The all-purpose, S-shaped stainless-steel blade chops, blends, mixes, and purées. Other attachments include disks for shredding, grating, or slicing; a plastic blade for kneading dough; and a disk for cutting julienne strips. A feed tube in the lid that fits snugly over the work bowl enables you to add ingredients while the food processor is running. You simply add ingredients to the tube and use the plunger to gently push them down onto the cutting surfaces of the disks. If you plan to mix dense dough, make sure your processor's motor is powerful enough, or the motor may dangerously overheat.

b MINI PREP

A compact version of a food processor, the mini prep is ideal for handling smaller-scale tasks in lesser quantities than a full-sized food processor, such as chopping fresh herbs or grinding nuts.

c BLENDER

A blender consists of a heavy metal or plastic base that contains an electric motor. A tall, narrow container sits on top of the base, allowing the motor to spin a small propeller-type blade at the bottom of the container. The containers can handle a greater volume of liquid than a food processor, typically 5–8 cups (40–64 fl oz/1.25–2 litres). Most blenders have lids with removable center caps that let you pour in liquid while the motor is running. The blender is an excellent appliance for puréeing soups and blending cold drinks such as milkshakes or fruit smoothies. You can also use a blender to chop herbs or transform bread into crumbs. Choose a model with a strong motor and a glass jar, which won't absorb flavors or odors and transfer them to other preparations. Blenders can have as many as 16 or more speeds, although some, including many super-powered bar blenders, have only 2 speeds.

d IMMERSION BLENDER

Also called a hand or stick blender, an immersion blender features a powerful blade at the end of a long shaft, which enables you to immerse the blade into a container to blend ingredients without needing to transfer them to a blender or food processor. Immersion blenders usually have just 2 speeds, and the blade must be completely immersed in the food to prevent spattering. Some also have whisk attachments or small containers for blending small amounts of food.

e HANDHELD MIXER

This small, light, portable machine can be used with nearly any bowl or pan, even those set over a pan of simmering water on the stove top. It works well for mixing most batters and soft doughs, but will not work well with stiff bread or pizza doughs. Handheld mixers usually come with a set of detachable twin beaters for all-purpose mixing as well as a whip for incorporating maximum air into egg whites and cream.

f STAND MIXER

This stationary, motor-driven electric mixer is good for combining large amounts of food and heavy batters. The basic set of attachments usually includes one or more stainless steel work bowls, which lock securely to the base; a wire whisk for beating egg whites or whipping cream; a paddle for creaming butter and sugar and mixing batters; and a dough hook for kneading bread dough. You can extend the versatility of a top-of-the-line model with a range of accessories that use the motor's powerful action to slice or shred; grind meat and stuff sausages; extrude or cut fresh pasta dough; juice citrus fruit; or even make ice cream.

Outfitting your kitchen

Stocking a kitchen with an array of tools and equipment that are useful for the way you cook is a lifelong process. Once you have acquired the basics, you may wish to add a few extra items. But base these choices on the things you enjoy preparing, rather than what you think you ought to have. Gadgets, as opposed to tools, will quickly lose their initial appeal, while poorly made equipment will wear out or break. If you invest in quality tools and equipment at the outset, they will likely last for years.

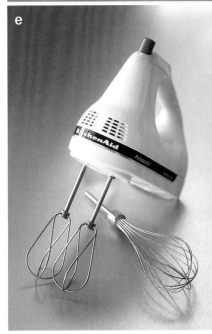

ELECTRICS

ELECTRICS

Specialty electrics

a COFFEE MACHINES

Coffee grinder (left) Seek out a grinder with a propeller-type blade that actually chops roasted coffee beans into ever-finer particles the longer you hold down the button. Many cooks keep a separate grinder for grinding spices.

Drip coffee maker (middle) Look for a good-quality electric coffee maker offering a range of features that best suit your needs, which can include a timer and a brew pause feature that halts the drip process. Some models replace the glass carafe with a vacuum bottle that keeps the coffee hot for hours.

Espresso machine (right) Try to find a machine that automatically heats water to the ideal brewing temperature and pumps it at high pressure through its metal filter filled with finely ground coffee. Good models come with interchangeable filters that yield both single and double shots, as well as a steam nozzle and stainless-steel pitcher for frothing milk.

b CONVECTION OVEN

A countertop convection oven offers a powerful fan that circulates precisely heated air through thermostat control. The result is a perfect baking setting for cookies, pizzas, and other pastries and breads, and quicker, more even roasting for poultry and meats.

c DEEP FRYER

Modern deep fryers eliminate much of the guesswork, mess, and fear home cooks used to experience when cooking French fries, calamari, and tempura. Models that control the oil temperature precisely are ideal for optimum cooking results and safety, has a sturdy base to keep it sitting securely on the kitchen counter, and includes a lid that guards against splattering and controls odors.

d INDOOR GRILL

With a heavy cast-aluminum cooking grid heated to searing temperatures by an electric element, this countertop grill enables you to achieve results similar to those delivered by an outdoor grill, including a well-browned surface with perfect grill marks.

e ELECTRIC CITRUS JUICER

If you use a large amount of citrus juice in your kitchen, consider purchasing an electric citrus juicer. It features a metal or plastic reamer that, when pressed, rotates rapidly to extract the juice of a citrus half. Look for a model that can accommodate both small limes and large grapefruits as well as everything in between.

f PANINI PRESS

Functioning like a waffle iron (below), this counter top device makes it easy to prepare the crisp, hot-pressed, Italian-style sandwiches known as panini, as well as other grilled sandwiches. Two ridged, heated nonstick plates cook the sandwiches from both sides at once, while the top portion is weighted to help flatten the sandwich. The best models have an adjustable hinge to accommodate different shapes and thicknesses. Also look for variable heat controls and an adjustable angle that allows fat to drain away into a grease tray, letting you use the press as a countertop grill.

g RICE COOKER

Also called a rice steamer, this appliance takes the guesswork out of cooking rice. The cooker, which sits on your kitchen counter, is fitted with an insert into which you pour measured amounts of rice and water before setting the timer. Some models also include additional inserts for steaming other vegetables. Depending on their size, rice cookers typically can prepare anywhere from 2–24 cups (10 oz–7.5 lb/315 g–375 kg) of rice.

h SLOW COOKER

Ranging in size from 1–7 quarts (1–7 litres), these handy covered electric pots slowly cook moist dishes such as stews, soups, and braises using their built-in heating elements, allowing safe, unattended slow cooking. Fill a slow cooker in the morning with soup or stew ingredients, set the timer and the heat level, and come home to a ready-to-eat hot meal. Newer models feature a removable insert that lets you brown meats, poultry, or vegetables on the stove top before returning it to the base for the hours-long cooking process, letting you contribute additional flavor.

i TOASTER

Toasters function very simply, lowering sliced bread into slots with heating coils on both sides, which quickly and evenly brown the surfaces. Look for a toaster that's solidly built, as the coils on less expensive models can come loose over time, causing uneven toasting. Most toasters include dials that let you adjust the heat level or toasting time. For bagels, look for a toaster with extra-wide slots that can accommodate their thickness.

j WAFFLE IRON

Waffle irons come in a variety of shapes, including squares, circles, and hearts, and some models have extra-deep grids for Belgian-style waffles. Most of today's waffle irons feature nonstick surfaces, making them much easier to use. Do not immerse an electric waffle iron in water, and do not wash the grids after use; simply brush out any crumbs still clinging to the grid or wipe the cooled machine with a paper towel.

k ICE CREAM MAKER

Lovers of frozen desserts find electric ice cream makers indispensable. Models range from sophisticated (and costly) units that both freeze and churn ice cream, sorbets, and other frozen desserts electronically to more simple types that use a refrigerant-filled work bowl that you prechill in the freezer. The latter requires a bit of planning, but after filling the bowl with your dessert mixture and putting it inside the appliance, an electric motor churns it to the desired smooth, frozen consistency.

Grilling tools

Many food enthusiasts love the beautiful, smoky, flavorful results they get from cooking food outdoors over an open fire. Grilling is often portrayed as a simplistic cooking method, although this is far from the truth. This techinque calls for know-how, skill, good recipes, and, as always, the rights tools for the tasks at hand.

Basic grilling tools

The two most popular types of outdoor grills are the propane- or natural gas–fueled gas grill, and the kettle-type charcoal grill. These grills work for both direct-heat grilling (cooking foods over high, direct heat in an uncovered grill) or indirect-heat cooking (cooking food by reflected heat in a covered grill). A gas grill's advantages are that the heat can be controlled by simply adjusting a dial and that cleanup is relatively easy. A charcoal grill is preferred by some for its ability to reach high temperatures and the desirable, smoky flavor imparted by the charcoal or hardwood fuel it uses. Purists believe that smoking should only be done on a charcoal grill, but many cookbooks feature modified recipes that allow you to smoke foods on a gas grill as well.

a GAS GRILL

A gas grill can be fueled by a natural-gas line run from your home or by propane in refillable tanks. The flames of a gas grill burn under a bed of heat-absorbent crushed lava rocks or ceramic briquettes, which turn red-hot and cook food placed on the rack or grid above them. More sophisticated models include multiple controls, allowing you to heat only parts of the bed for indirect-heat cooking, separate burners for cooking sauces or heating griddles, and built-in metal boxes that hold and heat wood chips for smoking. If you want to cook especially large cuts of meat or poultry, choose a grill with a high hood, which turns the grill into an outdoor oven, and includes a rotisserie attachment that lets you cook food on a spit that rotates above the cooking rack or grid. Some models also come with a narrow raised rack at the back of the grill that keeps food warm, and a cabinet underneath that conceals the propane tank.

b CHARCOAL GRILL

Consisting of a metal pan that holds a bed of glowing charcoal beneath a metal rack or grid, charcoal grills come in many shapes and sizes. These include the small, inexpensive, cast-iron Japanese hibachi and the flat-bottomed brazier, which starred in many backyard barbecues in the 1950s. More versatile than the brazier is the popular kettle grill, which has a deep, hemispherical fire pan and domed cover that makes it fuel efficient and suitable for cooking with direct or indirect heat. Vents on the fire pan and cover allow for control of the fire's temperature. Charcoal briquettes are the most widely available fuel choice for charcoal grills. These compact, uniform, pillow-shaped lumps of fuel are made by compressing pulverized charcoal with binding agents and additives that facilitate lighting and burning. They are easy to use, providing steady, spark-free heat, but the binding agents they include can give grilled food an unpleasant taste if not used correctly. Hardwood charcoal, which is also sold in bags, makes a hotter, cleaner-burning fire than briquettes. Be aware that using hardwood charcoal requires extra caution, since it may throw off some sparks when first lit. Hardwood briquettes are made from lumps of fragrant hardwood such as hickory, alder, oak, apple, pecan, cherry, or mesquite, burned until almost pure carbon. Choose relatively small, uniform pieces to ensure that the charcoal heats evenly.

c CHIMNEY STARTER

If you grill frequently over charcoal, you should have a chimney starter. Resembling a large coffee can with a handle and holes circling the bottom, it lights coals quickly without the use of lighter fluid. Newspaper is stuffed into the bottom of the chimney to create kindling, then charcoal briquettes or hardwood charcoal chunks are piled on top. When the newspaper is lit, the flame burns upward inside the chimney, igniting the charcoal. For more on using a chimney starter, turn to entry 164.

Caring for your grill

Grills are low-maintenence tools, but they do require some attention. With regular care, high-quality grills will cook efficiently and cleanly for years. After cooking, while the grill is still hot, use a long-handled wire brush to scrape off any food particles stuck to the rack. Cover the grill and allow the dying coals or gas flames to burn off the residue. Don't let ashes accumulate in a charcoal grill; clean out the fire bed often. Wait until the ashes are completely cold, scoop them out, and discard in a nonflammable container. Always consult the owners' manual that comes with the grill before cooking on it for the first time. Be sure to note the proper cleaning instructions and clean the grill regularly.

GRILLING TOOLS

GRILLING TOOLS

Grilling accessories

a LONG-HANDLED TOOL SET

Although grill cooks employ some of the same kinds of tools they use inside the kitchen to baste, lift, turn, and serve food, the intense heat of the grill and the often large or cumbersome items cooked on it make it necessary to have a separate set of tools specifically designed for outdoor use. These are distinguished by extra-long, heatproof handles, coupled with sturdy construction. Many grill tool sets include leather loops at the end of their handles, which let you hang them conveniently close to the grill, or carrying and storage cases that enable you to handle the tools easily.

Tongs (left) Grill tongs should be long and extra sturdy to give you a good, safe grip on heavy or unwieldy cuts of meat, poultry, or vegetables. For charcoal grilling, be sure to have a second set of tongs that are reserved specifically for moving the coals around the fire bed.

Spatula (middle) Choose a spatula with a wider, longer blade than you might use on the stove top. A sturdy model is handy not only for flipping burgers, steaks, fish fillets, or chops, but is also useful to free food from the grill rack when it sticks.

Fork (right) Two-pronged grill forks are useful for moving and turning large or awkwardly shaped pieces of food on the grill. Be careful not to puncture the food too deeply with the prongs, causing a loss of juices. Some grill sets also feature long-handled basting brushes for applying marinades and glazes to food as it cooks. Choose a wide brush with natural or heatproof silicone bristles. Avoid brushes with plastic bristles, which will likely melt in the grill's intense heat.

b GRILLING MITT

To shield not just your hand but also your wrist and forearm from the grill's heat, look for mitts made from thick, flame-retardant materials with extra-long cuffs. Some grill cooks are also discovering the merits of long mitts made from heat-resistant silicone, which withstands temperatures up to 500°F (260°C).

c GRILL-CLEANING BRUSH

The best tool for cleaning a grill is a stiff, rustproof wire brush, which can be used either before or after cooking, when the grill is hot, to remove any residue. The tool's long handle keeps your hand and arm far from the heat source. Some models also include a sturdy, angled metal plate, which you can use to scrape clinging bits from the individual rods of the cooking grid. Some grill-cleaning tools also feature a wire mesh or cellulose pad on the reverse side of the brush for scrubbing off any stubborn, cooked-on foods from the grill grate. It's best to use this side of the grill brush when the grill is cooling off and the heat is not as intense.

d FISH BASKET

Shaped to fit the profile of a large, whole fish, this hinged, two-piece wire grid attached to a long handle latches shut over fish fillets or whole fish to hold them securely on the grill and make them easy to cook and turn without falling apart.

e VEGETABLE BASKET

Use this hinged wire grid, which comes in a range of sizes and shapes, to grill small vegetables such as asparagus, mushrooms, or cherry tomatoes, which might otherwise fall into the fire.

f SMOKER BOX

This small metal box is perforated with holes and has a tight-fitting lid. Fill it with wood chips that you've presoaked in liquid, or with other aromatics such as dried herbs, then place it directly on the lava rocks, ceramic briquettes, or lit coals to add smoky flavor to foods cooked on your gas grill. If you don't have a smoker box, an aluminum foil packet can hold the chips. For more information on using wood chips, turn to entries 162 and 163.

g SKEWERS

Depending on the particular types of recipes you're preparing, you can choose from large or small skewers that are made from metal or bamboo.

Metal (left) Invest in sturdy stainless-steel skewers if you grill brochettes or kebabs frequently. Wide, flattened skewers and double-pronged models provide extra support, preventing pieces of food from spinning on the skewer when you need to turn them on the grill.

Bamboo (right) Bamboo skewers are simple and inexpensive, come in a variety of lengths, and are well suited to small kebabs and Asian recipes, such as satay, that cook for just a short time. Bamboo skewers tend to burn during grilling, but soaking them in a pan or dish of water for about 30 minutes before using them will lessen this tendency.

h WOOD CHIPS

Scattered over the glowing coals of an outdoor fire, or placed in a smoker box or foil packet to use with a gas grill, wood chips add hints of their distinctive smoky flavor to grilled foods. Fruit woods such as apple, cherry, almond, grape, or olive have subtle aromas, while stronger woods such as mesquite or hickory give off more assertive smoke. For the best results, use wood chips during slow, indirect-heat cooking, although they'll add some flavor to quickly grilled foods. You can use the chips dry for stronger flavors, or soak them in water, beer, or wine to produce a more subtle aroma.

i WOOD PLANKS

Made of fragrant wood such as cedar or alder, these thin planks have become a popular accessory for grilling fish, especially salmon fillets, to which they add their own smoky fragrance. Before using, the planks should be soaked in water for at least an hour. After cooking, the plank and fish can be transferred together to a serving platter; some planks come as part of a set with a serving holder into which the wood neatly fits. If the planks are not too charred, they can be used more than one time. For more on using wood planks, turn to entry 171.

Measuring tools & timers

Some cooks add "a little of this" without measuring, and cook their food "until it's done" with fine results. However, many recipes require more precise measurements and timing. For that reason, it's a good idea to stock your kitchen with accurate measuring tools, thermometers, and timers.

Measuring tools

a LIQUID MEASURING CUPS

Resembling pitchers with calibrated measurements of fluid ounces and cups printed vertically on their sides, the best liquid measuring cups are made of heatproof tempered glass. They have pour spouts in their rims opposite a comfortable handle and are available in a variety of sizes to suit your needs. A cup with a 2-cup (16–fl oz/500-ml) capacity is the most versatile.

b DRY MEASURING CUPS

Dry measuring cups come in sets of graduated volumes, typically ranging from ¼ cup (2 fl oz/60 ml) to 1 cup (8 fl oz/250 ml). They are usually made of stainless steel, heavy-duty plastic, or polycarbonate, with a straight rim that enables you to level the ingredient being measured for an accurate quantity.

c MEASURING SPOONS

Sets of measuring spoons typically include spoons in increments of ¼ teaspoon, ½ teaspoon, 1 teaspoon, and 1 tablespoon for measuring both dry and liquid ingredients. As with dry measuring cups, level off dry ingredients in the spoon with a flat edge for accuracy.

d KITCHEN SCALES

A kitchen scale can be convenient, especially for baking recipes, because it measures ingredients more accurately than measuring by volume. Choose a scale, whether manual or digital, capable of weighing up to 10 pounds (5 kg) in increments no larger than ¼ ounce (7 g), and that also provides corresponding metric measurements. The weighing bowl of a manual scale should be large enough to handle at least 2 cups (10 oz/315 g) of flour or an equivalent item. Digital scales should allow you to weigh ingredients in any bowl or container.

Thermometers

a INSTANT-READ

Every kitchen should have an instant-read thermometer, which enables you to determine at a glance the precise degree of doneness for meat, poultry, or fish as it is cooking.

Dial type (left) This traditional-style thermometer features a calibrated dial and a pointer turned by a coil made of heat-sensitive metal.

Digital (right) A battery-operated digital thermometer provides the fastest, most accurate reading, presented in numerals on its face. Choose a model with the largest, easiest-to-read display.

b CANDY/OIL

This model is specifically designed to measure the temperature of sugar syrups or hot oil when you're making candy or deep-frying. A clip that slides along the shaft secures it to the side of a pan or pot to give you safe, accurate readings. These thermometers are available with both dial or digital displays.

c DIGITAL PROBE

This thermometer features a probe that is inserted into the food, then is attached to a remote console via a long, heat-resistant cord. The console, which sits outside of the oven, allows you to program the desired degree of doneness and, when reached, makes an audible sound to alert you when the food is ready.

d OVEN

Use one of these tools to take the true temperature of your oven, so you can tell whether the dial settings are accurate. Look for a model that can hang from an oven rack or that stands well above it, so that it reads the air temperature rather than the heat of the metal. Once you know the true temperature inside your oven, you can adjust the dial accordingly.

Timers

Timers are an essential part of a well-stocked kitchen. They remind you when it's time to check on food as it cooks to ensure it doesn't overcook or burn. Some cooks even like to wear a timer around their neck, less they get distracted by other household tasks.

a MANUAL

Traditional manual timers are typically spring-activated models with dials that you turn to the desired length of time. When that time has elapsed, the timer buzzes or rings like an alarm clock. They can be found in an array of colors.

b ELECTRONIC

These timers feature a digital display that beeps when the time is up. Some include multiple displays to help you keep track of the timing for more than one dish. Some sit on the counter, while others use a magnetic strip to stick to appliances.

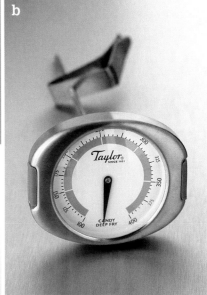

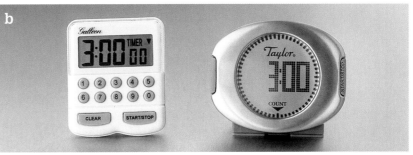

MEASURING TOOLS & TIMERS

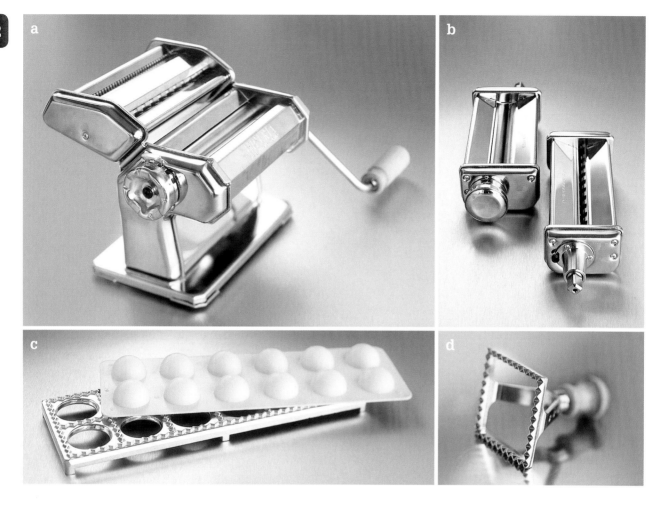

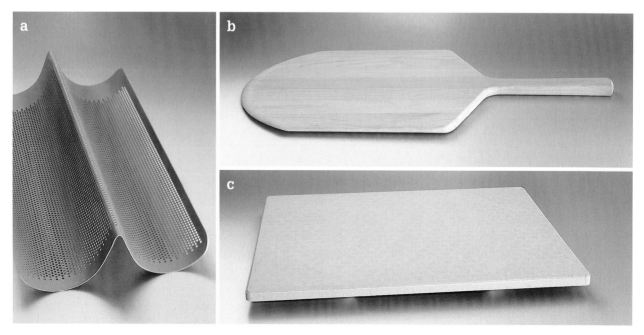

Pasta & bread equipment

More and more home cooks are discovering the pleasures of making pasta and bread from scratch. With the help of a pasta machine, simple shaping tools, and basic baking equipment, you can get results as good as you would find in an Italian deli or boutique bakery.

Pasta equipment

a PASTA MACHINE

A pasta machine simplifies kneading, rolling, and cutting pasta. The classic Italian-style pasta machine consists of two sets of rollers turned by a hand crank that you move from one set to the other as needed. The machine is affixed to the countertop or work surface with a vicelike tool, which holds it securely while you work. The first set of rollers, made of smooth, heavy stainless steel, kneads and rolls the pasta. After kneading a few times, the pasta dough is then rolled through progressively narrower settings until it becomes a thin sheet of dough (for more on rolling out pasta dough, see entries 225 and 227). Next, one of the interchangeable cutting attachments is affixed to the machine for cutting narrow strands, such as linguine, or wider strips, such as fettuccine. Roll the dough sheets through the cutting teeth to make the desired strands. You can purchase separate attachments for cutting fresh angel hair and spaghetti or for forming and shaping ravioli. (For more information on cutting pasta with a machine, turn to entry 226). It is also possible to find electric pasta machines that work the same way as manual pasta machines—only faster and with less effort. Some pasta machine manufacturers also produce an electric motor, which can be attached to the crank mechanism of a manual pasta machine to speed up the rolling and cutting process.

b CUTTING ATTACHMENTS

If you enjoy making pasta frequently, a convenient option is to purchase attachments for a stand mixer (see entry 25f), which gives the machine greater versatility in the home kitchen. Attachments exist to prepare fresh pasta dough sheets and to cut them into shapes such as spaghetti, fettuccine, or angel hair. There are also attachments that help you to fill and cut ravioli.

c RAVIOLI MOLD

Also called a ravioli plaque, this simple manual device helps you create uniform ravioli. Drape one rolled-out sheet of fresh pasta dough over the metal frame, which includes regularly spaced holes, each surrounded by a circular or square raised ridge. Place the plastic mold on top and press down to make depressions in the pasta. Spoon the filling into each depression, and moisten the dough around each spoonful. Then, drape another pasta sheet on top and roll across the plaque with a rolling pin, pressing down so that the filling is sealed and the raised ridges cut through to form individual ravioli.

d PASTA STAMP

Found in a range of sizes and shapes, with both smooth and fluted edges, this device cuts individual ravioli or other filled pastas in the same way that a cookie cutter cuts rolled-out cookie dough.

Bread & pizza equipment

a FRENCH BREAD PAN

If you enjoy baking bread at home, consider investing in a French bread pan. With the help of this pan, you can produce the same quality results that you would see at a French neighborhood bakery. The pan's long half-cylindrical shape holds and forms two baguettes, batards, or other traditional long country loaves side by side. Perforations in the nonstick, commercial-grade aluminum surface keep the oven's air circulating freely all around the dough to produce a crisp, golden-brown crust with the tiny indentations you see on the bottoms of many classic French breads.

b BAKER'S PEEL

Professional bread bakers use this tool—essentially a broad, flat wooden paddle with a tapered edge—to slide loaves in and out of large ovens. At home, you'll find that a peel helps you slide a loaf of bread or a fully loaded pizza onto a hot baking stone in the oven and retrieve it when it's done.

c BAKING STONE

Also called a pizza stone, baking tile, or quarry tile, this flat rectangular, square, or round piece of unglazed stoneware is used principally for baking breads and pizzas to produce crisp crusts. The stone works by recreating the intense, dry heat of a professional oven. Appreciated for its efficient heat absorption and distribution, a baking stone is usually placed on the lowest rack of the oven—or, depending on your type of oven, directly on the oven floor—and preheated for at least 45 minutes or up to 1 hour before using. The best baking stones are made of the same type of clay used to line kilns, as they are less apt to crack than ordinary clay baking stones. After each use, wipe the cooled stone clean with a damp cloth or paper towels. Do not immerse it in water or use soap, which could get trapped inside the stone's pores.

techniques

Learning basic cooking skills, such as wielding a knife, using a pastry bag, and identifying fresh herbs, is the first step in becoming a good cook. In the following pages, you will find over 250 such techniques, from carving a roast, to shucking clams and oysters, to whipping egg whites to form soft peaks. We've also included a handful of staple recipes that are destined to become a core part of your cooking repertory. You will also find this section is helpful when you encounter a confusing element in a cookbook and need a step-by-step guide to help accomplish the task.

Whipping cream

1 Pour the cream into a bowl

Pour cold heavy (double) cream into a glass or stainless-steel bowl. For the best results, chill the bowl first. Add any flavorings called for in the recipe. Sugar and pure vanilla extract are common additions.

2 Whip the cream to soft peaks

Fit a mixer with the whip attachment. Beat the cream mixture on medium-high speed just until soft (slightly bent) peaks form in the cream when you stop the mixer and lift the whip, about 3–4 minutes.

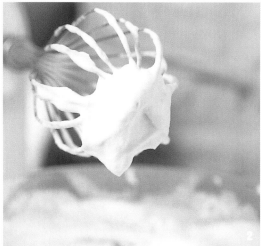

TROUBLESHOOTING

Cream that has been whipped too long becomes stiff, grainy, and has a curdled appearance, but it can be fixed.

3 Fix overwhipped cream, if needed

To fix overwhipped cream, add a small amount of unwhipped cream and beat it gently to bring back the soft peaks.

Creaming butter

1 Combine the butter and sugar
Fit a stand mixer with the paddle attachment or a handheld mixer with the twin beaters. Add the room-temperature butter and sugar called for in your recipe to a large mixing bowl.

2 Cream the mixture
Beat the butter mixture on medium speed until light and fluffy, about 2 minutes. The mixture will change from light yellow to ivory, and it will have the consistency of stiffly whipped cream.

Sifting dry ingredients

1 Add flour to the sieve/sifter
Place a fine-mesh sieve or a flour sifter in a large work bowl. Add the measured dry ingredients to the sieve or sifter according to your recipe. (Some recipes call for flour to be measured after it is sifted.)

2 Sift ingredients into a bowl
If using a sieve, gently tap the edge to encourage the ingredients to fall into the bowl. If using a sifter, squeeze the handle until the ingredients have passed through.

Working with vanilla beans

1 Split the pod lengthwise
Hold the vanilla bean pod in place with one hand. With a paring knife, carefully cut down the center of the bean lengthwise.

2 Scrape out the seeds
Using the tip of the knife, scrape the vanilla seeds from the inside of each pod half. The seeds will stick, so you may need to scrape twice to reach all the seeds.

Separating eggs

1 Crack the egg
Eggs are easiest to separate when they are cold. Have ready 3 clean, grease-free bowls. To reduce shell fragments, crack the side of the egg sharply on a flat surface rather than the rim of a bowl.

2 Pull the shell halves apart
Hold the cracked egg over an empty bowl and carefully pull the shell apart, letting the white (but not the yolk) start to drop into the bowl below.

3 Pass the yolk back and forth
Transfer the yolk back and forth from one shell half to the other, letting the remaining egg white fall into the bowl below. Be careful not to break the yolk on a sharp shell edge.

4 Put the yolk in another bowl
Gently drop the yolk into the second bowl. Keeping the whites free of any yolk is key if you plan to whip the whites. A trace of yolk (or other fat) will prevent the whites from foaming and forming peaks.

TROUBLESHOOTING
If a yolk breaks into the white as you separate the egg, the egg white cannot be used for whipping. Reserve the white for another use (like making an omelet or scrambled eggs) or discard it. Be sure to rinse the bowl before separating any remaining eggs.

5 Transfer the white to a clean bowl
If the egg separates cleanly, pour the white into the third bowl. To avoid mishaps, break each new egg over the first empty bowl and transfer the whites each time.

Whipping egg whites

1 Beat the egg whites
Fit a stand mixer with the whip attachment or a handheld mixer with the twin beaters. Beat room-temperature egg whites with a pinch of cream of tartar (for stability) on medium speed until foamy and the cream of tartar dissolves, about 1 minute. Alternatively, use a copper bowl (see entry 9e) and omit the cream of tartar.

2 Look for soft peaks
If your recipe calls for egg whites whipped to the soft-peak stage, beat on medium-high speed until the whites look opaque but moist, 2–3 minutes. Stop beating and lift the whip: The whites should form slightly bent peaks.

3 Beat to stiff peaks
If your recipe calls for egg whites with stiff peaks, continue to beat until the whites look glossy, 1–2 minutes longer. When the whip is lifted, they should hold a firm, straight peak. Take care not to overbeat.

TROUBLESHOOTING
Overbeaten egg whites appear grainy and can separate. If you beat the egg whites to this stage, you'll need to discard them and start again with fresh egg whites.

Tempering eggs

1 Combine the mixtures
Tempering eggs is common when making custards such as for pastry cream or ice cream. In a heatproof bowl, mix together eggs or yolks with cream or milk according to your recipe. Add a small amount of the hot mixture while whisking constantly.

2 Heat the mixtures together
After some of the hot mixture has been blended into the eggs, pour the tempered egg mixture back into the saucepan, whisking constantly.

Citrus curd

These thick, citrus-flavored mixtures can be used as fillings for layer cakes or cake rolls, or combined with whipped cream for fluffy frostings. The addition of egg yolks along with whole eggs gives the curd a particularly rich flavor.

INGREDIENTS

3 or 4 lemons, 4 or 5 limes, or 2 or 3 oranges, preferably organic

2 large eggs plus 2 large egg yolks

1 cup (8 oz/250 g) granulated sugar

6 tablespoons (3 oz/90 g) unsalted butter, at room temperature

MAKES ABOUT 1½ CUPS
(12 FL OZ/375 ML)

1 Zest the fruit
Wash the fruit. With a rasp grater positioned over a bowl, carefully draw the fruit across the grater, removing just the colored portion of the peel, called the *zest*. Take care not to remove the white *pith* below, as it is bitter. Measure out 2 teaspoons zest and set aside.

2 Juice the fruit
Cut the fruit in half crosswise. Using a citrus reamer or a citrus press held over a bowl, juice each half. Pour the juice through a fine-mesh sieve held over a measuring cup or bowl to remove the pulp and seeds. Measure out ½ cup (4 oz/125 ml) juice and set aside.

To freeze citrus curd, put the chilled curd into an airtight container. Press plastic wrap directly onto the surface of the curd and cover tightly. Freeze for up to 1 month. Because the curd has a dense texture and low moisture, there is no need to thaw it before using.

6 Check the consistency
To test the consistency of the citrus curd, pull the spoon or spatula out of the mixture and draw your finger across the back; a trail should remain that does not fill in immediately. (You can also test the curd with an instant-read thermometer; it should register 165°F/74°C when it's inserted into the mixture.)

3 Combine the ingredients
Pour water to a depth of 1 inch (2.5 cm) into a saucepan. In a metal bowl large enough to fit on top of a saucepan to create a double boiler, combine all the ingredients except the butter and zest. Whisk the ingredients until well blended.

4 Add the butter
Cut the butter into 12 equal pieces and add them to the mixture without stirring. Place the saucepan over medium-low heat until the water is barely simmering.

5 Cook the citrus curd
Place the bowl with the egg mixture on top of the saucepan and cook, stirring constantly with a wooden spoon or silicone spatula, until the curd is thick, about 8 minutes. To ensure a smooth curd, make sure you reach the bottom and sides of the bowl when stirring.

7 Strain and cool the curd
Hold a fine-mesh sieve over a bowl and pour the curd through the sieve. You can use the wooden spoon or silicone spatula to help the mixture through. Any stray lumps will be trapped in the sieve. Stir the citrus zest into the curd. Press a piece of plastic wrap directly onto the surface of the curd (this helps prevent a skin from forming) and poke a few holes in the plastic with a thin skewer or toothpick to allow the heat to escape. Refrigerate until the curd is well chilled and set, about 3 hours.

Making a meringue

1 Beat the egg whites until foamy
Fit a mixer with the whip attachment or choose a balloon whisk. Beat the egg whites with cream of tartar, if called for in the recipe, until dissolved and foamy, about 1 minute.

2 Look for soft peaks
Continue to beat on medium speed until the egg whites begin to thicken, 2–3 minutes. Increase the mixer speed to medim-high and beat until the egg whites form slightly bent peaks when you lift the whip.

3 Sprinkle in the sugar while beating
Increase the mixer speed to high and slowly sprinkle in sugar as called for in the recipe, beating the mixture for about 15 seconds after each addition.

4 Beat until stiff peaks form
When all the sugar has been added, continue to beat until the egg whites form stiff glossy peaks with tips that barely droop when the whip is raised, about 1 minute.

Folding together two mixtures

1 Add some of the light mixture
Folding is a crucial technique that combines two ingredients or mixtures with different densities. Pile one-third of the lighter mixture (here, beaten egg whites) on top of the mixture that is to be folded.

2 Cut the spatula down the center
Using a flexible silicone spatula and holding it vertically, slice down through the center of the mixtures to the bottom of the bowl.

3 Bring the spatula up one side
Turn the spatula horizontally, so it lies on the bottom of the bowl. Pull the spatula along the bottom of the bowl and up the side, keeping it flat against the side of the bowl.

4 Fold the batter
Pull the spatula up and over the lighter mixture on top, bringing some of the heavier mixture from the bottom with it. Rotate the bowl a quarter turn.

5 Finish the folding process
Repeat this folding action, rotating the bowl each time, until no white streaks remain. Once the batter is lightened, fold in the rest of the light mixture by repeating steps 1–5.

TROUBLESHOOTING
It's natural for the batter to deflate slightly during folding, but overly deflated batter will affect the texture of the baked item. Be sure to work quickly and stop folding when the mixtures are just combined.

Pastry cream

A basic custard that is used for filling a variety of cakes and pastries, pastry cream is a versatile kitchen staple. Use it to fill cream puffs or éclairs (see entry 45) or as a filling in a fresh fruit tart. It is also the classic filling for Boston Cream Pie.

1 Steep the vanilla bean in milk
In a heavy-bottomed saucepan over medium heat, warm the milk, vanilla bean pod, and vanilla seeds until tiny bubbles form along the edges of the pan. Remove from the heat and let the milk mixture steep for a minute or two.

2 Whisk the yolks and sugar
In a large heatproof bowl, whisk together the eggs yolks and sugar until blended. Add the cornstarch and whisk until blended and smooth.

INGREDIENTS

1½ cups (12 fl oz/375 ml) whole milk

1 vanilla bean, split, with the seeds scraped out

4 large egg yolks

½ cup (4 oz/125 g) granulated sugar

2 tablespoons cornstarch (cornflour)

2 tablespoons unsalted butter, at room temperature

MAKES ABOUT 1½ CUPS
(12 FL OZ/375 ML)

5 Strain out the solids
Pour the hot pastry cream mixture through a fine-mesh sieve placed over a clean, heatproof bowl. Discard the vanilla bean in the sieve. Add the butter to the strained pastry cream and stir gently until the butter melts.

FLAVORED PASTRY CREAMS

Chocolate Pastry Cream

Follow the recipe to make Pastry Cream. In step 5, stir in 6 oz (185 g) finely chopped semisweet (plain) chocolate with the butter until the chocolate melts. Proceed with the recipe.

Mocha Pastry Cream

Follow the recipe to make Pastry Cream. In step 1, add 1 teaspoon instant espresso powder to the milk. In step 5, stir in 6 oz (185 g) finely chopped semisweet (plain) chocolate with the butter until the chocolate melts. Proceed with the recipe.

Lemon Pastry Cream

Follow the recipe to make Pastry Cream. In step 2, whisk 2 teaspoons grated lemon zest with the yolks and sugar. Proceed with the recipe.

3 Temper the eggs
While whisking constantly, slowly add about one-fourth of the warm milk mixture to the egg mixture to slightly warm, or *temper*, the eggs.

4 Cook the pastry cream
Pour the tempered eggs back into the saucepan, place over medium heat, and stir constantly with a whisk until the mixture thickens and comes to a boil, 2–3 minutes.

6 Chill the pastry cream
Press a piece of plastic wrap directly on the surface of the pastry cream (this helps prevent a skin from forming), and poke a few holes in the plastic with a thin skewer or a toothpick to allow the heat to escape. Refrigerate until the pastry cream is well chilled, about 2 hours.

Choux pastry

Choux (pronounced "shoo") pastry is a thick batter that is cooked on the stove top and then fashioned into a variety of shapes using a pastry bag. After baking in a hot oven, the choux is transformed into delicate shells for cream puffs or éclairs.

1 Boil the liquid
Position 2 racks evenly in the oven, and preheat to 425°F (220°C). Line 2 half-sheet pans with parchment (baking) paper or aluminum foil. In a saucepan over medium-high heat, combine the milk, water, butter, and salt and bring to a full boil.

2 Add the flour all at once
When the butter melts, remove the pan from the heat and add the flour all at once. Stir vigorously with a wooden spoon until blended.

INGREDIENTS

½ cup (4 fl oz/125 ml) whole milk

1 cup (8 fl oz/250 ml) water

6 tablespoons (3 oz/90 g) unsalted butter, cut into ½-inch (12-mm) pieces

¼ teaspoon salt

1 cup (5 oz/155 g) all-purpose (plain) flour

4 large eggs

MAKES ABOUT 15 LARGE PUFFS OR 10 LOGS

6 To shape logs:
Fit a pastry bag with a ¾-inch (2-cm) plain tip and pipe out logs 4 inches (10 cm) long and 1 inch (2.5 cm) wide. Space the logs at least 2 inches (5 cm) apart to allow for expansion.

3 Cook the mixture
Return the pan to medium heat and continue stirring until the mixture leaves the sides of the pan and forms a ball. Remove from the heat and let cool for 3–4 minutes, or until about 140°F (60°C) when tested with an instant-read thermometer.

4 Add the eggs
Crack the eggs into a small bowl and check for shells. Add about 1 egg and beat with a wooden spoon until incorporated. Stir in the remaining 3 eggs, about one at a time, beating vigorously after each addition so that the batter returns to a smooth paste. Let the paste cool for about 10 minutes.

5 To shape puffs:
Fit a pastry bag with a ⅝-inch (1.5-cm) plain tip and fill the bag with the paste. For each puff, pipe about 1 tablespoon of the paste onto the prepared pan, forming a mound about 2 inches (5 cm) in diameter. Space the mounds at least 2 inches apart to allow for expansion.

7 Bake and vent the pastries
Bake the puffs or logs for 15 minutes, then reduce the heat to 375°F (190°C) and continue baking until golden brown, 5–10 minutes longer. Remove the baking sheet from the oven and immediately prick the side of each puff or log with the tip of a paring knife. Return the pastries to the turned-off oven, leave the door open, and let them dry out in the oven for 10–15 minutes. Let the pastries cool completely on the pans on wire racks before filling.

Filling a pastry bag

1 Fit the tip into the bag
Firmly push the desired decorating tip down into the small hole in the pastry bag. If you're using a device called a *coupler* to hold the tip in place, screw it on tightly.

2 Form a cuff in the pastry bag
Using both hands, fold down the top of the bag to form a cuff. The cuff should be about one-third the length of the bag. To make it easier to fill, you can also fold the cuff over a tall glass, with the tip inside the glass.

3 Fill the bag
Place one hand under the cuff of the pastry bag. Using a silicone spatula, scoop the filling or frosting mixture into the large opening in the bag, filling it no more than half full.

4 Push the mixture to the tip
Unfold the cuff. Push the filling or frosting down toward the tip, forcing out any air at the same time. Trapped air bubbles can cause problems when piping.

5 Twist the bag
To further ensure against air bubbles, and to keep the mixture flowing steadily, twist the bag several times at the location where the filling ends.

6 Hold the filled pastry bag
With your dominant hand, hold the bag where you just made the twist. With your non-dominant hand, hold the bag near the tip and proceed to pipe.

Piping frosting with a pastry bag

1 Hold the bag at an angle
Fill the pastry bag with the desired frosting. Use your upper hand to apply pressure, and the lower hand to guide the tip. Hold the bag with the tip 1 inch (2.5 cm) above and at a 60-degree angle to the cake.

2 To pipe rosettes:
Using the star tip, apply gentle pressure to pipe a mound of frosting ½ inch (12 mm) wide. Pull the bag up, lessening the pressure and reducing the angle. Repeat to form a row of rosettes.

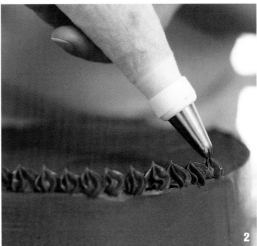

3 To pipe shells:
Using the fluted tip, pipe a mound of frosting about ½ inch (12 mm) long. Pull the bag up, lessening the pressure and reducing the angle slightly. Repeat to form a row of shells.

4 To pipe dots:
Using a small plain tip, pipe a small mound of frosting, lifting up the bag to make a point on the top. Repeat to form the desired pattern of dots.

Curling chocolate

1 Run a peeler over the chocolate
Soften the chocolate by holding it in your hands for a minute or two. Holding the chocolate with one hand, use a vegetable peeler to scrape curls 1½–2 inches (4–5 cm) long.

2 Let the curls fall onto a pan
Turn the chocolate block so that you scrape from all sides, letting the chocolate curls fall in a single layer onto a rimmed baking sheet lined with parchment (baking) paper.

Chopping chocolate

1 Cut the chocolate into chunks
With one hand, grasp the handle of a serrated or chef's knife. With your other hand placed midpoint on the back of the blade, cut the chocolate into medium-sized pieces, gradually moving the knife across the block of chocolate.

2 Chop the chocolate into pieces
Moving your other hand slightly closer to the front of the blade, rock the knife to cut the chocolate into small, even pieces. The smaller, uniform pieces will melt evenly.

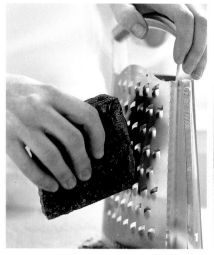 

Grating chocolate

1 Grate the chocolate
Holding a box grater-shredder with one hand, quickly run a block of chocolate over the shredding holes with the other hand. Be sure the chocolate is cool to the touch (it will melt easily).

2 Transfer the gratings to a plate
Let the gratings fall onto a work surface. When you're ready to transfer them, scoop them up with a bench scraper or quickly pick them up with cool hands, as they will easily melt.

Melting chocolate

1 Put chopped chocolate in a bowl
Chop the chocolate into small pieces. Using a bench scraper, transfer the chopped chocolate to a metal bowl or the top part of a double boiler. Add other ingredients, such as butter, if called for in the recipe.

2 Set up a double boiler
Fill a saucepan or the bottom part of a double boiler with about 1½ inches (4 cm) of water and heat until it barely simmers. Place the bowl or pan on top, making sure it doesn't touch the water below.

3 Melt the chocolate
Heat the chocolate, stirring often with a silicone spatula, until melted and smooth, 3–4 minutes. Using pot holders, lift out the bowl and use the chocolate as directed.

TROUBLESHOOTING
Chocolate can seize when it comes into contact with moisture. Take care to keep water (including steam) away from the chocolate.

Chocolate ganache

When freshly made, this smooth mixture of chocolate, cream, and butter is a thick, pourable sauce that makes a delicious accompaniment to cake slices. When cooled and set, ganache can be used as an icing for cakes and cookies.

INGREDIENTS

8 oz (250 g) semisweet (plain) or bittersweet chocolate

2 tablespoons unsalted butter

⅔ cup (5 fl oz/160 ml) heavy (double) cream, plus more as needed to adjust the consistency

1 teaspoon pure vanilla extract

MAKES ABOUT 1½ CUPS
(12 FL OZ/375 ML)

1 Chop the chocolate
Grasp a serrated or chef's knife in one hand and position your other hand on the midpoint of the back of the blade. Cut off medium-sized pieces from the block of chocolate. Move your hand close to the front of the blade and rock the knife back and forth to cut the chocolate into even pieces. The smaller the pieces, the easier they will melt.

2 Combine the butter and cream
Cut the butter into 2 equal pieces. In a heavy saucepan over medium-low heat, combine the ⅔ cup cream and butter. Heat until the butter is melted and tiny bubbles have formed along the edges of the pan.

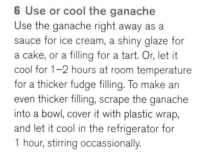

If your finished ganache looks curdled, or broken, heat it again over a double boiler and let it melt, taking care that it does not boil. Chill for 30 minutes in the refrigerator and whisk to bring it back to the desired consistency.

6 Use or cool the ganache
Use the ganache right away as a sauce for ice cream, a shiny glaze for a cake, or a filling for a tart. Or, let it cool for 1–2 hours at room temperature for a thicker fudge filling. To make an even thicker filling, scrape the ganache into a bowl, cover it with plastic wrap, and let it cool in the refrigerator for 1 hour, stirring occassionally.

3 Test the temperature
The mixture should register about 160°F (71°C) on an instant-read thermometer. Do not allow the mixture to boil, or it could scorch and give the finished ganache a burned taste.

4 Add the chopped chocolate
Remove the pan from the heat and add the chopped chocolate. Let the chocolate sit in the hot cream for about 30 seconds to soften, then add the vanilla extract. (Here, you can also add other flavors, like orange or almond, to make a different-flavored ganache.)

5 Mix the ganache
Using a straight whisk, stir the mixture in a circular motion until all the chocolate is melted and the mixture is smooth. Try not to incorporate a lot of air.

7 Whip the mixture, if desired
Whipped ganache makes a fluffy, easy-to-spread frosting. Using a whisk, a stand mixer with the whip attachment, or a handheld mixer with twin beaters, whip the chilled ganache until it changes from a dark to a medium chocolate color and increases in volume, about 30 seconds. The whipped mixture firms up quickly, so use it as soon as possible.

Classic puff pastry

The key to success with this butter-enriched dough lies in a simple secret: Start with cold ingredients and return the dough to the refrigerator often as you work. Use the dough to make a variety of rich, flaky pastries and desserts.

INGREDIENTS

3 cups (15 oz/470 g) plus 2 tablespoons unbleached all-purpose (plain) flour

1 cup (4 oz/125 g) cake (soft-wheat) flour

1 teaspoon salt

2 tablespoons cold unsalted butter, cut into small pieces, plus one 1-lb (500-g) block unsalted butter

About 1 cup (8 fl oz/250 ml) ice water

MAKES ABOUT 2 LB (1 KG) DOUGH

1 Work the butter into the flour
In a large bowl, stir together the 3 cups (15 oz/470 g) all-purpose flour, the cake flour, and the salt. Scatter the butter pieces over the flour and work in with a pastry blender or your fingers until the mixture is crumbly.

2 Add the water
Make a well in the center and pour in the ice water. Using a wooden spoon, gradually stir in the flour until it becomes a fully incorporated rough mass that holds together. If necessary, add more ice water, 1 tablespoon at a time. Turn the dough out onto a lightly floured work surface and knead for 15–20 seconds until smooth but not sticky.

6 Brush off the excess flour
Since too much flour on the dough can dry it out, brush off the excess flour with a pastry brush. Wrap the dough in plastic wrap and refrigerate for 20–30 minutes. Turn the rectangle lengthwise, with the folded side to your left, roll out the dough again into a 24-by-8-inch (60-by-20-cm) rectangle, and fold it into thirds. This is called a *turn;* repeat to make 4 more turns, refrigerating for 20–30 minutes between each turn.

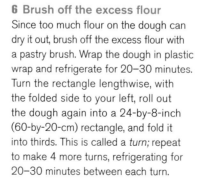

3 Form the butter package

Using a rolling pin or the heel of your hand, knead or beat the butter on a work surface to flatten it and warm it until smooth and pliable. Sprinkle the butter with the 2 tablespoons flour and gently beat the butter with the rolling pin to press the flour into the butter. Shape the floured butter into a 6-inch (15-cm) square about ¾ inch (2 cm) thick.

4 Fold the dough over the butter

On a lightly floured surface, and using a ruler as a guide, roll out the dough into a 12-inch (30-cm) square. Place the butter at a diagonal in the center of the dough. Fold over the dough corners to meet in the center, covering the butter completely. Pat with your hands to form a compact square. Roll the dough into a rectangular strip 24 inches (60 cm) long by 8 inches (20 cm) wide.

5 Fold the dough into thirds

With a short side facing you, fold the bottom third of the dough up, then fold the top third of the dough down over it, as if folding a letter.

7 Chill the dough

After the final turn, wrap the dough in plastic wrap, place in a plastic bag, and refrigerate for at least 4 hours or up to overnight before shaping.

Quick puff pastry

If you don't have time to make Classic Puff Pastry (see entry 53), this quick version is great in a pinch. The layers of flaky pastry will not be as numerous or pronounced, but the flavors will be equally rich. Be sure to use good-quality butter.

INGREDIENTS

1½ cups (7½ oz/235 g) unbleached all-purpose (plain) flour

½ cup (2 oz/60 g) cake (soft-wheat) flour

½ teaspoon salt

½ lb (250 g) cold unsalted butter

½ cup (4 fl oz/125 ml) ice water

MAKES ABOUT 1 LB (500 G) DOUGH

1 Combine the dry ingredients
In the bowl of a stand mixer fitted with the paddle attachment, stir together the all-purpose and cake flours and the salt on low speed.

2 Scatter the butter over the flour
Cut the butter into ½-inch (12-mm) cubes. Scatter the butter cubes over the flour mixture. Mix on low speed just until the butter is coated with the flour, about 1 minute.

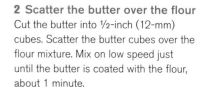

6 Turn and fold again
Turn the rectangle lengthwise, with the folded side to your left, and repeat the process again, rolling the dough into a 12-by-7-inch (30-by-18-cm) rectangle and folding it into thirds. Turn again and repeat the rolling and folding a third time. If the dough seems to be warming up too fast and the butter softening, place it in the refrigerator to chill for 20–30 minutes.

3 Pour in the water
Gradually pour in the water and mix for a few seconds just until the water is absorbed. The butter should still be in large pieces. Use your hands to gently pat the mixture into a loose ball.

4 Roll out the dough
Transfer the dough to a lightly floured work surface, dust it lightly with flour, and pat it into a rectangle that is ¾ inch (2 cm) thick. Using a ruler as a guide, roll out the dough into a 12-by-7-inch (30-by-18-cm) rectangle that's about ½ inch (12 mm) thick.

5 Fold the dough into thirds
With a short side facing you, fold the bottom third of the dough up, then fold the top third of the dough down over it, as if folding a letter.

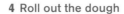

7 Chill the dough
After the third turn, wrap the dough in plastic wrap, place in a plastic bag, and refrigerate for at least 4 hours or up to overnight before shaping.

Working with filo dough

1 Ready your equipment
Filo dough, used to make a variety of flaky appetizers and desserts, dries out quickly when exposed to the air, so make sure you have all your ingredients and tools ready before starting.

2 Prepare the filo sheets
Tear off 2 sheets of plastic wrap, each about 2 feet (60 cm) long, and place them on the work surface, overlapping them side by side. Remove the thawed filo dough from its box and unroll it onto the plastic wrap.

3 Cover the dough
To keep the dough from drying out, cover it with 2 additional 2-foot-long sheets of plastic wrap, overlapping them in the center. Rinse 2 kitchen towels and wring them out. Place on top of the plastic wrap.

4 Work with one layer at a time
Carefully remove 1 filo sheet from the stack and place it on a work surface. Immediately re-cover the remaining filo sheets. Don't worry if the filo cracks a little.

5 Brush with butter
Using a pastry brush, cover the entire filo sheet lightly with melted butter or clarified butter (see entry 106), dabbing it on and covering the edges well. Add additional layers of filo if called for in the recipe.

6 Cut the filo into strips
The easiest way to cut filo is to use a straight edge, such as a ruler, and a pizza cutter to make even strips or squares.

Caramelizing sugar

1 Add the ingredients
Pour granulated sugar and any other ingredients, if called for, into a deep, heavy saucepan. (Here, 1 cup/8 oz/250 g sugar is combined with 2 tablespoons water and 1 teaspoon lemon juice.)

2 Add the optional corn syrup
Add corn syrup, if called for, to the saucepan (here, 1 tablespoon). The corn syrup helps dissolve the sugar and will also help prevent it from crystallizing.

3 Stir the mixture
Using a wooden spoon, mix the ingredients together. At this stage, the mixture will look cloudy and grainy.

4 Cook the sugar
Place the saucepan over medium heat and stir constantly until no grains of sugar are visible, 1–2 mintues. Raise the heat to medium-high and continue to cook, without stirring.

5 Check the color
As soon as you see the color turn a rich amber, or the mixture registers 320°–360°F (160°–182°C) on a candy thermometer, about 2–4 minutes, immediately remove the pan from the heat.

TROUBLESHOOTING
You must watch the caramel vigilantly as it cooks, as it can turn dark within seconds. If the caramel looks very dark brown, it is burnt and will have an unpleasant flavor. The lighter the color, the more mild the flavor will be.

Candying citrus zest

1 Remove the zest from the fruit
Using a vegetable peeler, remove the colored part of the peel, called the *zest*, from the fruit in long, wide strips. Leave as much of the bitter white *pith* on the fruit as you can.

2 Cut the zest into matchsticks
Cut the zest into matchstick-sized strips. Discard any small or odd-shaped pieces. Blanch the strips in water to cover, then drain and rinse under cold water to halt the cooking process.

3 Simmer the zest strips
For each fruit zested, simmer with ⅓ cup (3 fl oz/80 ml) water, 1 tablespoon cider vinegar, and ¼ cup (2 oz/60 g) granulated sugar until softened, about 10 minutes.

4 Use or store the candied zest
Let cool slightly, then transfer the zest and syrup to a bowl until ready to use. Drain before serving.

Sugaring flower petals

1 Paint the flowers with egg whites
In a small bowl, whisk a small amount of pasteurized egg whites until foamy. Dip a clean paintbrush into the egg whites and lightly and evenly coat a pesticide-free edible flower petal.

2 Sprinkle with sugar
Pour some superfine (caster) sugar into another small bowl. Sprinkle the egg white–coated petal lightly and evenly with a thin coating of the sugar.

3 Shake off the excess
Gently shake any excess sugar back into the bowl. Place the finished petal on a wire rack topped with parchment (baking) paper.

4 Let the petals dry
Repeat to coat any remaining petals, then let stand in a cool place to dry completely, at least 4 hours or up to overnight.

Proofing yeast

1 Add yeast to warm water
Dissolve active dry yeast in a small amount of warm liquid (105°–115°F/40°–46°C). Fresh yeast cake should be crumbled into lukewarm liquid (90°–100°F/33°–38°C). If the water is too hot, it will kill the yeast. If it is too cold, the yeast will not be efficiently activated. Some recipes call for adding sugar or honey to help feed the yeast.

2 Check for activity
Let the mixture stand for 5–10 minutes until bubbling and foamy. If the yeast does not bubble, start over with fresh yeast.

Making a sponge

1 Add flour to the proofed yeast
A *sponge*—typically a mixture of flour, liquid, and yeast—adds a deeper flavor and better texture to finished bread. To make a sponge, first proof the yeast in a large mixing bowl. Add the flour and any other ingredients called for in the recipe and stir with a wooden spoon until smooth.

2 Cover and let the sponge stand
Cover the bowl with plastic wrap and let stand for at least 3 hours at cool room temperature or up to overnight in the refrigerator, or according to your recipe.

3 Bring sponge to room temperature
When the sponge is ready, it will have risen, be bubbly, and have a slightly sour or fermented smell. If the sponge has been refrigerated, bring it to room temperature for 1 hour before finishing the dough.

TROUBLESHOOTING
Check on the sponge periodically during proofing. If it doesn't look bubbly or smell sour, discard it and start again with fresh ingredients.

Mixing & kneading bread dough by hand

1 Add flour to the sponge
Make a sponge (see entry 60) and let stand
for at least 3 hours or according to your
recipe. Add the flour, then the salt to the
sponge. If the salt comes in direct contact
with the yeast, it can deactivate it.

2 Stir together the dough
Using a wooden spoon or your hands, stir the
dough until if forms a rough mass. Using a
plastic pastry scraper, scrape the dough onto
a floured work surface. Invert the bowl over
the dough and let it rest for 10–15 minutes.

3 Knead the dough
Uncover the dough and knead it by using
the heel of one hand to push the dough
away from you and then pull it back with your
fingertips. Turn and repeat until the dough
is smooth and elastic, 5–7 minutes.

4 Transfer the dough to an oiled bowl
Form the dough into a ball, transfer to
a lightly oiled bowl, and cover the bowl
with plastic wrap.

1 Add the ingredients to a mixer
Fit a stand mixer with the hook attachment.
Transfer the sponge, if using, to the bowl of
the stand mixer. Then, add the flour and any
other ingredients called for in the recipe.

2 Knead the dough
Turn the mixer on low speed and knead,
adding flour as neccessary, until the dough
comes away from the sides of the bowl.
Continue kneading until smooth and
elastic, 5–7 minutes.

3 Transfer to a floured work surface
Remove the bowl from the mixer and use
your hand or a spatula to ease the dough
onto a floured work surface.

4 Place the dough in an oiled bowl
Form the dough into a ball by tucking the
sides of the dough underneath and lightly
pinching them together. Rotate, tucking and
pinching, until a ball forms. Place the ball
in an oiled bowl and cover with plastic wrap.

Proofing & shaping bread dough

1 Let the dough rise
Let the dough rise in a warm, draft-free spot until it doubles in bulk. This can take 1–2 hours or more, depending on the temperature of the room.

2 Punch down the dough
Punching down the dough releases gases that have built up during rising. Simply press down on the dough a few times with your fist until it has lost most of its air. Then, turn the dough out onto a lightly floured surface.

3 Divide the dough
If your recipe calls for dividing the dough into portions, use a bench scraper or a sharp knife to cut it. You can cover the portions of dough you aren't using with a damp kitchen towel so they won't dry out.

4 Shape the dough
Working with one portion at a time, shape the dough as specified in your recipe. Here, we show the beginning stages of shaping the dough into a baguette. Transfer the finished shaped dough onto a baking pan sprinkled with cornmeal.

Slashing bread dough

1 Angle the knife blade
Hold the knife blade at a shallow angle (about 45 degrees) so that you slit under the surface of the dough, rather than cut too deeply.

2 Slash the dough
Slashing the dough, or cutting slits in it, allows the carbon dioxide and steam that builds up during baking to be released. Keeping the knife at an angle, make 2–5 slits depending on the shape of your dough, or according to your recipe.

BREADS & BATTERS

Pizza dough

Pizza dough, like bread dough, needs a lot of manipulation to develop the gluten and help the dough to rise. Bread flour is made from hard wheat and has just the right amount of gluten for this crisp-crust pizza dough.

INGREDIENTS

2 packages (5 teaspoons) active dry yeast

2¼ cups (18 fl oz/560 ml) warm water (105°–115°F/40°–46°C)

2 teaspoons malt syrup or granulated sugar

¼ cup (2 fl oz/60 ml) olive oil

5 cups (25 oz/780 g) bread (strong) flour, plus extra as needed

1 tablespoon sea salt

All-purpose (plain) flour for rolling and shaping

MAKES TWO 12- TO 14-INCH (30- TO 35-CM) PIZZA CRUSTS

1 Proof the yeast
Pour the yeast into the warm water in a bowl and gently stir until the yeast dissolves. Let the yeast and water stand until foamy, about 5 minutes. (If the yeast doesn't foam, it is either inactive or you have used water that is too cold or too hot; start over with fresh yeast.)

2 Add the other ingredients
When you have determined that the yeast is active, add the malt syrup, oil, flour, and salt. The salt will kill the yeast if it comes in direct contact with it, so make sure to add the salt last.

6 Divide and shape the dough
Turn the dough out of the bowl onto a lightly oiled worked surface. Cut it in half with a sharp knife or bench scraper. Gently shape each half into a loose ball by moving the dough in a circle and pushing the sides down toward the bottom so that the ball tightens a little.

3 Mix the dough
Using a wooden spoon or your hands, stir the dough until if forms a rough mass. Using a plastic pastry scraper, scrape the dough onto a lightly floured work surface.

4 Knead the dough
Knead the dough until soft, smooth, and elastic, 8–10 minutes, adding flour to the work surface as needed to prevent the dough from sticking to it.

5 Let the dough rise
Form the dough into a ball and transfer it to a clean, lightly oiled bowl. Cover the bowl with plastic wrap or a clean kitchen towel. Let the dough rise in a warm, draft-free spot until it doubles in bulk, 1½–2 hours. (Alternatively, place the covered bowl in the refrigerator overnight. Let the dough come to room temperature before shaping.)

7 Roll out the dough
Cover one of the dough balls with a damp towel. Lightly dust the other dough ball with all-purpose flour. Using a rolling pin or your hands, roll or stretch the dough into a 12- to 14-inch (30- to 35-cm) round and transfer to a baker's peel (see entry 33b) or the top of an inverted baking pan. Top the pizza dough as desired and bake using the directions at right, or according to your recipe. Repeat with the remaining dough ball.

To bake a pizza, place a baking stone (see entry 33c) on a rack in the lower third of the oven. Preheat the oven to 500°F (260°C) for at least 30 minutes. Slide the topped pizza onto the hot stone and bake until the crust is crisp and brown, 10–15 minutes. Cut into wedges to serve.

Baking-powder biscuits

These old-fashioned biscuits can be rolled and cut out into any shape. Round is the classic form, but you can also roll out the dough into a rectangle and cut the biscuits into squares. This way, there are no dough scraps to reroll.

1 Stir together the dry ingredients
Preheat the oven to 425°F (220°C). Line a half-sheet pan with parchment (baking) paper or butter the pan lightly. In a bowl, stir together the flour, baking powder, and salt.

2 Incorporate the butter
Add the butter pieces to the flour mixture. Using a pastry blender or 2 knives, cut in the butter just until the mixture forms large, coarse crumbs the size of small peas.

INGREDIENTS

2 cups (10 oz/315 g) all-purpose (plain) flour

2½ teaspoons baking powder

½ teaspoon salt

6 tablespoons (3 oz/90 g) cold unsalted butter, cut into ½-inch (12-mm) pieces

¾ cup (6 fl oz/180 ml) whole milk

MAKES ABOUT 10 BISCUITS

You can also make these into drop biscuits by dropping the dough by tablespoonfuls onto a parchment-lined pan. Baked this way, the biscuits will be slightly irregular in shape and more rustic looking, but the peaks in the batter will get browned and crisp, while the insides will stay moist.

6 Place the biscuits on a pan
Place the dough rounds on a half-sheet pan lined with parchment (baking) paper or a nonstick baking mat, spacing them about 1 inch (2.5 cm) apart. Gather up the dough scraps, roll or pat them out again, cut out more dough rounds, and place them on the pan.

3 Pour in the milk
Pour in the milk and mix with a fork or silicone spatula just until the dry ingredients are moistened. Take care not to overmix the batter, which could create tough biscuits.

4 Shape the dough into a round
Turn the dough out onto a lightly floured work surface and knead gently a few times until it clings together. Using a light touch, roll or pat out the dough into a round about ¾ inch (2 cm) thick.

5 Cut out the biscuits
Using a 3-inch (7.5-cm) round biscuit cutter with straight or fluted sides, cut out dough rounds, pressing straight down and lifting straight up.

7 Bake the biscuits
Bake the biscuits until lightly browned, 15–18 minutes. Serve the biscuits right away, or let them cool slightly on a wire rack before serving.

Currant-cream scones

Cream scones have a flaky, slightly cakelike texture. The secret to making tender scones is to use a light touch, work quickly, and put them into the oven immediately after cutting. Scones can be flavored with a variety of fruits and spices.

1 Cut in the butter

Position a rack in the middle of the oven and preheat to 425°F (220°C). In a bowl, stir together the flour, the ¼ cup (2 oz/60 g) sugar, the baking powder, salt, and lemon zest. Using 2 knives or a pastry blender, cut in the butter until the mixture forms large, coarse crumbs the size of small peas.

2 Add the cream

Stir in the currants. Pour the ¾ cup (6 fl oz/180 ml) cream over the dry ingredients and mix with a fork or silicone spatula just until the dry ingredients are moistened.

INGREDIENTS

2 cups (10 oz/315 g) all-purpose (plain) flour

¼ cup (2 oz/60 g) plus 1 tablespoon granulated sugar

1 tablespoon baking powder

½ teaspoon salt

2 teaspoons grated lemon zest

6 tablespoons (3 oz/90 g) cold unsalted butter, cut into ½-inch (12-mm) pieces

½ cup (3 oz/90 g) dried currants

¾ cup (6 fl oz/180 ml) plus 2 teaspoons heavy (double) cream

1 teaspoon ground cinnamon

MAKES 6 SCONES

5 Brush the wedges with cream

In a small bowl, stir together the cinnamon and remaining 1 tablespoon sugar. Using a pastry brush, coat the wedges with the remaining 2 teaspoons cream and then sprinkle evenly with the cinnamon sugar.

3 Roll the dough into a round
Turn the dough out onto a lightly floured work surface and press together gently until the dough clings together in a ball. Using a light touch, roll or pat the dough into a round about ½ inch (12 mm) thick and 6½ inches (16.5 cm) in diameter.

4 Cut the round into wedges
Using a sharp knife, cut the round into 6 wedges, or use a 3-inch (7.5-cm) biscuit cutter to cut out dough rounds. Place the wedges 1 inch (2.5 cm) apart on a half-sheet pan lined with parchment (baking) paper.

6 Bake the scones
Bake the scones until golden brown, 13–17 minutes. Transfer to a wire rack to cool slightly. Serve warm.

SCONE VARIATIONS

Lemon-ginger scones
Follow the recipe for Currant-Cream Scones, but replace the currants with ⅓ cup (2 oz/60 g) diced crystallized ginger in step 2.

Dried cranberry scones
Follow the recipe for Currant-Cream Scones, but replace the lemon zest with orange zest in step 1, and the currants with ½ cup (2 oz/60 g) chopped dried cranberries in step 2.

Cherry-almond scones
Follow the recipe for Currant-Cream Scones, but replace the currants with ½ cup (2 oz/60 g) dried tart cherries and ½ cup (2½ oz/75 g) chopped almonds in step 2.

Scones with lemon curd
In England, scones are traditionally served with clotted cream and lemon curd. To make lemon curd, follow the recipe for Citrus Curd (entry 41) using organic lemons.

Buttermilk pancakes

Pancakes, or "flapjacks," are a favorite part of weekend breakfasts. Buttermilk lends its tangy flavor to this recipe. To keep the cooked pancakes warm while you cook the rest of the batter, put them on a baking sheet in a 200°F (95°C) oven.

1 Combine the ingredients
In a large mixing bowl, whisk together the flour, sugar, baking powder, baking soda, and salt. In a large glass measuring cup or small bowl, lightly beat the eggs, then add the buttermilk and melted butter and whisk to combine. Pour the buttermilk-egg mixture into the bowl with the dry ingredients.

2 Mix the batter
Gradually whisk from the center outward until the ingredients are well combined but the batter is still a little lumpy; do not overmix the batter or the pancakes will be heavy.

INGREDIENTS

2 cups (10 oz/315 g) all-purpose (plain) flour

2 tablespoons granulated sugar

2 teaspoons baking powder

1 teaspoon baking soda (bicarbonate of soda)

1 teaspoon salt

2 large eggs

2 cups (16 fl oz/500 ml) buttermilk

¼ cup (2 oz/60 g) unsalted butter, melted, plus butter for stacking the cakes, optional

1–2 tablespoons canola oil

MAKES 4 SERVINGS

5 Flip the pancakes
Cook until the surface of the pancake is covered with tiny bubbles, the bottom is browned, and the edges look dry, about 2 minutes. Flip each pancake over and continue to cook until the second side is golden brown, about 2 minutes longer.

FLAVORING PANCAKES

Blueberry pancakes

Follow the recipe for Buttermilk Pancakes. In step 4, while the batter is still liquid, sprinkle the top of each pancake with 1–2 tablespoons thawed frozen or fresh blueberries and proceed with the recipe.

Chocolate-chip pancakes

Follow the recipe for Buttermilk Pancakes. In step 4, while the batter is still liquid, sprinkle the top of each pancake with 1–2 tablespoons semisweet (plain) chocolate chips and proceed with the recipe.

Cornmeal pancakes

Follow the recipe for Buttermilk Pancakes, but reduce the all-purpose (plain) flour to 1½ cups (7½ oz/235 g) and add ½ cup (3 oz/90 g) cornmeal.

See entry 69 for topping suggestions

3 Oil the cooking surface
Heat a nonstick or cast-iron griddle or a large, heavy nonstick frying pan over high heat until a few drops of water flicked on the surface bounce across it. Use a pastry brush to lightly coat the entire cooking suface with oil.

4 Ladle the batter onto the pan
Fill a ¼-cup (2–fl oz/80-ml) ladle with batter to just below the lip. Pour the batter onto the griddle. If necessary, use the bottom of the ladle to nudge the batter into a circle. Repeat to form as many pancakes as you can fit on the griddle. If the pancakes touch, separate them with the edge of a metal spatula.

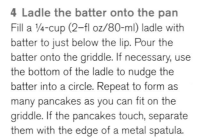

6 Stack the pancakes
Repeat steps 3–5 with the remaining batter, re-oiling the cooking surface as needed. Use a spatula to transfer the pancakes to a plate, stacking them on top of each other with pats of butter in between the layers, if desired.

Classic waffles

Waffle batter is easy to make, requiring ingredients you probably have on hand in the pantry. The only special equipment needed is a waffle maker. Be sure to read the manufacturer's instructions for use and clean-up before you start.

INGREDIENTS

2 large eggs

1¾ cup (14 fl oz/430 ml) buttermilk

¼ cup (2 fl oz/60 ml) canola oil

1½ cups (7½ oz/235 g) all-purpose (plain) flour

1 tablespoon granulated sugar

2 teaspoons baking powder

½ teaspoon ground cinnamon, optional

¼ teaspoon baking soda (bicarbonate of soda)

⅛ teaspoon fine sea salt

MAKES 4 SERVINGS

1 Whisk the eggs
Preheat a waffle iron according to the manufacturer's instructions. In a large mixing bowl, whisk the eggs until evenly mixed and frothy.

2 Add the wet ingredients
Add the buttermilk to a large glass measuring cup and then add the oil. Pour the buttermilk-oil mixture into the bowl with the eggs and whisk until blended.

5 Pour the batter onto the iron
When the waffle iron is hot, pour some batter evenly over the grid, easing it toward, but not into, the corners and edges with a wooden spoon or silicone spatula. Close the waffle iron and bake according to the manufacturer's instructions or until the waffle is golden brown, about 4 minutes.

3 Add the dry ingredients

Add the flour, sugar, baking powder, cinnamon (if using), baking soda, and salt and mix just until the large lumps disappear (small lumps are fine).

4 Transfer the batter

Using a silicone spatula, transfer the batter to a glass measuring cup or another container with a spout, which will help you pour the batter onto the waffle maker.

6 Lift out the waffles

When the waffles are done, use a fork to carefully lift them out of the waffle iron. Repeat to bake the remaining batter. To keep the finished waffles warm while you bake the rest of the batter, transfer them to a baking sheet or platter set in a 200°F (95°C) oven.

WAFFLE OR PANCAKE TOPPINGS

Summer fruit compote

In a nonaluminum saucepan over medium-high heat, bring ½ cup (4 oz/125 g) sugar and 2 tablespoons water to a boil and cook until golden brown, about 6 minutes. Let cool for 5 minutes. Meanwhile, add 1 mango, pitted and cut into ½-inch (12-mm) dice; 2 ripe plums, pitted and cut into ½-inch dice; and the seeds from 1 vanilla bean to a glass bowl. Add the cooled sugar syrup, mix gently, and let steep for 20 minutes before serving. Makes about 3 cups (24 oz/750 g).

Orange butter

In a bowl, mix together 4 tablespoons (2 oz/60 g) room-temperature unsalted butter, 1 tablespoon fresh orange juice, 1 teaspoon pure vanilla extract, a pinch of granulated sugar, and a pinch of salt until well blended and fluffy. Makes about ⅓ cup (3 fl oz/80 ml).

Bing cherry syrup

In a nonaluminum saucepan over high heat, combine ½ cup (3½ oz/105 g) firmly packed brown sugar, ½ cup (4 oz/125 g) granulated sugar, and 1 cup (8 fl oz/250 ml) warm water and stir until the sugar dissolves. Bring to a boil and cook, uncovered, for 5 minutes. Add 1½ cups (9 oz/280 g) stemmed and pitted large ripe Bing cherries, reduce the heat to low, and simmer until the cherries are cooked, 8–10 minutes. Remove from the heat and stir in 1 teaspoon pure almond extract. Let cool. Makes about 1½ cups (12 fl oz/375 ml).

Sweet crêpes

Crêpes are very thin, French-style pancakes that can be filled or sauced with a variety of sweet or savory mixtures. Unlike other pancakes, crêpes do not contain any leavening agents, so they do not puff up when they cook.

INGREDIENTS

½ cup (4 fl oz/125 ml) water

½ cup (4 fl oz/125 ml) whole milk

1 cup (5 oz/155 g) all-purpose (plain) flour

2 teaspoons sugar

1 teaspoon pure vanilla extract

2 large eggs

Melted unsalted butter for greasing the pan

MAKES 4 SERVINGS

Sweet crêpes can be topped with prepared chocolate-hazelnut (filbert) spread, jam or marmalade, or a variety of other sweet toppings. To make savory crêpes, omit the sugar and vanilla extract and add a pinch of salt. Fill savory crêpes with vegetables, cheese, or meat mixtures.

1 Add ingredients to the blender
To make the crêpe batter, in a blender, combine the water, milk, flour, sugar, and vanilla. Crack the eggs into a small bowl. Check for shells and then add the eggs to the blender.

2 Blend until smooth
Blend the mixture until very smooth and free of lumps. Pour the batter into a large liquid measuring cup or a bowl and refrigerate, covered, for at least 1 hour or up to 1 day.

6 Flip the crêpe
Use a small offset spatula to lift the edge of the crêpe, then carefully grasp the edge and quickly flip the crêpe over in the pan. Cook for another 10 seconds, until the second side is slightly browned and set.

3 Grease the pan

Using a pastry brush dipped in the melted butter, lightly grease the entire surface of a 9-inch (23-cm) crêpe pan or nonstick frying pan and place over medium heat.

4 Swirl the batter in the pan

Fill a ¼-cup (2–fl-oz/60-ml) ladle with batter to just below the lip. Holding the pan at an angle above the burner, pour the batter into the pan close to one edge. Quickly swirl the pan so that the batter covers the entire bottom of the pan. This should happen very fast since the batter will start to cook upon contact with the hot pan.

5 Cook the crêpe

Cook, shaking the pan from time to time, until the crêpe begins to bubble, the bottom is lightly browned, and the batter looks set, about 1 minute.

7 Stack the crêpes

Transfer the finished crêpe to a plate. Repeat steps 3–6 to cook the rest of the batter, stacking the crêpes on the plate between squares of waxed paper.

Preparing round cake pans

1 Butter the pan
Place a small amount of soft unsalted butter on a piece of waxed paper and spread it over the bottom and sides of a round cake pan, generously coating the entire surface.

2 Fold parchment into a triangle
Cut out a square of parchment (baking) paper that is 2 inches (5 cm) larger than the diameter of your pan. Fold it into quarters to make a smaller square. Fold the square in half to make a triangle.

3 Form a crease in the paper
Position the point of the triangle in the center of the pan, unfold it slightly, and press it into the pan so that a crease forms along the edge.

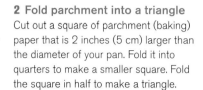

4 Cut the parchment paper
Remove the creased parchment paper from the pan. Use scissors to cut along the crease. Unfold the paper, which should form a circle that fits in the bottom of the pan.

5 Butter the parchment paper
Place the cut parchment paper back in the bottom of the buttered pan. Again, place a small amount of soft butter on a piece of waxed paper and spread the butter evenly over the paper.

6 Flour the pan
If the recipe calls for a floured pan, add about 2 tablespoons flour to the pan, then tilt and shake it so the flour coats the butter evenly. Invert the pan over the sink and tap it to release the excess flour.

Preparing tube pans

1 Butter the pan
If the recipe calls for a buttered pan, place a small amount of soft unsalted butter on a piece of waxed paper and spread it over the bottom, sides, and center tube of the pan.

2 Dust with flour
If the recipe calls for a floured pan, add about 2 tablespoons flour to the pan, then tilt and shake it so the flour coats the butter evenly. Tap out the excess flour.

Preparing sheet pans

1 Butter the pan and line with parchment
Place a small amount of soft unsalted butter on a piece of waxed paper and spread it over the bottom and sides of the pan. Cut parchment (baking) paper to fit and place in the pan.

2 Dust with flour
Butter the parchment paper. If the recipe calls for a floured pan, add about 2 tablespoons flour to the pan, then tilt and shake it so the flour coats the butter evenly. Tap out the excess flour.

Beating eggs & sugar

1 Beat the eggs and sugar
Using a handheld mixer with twin beaters or a stand mixer with the whip attachment, beat the eggs and sugar on medium-high speed. The mixture will change from bright to pale yellow as you beat.

2 Check for ribbon stage
After about 3 minutes, depending on how many eggs you are beating, the mixture will be close to *ribbon stage*. To check, pull the beaters out of the mixture; the batter should fall back on itself like a ribbon.

Releasing round cakes after baking

1 Cool the cake in the pan
Transfer the just-baked cake to a wire rack and let it cool in the pan for 15 minutes, or according to your recipe. Wire racks allow air to circulate, which speeds cooling and prevents sogginess.

2 Loosen the cake from the pan
Run a thin knife along the inside edge of the pan to loosen the cake, keeping the knife pressed against the pan sides so it won't cut into the cake.

3 Invert the pan
Place another wire rack upside down on the cake pan. Using pot holders, grasp the rack and pan together and invert them in one quick movement.

4 Lift the pan off the cake
When cool enough to touch, lift the pan away from the cake. The cake will release from the pan. Then, peel off the parchment (baking) paper, if present, and discard. Let the cake stand until cool to the touch, or according to your recipe.

CAKES

Releasing tube cakes after baking

1 Test for doneness
Insert a thin skewer or toothpick near the center of the pan. If it comes out clean, the cake is done. If it comes out wet or with crumbs clinging to it, bake for another 5 minutes and test again. Repeat until the skewer comes out clean.

2 Cool the cake in the pan
Using pot holders, carefully remove the cake from the oven and let cool on a wire rack. If you're baking an angel food cake, it needs to cool upside down: If the pan has feet, invert it onto a wire rack. If the pan does not have feet, you can invert the pan onto the neck of a wine bottle.

3 Loosen the cake in the pan
Run a thin knife around the sides and center tube of the pan. (If your tube pan has a fixed bottom, first loosen the cake from the pan sides with a knife, then use your fingers to gently pull the cake away.) Rotate the pan and keep working the cake out of the pan until it comes out cleanly.

4 Release the cake from the pan
Invert a large plate over the pan and invert the plate and pan together. Lift off the pan and the pan bottom, if it is not attached.

Releasing sheet cakes after baking

1 Cool the cake in the pan
Transfer the just-baked cake to a wire rack and let it cool in the pan for 25 minutes, or according to your recipe. Run a thin knife along the inside edge of the pan to loosen the cake.

2 Invert the cake onto a wire rack
Invert a wire rack on top of the cake and, using pot holders, invert the pan and rack together. Lift off the pan and peel off and discard the paper. Let the cake stand until cool to the touch.

Cooling & storing foam cakes

1 Cool the cake in the pan
Cakes made with the foam method, such as sponge cake or genoise, are often baked ahead of time and stored until ready to use. Let the baked cake cool on a wire rack for 10 minutes, or according to your recipe.

2 Invert the cake onto a wire rack
Run a thin knife along the inside edge of the pan to loosen the cake, keeping the knife pressed against the pan sides. Invert a wire rack on top of the cake, then invert the pan and rack together. Lift off the pan.

3 Peel off the parchment paper
Slowly and carefully peel off the parchment (baking) paper to speed cooling on the underside of the cake. Turn the cake top side up and let stand until cool to the touch, or according to your recipe.

4 Wrap the cake for storage
One at a time, wrap the cooled cake layers tightly in plastic wrap and store at room temperature for up to 2 days.

Rolling & storing sheet cakes

1 Unmold the sheet cake
To prevent cracking, sheet cakes intended for roulades or similar cake rolls should be rolled while still slightly warm and easy to shape. Release the sheet cake onto a wire cooling rack.

2 Dust the top of the cake
Cocoa powder or confectioners' (icing) sugar will keep the cake from sticking when it is rolled. Tap the side of a fine-mesh sieve filled with cocoa powder or sugar, to lightly dust the top of the cake.

3 Roll the cake in waxed paper
Cut two sheets of waxed paper that are slightly larger than the cake. Dust the paper with cocoa powder or confectioners' sugar. Place the cake, top side up, on the dusted paper. Top with the second sheet. Starting from a long side, roll up the cake.

4 Seal the cake in waxed paper
Fold the ends of the paper under the cake. Store at room temperature for up to 2 days.

Buttercream

This is a must-have recipe to add to any aspiring baker's repertoire. The classic smooth, creamy, full-flavored frosting can be used for a variety of layer cakes, cake rolls, or cupcakes and is always a crowd-pleaser. You can add flavorings or food coloring to fit the occasion.

INGREDIENTS

⅔ cup (5 oz/155 g) plus
2 tablespoons granulated sugar

¼ cup (2 fl oz/60 ml) water

1 tablespoon light corn syrup

3 cold large egg whites

¼ teaspoon cream of tartar

1¼ cups (10 oz/315 g) unsalted butter, at room temperature, cut into 2-tablespoon pieces

1 tablespoon pure vanilla extract

MAKES ABOUT 4½ CUPS
(36 FL OZ/1.1 L)

1 Cook the sugar syrup
In a small, heavy-bottomed saucepan, combine the ⅔ cup sugar, the water, and the corn syrup. Clip a candy thermometer onto the pan, making sure the stem is submerged in liquid. Partially cover and place over low heat until the sugar dissolves, about 5 minutes. Stir occassionally with a wooden spoon to make sure the sugar dissolves.

2 Boil until soft-ball stage
Raise the heat to high and let the syrup bubble vigorously, without stirring, until it is smooth and thick and registers 240°F (116°C) on the thermometer, about 5 minutes. Using a damp pastry brush, wipe down any sugar crystals that form on the pan sides. Remove from the heat.

5 Add the butter pieces
Increase the mixer speed to medium-high speed and add the butter, 1 piece at a time, beating until each portion is incorporated before adding the next one. If unbeaten butter sticks to the sides of the bowl, stop the mixer and use a silicone spatula to scrape it down into the rest of the mixture. Add the vanilla extract and beat until evenly combined.

CAKES

3 Whip the egg whites

Right away, fit a mixer with the whip attachment and beat the egg whites with the cream of tartar and the remaining 2 tablespoons sugar on medium speed until foamy, about 1 minute. Increase the speed to medium-high and continue beating until the peaks of the whites are slightly bent, or *soft peaks,* when the whip is pulled out of the mixture, about 2–3 minutes.

4 Beat in the hot sugar syrup

Reduce the mixer speed to low. Slowly pour the hot syrup in a thin stream into the egg whites. Pouring slowly prevents the sugar syrup from splashing onto the sides of the bowl. The outside of the bowl will feel hot to the touch. When all the syrup has been added, increase the mixer speed to medium-low and beat continuously for 5 minutes.

Chocolate buttercream

Follow the recipe to make Buttercream. In step 5, add 8 oz (250 g) chopped semisweet (plain) chocolate, melted and cooled, with the butter. Proceed with the recipe.

White chocolate buttercream

Follow the recipe to make Buttercream. In step 5, add 8 oz (250 g) finely chopped white chocolate, melted and cooled, with the butter. Proceed with the recipe.

Coconut buttercream

Follow the recipe to make Buttercream. In step 5, add 1 teaspoon coconut extract to the bowl with the vanilla extract. Proceed with the recipe.

Banana buttercream

Follow the recipe to make Buttercream. In step 5, reduce the vanilla extract to 1 teaspoon and add 2 tablespoons banana liqueur. Proceed with the recipe.

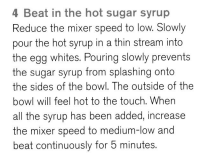

6 Adjust the consistency

When done, the buttercream should be soft enough to spread, but not so soft that it pours. If the butter is too cold and forms tiny lumps, put the bowl over (but not touching) hot water in a saucepan and stir vigorously until the lumps disappear and the buttercream is smooth, then continue to whip until fluffy. If the buttercream is too soft, refrigerate for 20 minutes, then whisk for a few seconds before using.

Cutting cakes into layers

1 Measure the height
Place the cake on a cool work surface. Hold a ruler alongside the cake to measure its height and note the midpoint. If the cake isn't even on all sides, try to find an average.

2 Mark the midpoint with toothpicks
Using toothpicks, mark the midpoint of the cake at 4–6 equally spaced intervals around the cake. The picks will guide you as you cut the cake into 2 equal layers.

3 Split the cake into layers
Using a long serrated knife and a sawing motion, cut the cake layer horizontally to make 2 layers. (Don't worry if the layers are uneven; they can be masked with filling or frosting.)

4 Place the layers on waxed paper
Place a large sheet of waxed paper on the work surface. Lift off the top cake layer and place it on the waxed paper.

5 Split the second layer
If you are cutting a second cake, follow steps 1–4 to split the second cake into 2 even layers and place them on another sheet of waxed paper.

6 Evaluate the layers
Look at the cake layers and determine the order in which they will be layered. You'll want to put any uneven layers in the center of the cake, and reserve one of the smooth cake tops for the top tier.

Filling & frosting a four-layer cake

1 Brush the layers with syrup
Have ready the frosting and filling for your cake. Using a pastry brush, brush each cake layer with a simple syrup, sometimes with flavor added, according to your recipe. Transfer one layer to a cake stand or plate.

2 Fill the layers
Slip 4 waxed-paper strips under the edges of the cake. Mound one-third of the filling on the first layer and using a large offset spatula, spread the filling evenly to the edges. Repeat with the remaining filling and layers.

3 Spread on the crumb coat
Using a clean offset spatula, spread a thin layer of frosting over the top and sides of the cake to seal in the crumbs and create a smooth surface.

4 Mound more frosting on the cake
Clean the spatula to remove any stray crumbs, then use it to mound half the remaining frosting on top of the cake.

5 Spread the frosting over the top
Using broad strokes, spread the frosting evenly over the top of the cake. Wipe the spatula frequently against the edge of the bowl to remove any excess.

6 Spread the frosting over the sides
Apply the remaining frosting in small batches to the sides of the cake, turning the plate or cake stand as needed to frost evenly. Finally, go over the top one last time to ensure it is smooth.

Cutting a dense cake

1 Unmold the cake
Dense cakes, like cheesecakes or chocolate tortes, are often baked in springform pans so they can be released easily. Run a thin knife along the inside edge of the pan to loosen the cake. Release and lift off the pan sides.

2 Warm the knife
A hot knife helps make a clean cut through a dense cake. Have ready a tall pitcher or glass filled with very hot water and a long, sharp knife. Dip the knife into the water and let sit for a few seconds to warm the blade.

3 Wipe the knife dry
Holding the sharp side of the knife away from you, wipe the blade dry with a paper towel or kitchen towel.

4 Cut the cake
Using the warm, dry knife, lightly score the top of the cake to indicate where you want to cut. Then, cut the cake along the score marks, dipping the knife in the hot water and wiping it clean after each cut.

Slicing a frozen torte

1 Mark the center
A torte is easiest to cut if solidly frozen, so be sure that it has been in the freezer for at least 3 hours. Lightly insert a toothpick or round wooden skewer to mark the center of the torte.

2 Score the slices
Starting at the center, and with the toothpick as a guide, use a chef's knife to score the slices gently. Cut down lightly on each mark, but don't cut all the way through the torte.

3 Warm the knife
Have ready a tall pitcher or glass filled with very hot water. Before each cut, dip the chef's knife into the water to warm it, which will ease slicing through the frozen layers.

4 Wipe the knife dry
Holding the sharp side of the knife away from you, wipe the blade dry with a paper towel or kitchen towel.

5 Cut the torte
Using the warm, dry chef's knife, cut the torte into individual slices along the score marks. The hot knife should easily cut through the cold ingredients.

6 Serve the slices
Use a triangular cake server to lift up each slice and place it on a plate. Return any remaining torte to the freezer right away.

Preparing cookie sheets

1 Cut the parchment paper
Cut a 16-by-14-inch (40-by-35-cm) rectangle of parchment (baking) paper and place on top of the cookie sheet.

2 Secure the parchment paper
Place a small amount of unsalted butter on a piece of parchment paper and dot the corners of the pan to "glue" the paper down.

Portioning cookie dough

1 Scoop up the dough
Line a cookie sheet with parchment (baking) paper or a silicone baking mat. Using an ice cream scoop or a large tablespoon, scoop up some of the dough.

2 Release the dough onto the sheet
Release the dough onto the prepared cookie sheet starting at one corner of the sheet. If necessary, use your fingers to smooth the dough into a compact ball.

3 Space out the dough portions
Repeat to place more dough balls on the baking sheet, spacing them 2–3 inches (5–7.5 cm) apart. The more butter in your recipe, the more the cookies will spread out when they are baking.

4 Store the baked cookies
Portioning and baking the dough in a methodical way will ensure evenly sized and shaped cookies. Store them at room temperature wrapped in plastic wrap with a square of waxed paper between each cookie.

Rolling out cookie dough

1 Dust the tools with flour
Lightly dust your work surface and rolling pin with flour. Keep a bowl of flour nearby in case you need more to prevent sticking.

2 Roll out the dough
Using gentle pressure and rolling from the center to the edges, roll out the dough disk. If the dough seems to be sticking to the rolling pin or work surface, lightly dust them with additional flour.

3 Turn the dough
After a few rolls, carefully turn the dough disk, lifting up and dusting with more flour under the dough, if necessary. This will help prevent the dough from sticking to the work surface. If the dough sticks, use a bench scraper to release it.

4 Finish rolling the dough
Continue to roll out the dough until it is about ⅛–¼ inch (3 mm–6 mm) thick, or according to the recipe. After you cut out the cookies, you can flatten the extra dough scraps into a disk and follow steps 1–3 to reroll the dough.

Cutting out sugar cookies

1 Cut out shapes
Using the cookie cutter of your choice, lightly dip it in flour, then press down firmly on the rolled-out dough to cut out a cookie. Remove the cutter but leave the cutout in place. Repeat to cut out as many cookies as possible, dipping the cutter in flour when needed to prevent sticking.

2 Transfer cookies to a cookie sheet
Use a metal spatula to loosen the cutout cookies and transfer them one at a time to prepared cookie sheets.

COOKIES & BARS

Rolling & cutting ice box cookies

1 Roll the dough into a log
Place the layered dough on waxed paper. With the long side facing you, roll the dough into a tight cylinder, using the waxed paper to help you roll. Chill the dough for at least 2 hours before slicing.

2 Slice the cookies
Using a large knife, cut the dough into slices about ¼ inch (6 mm) thick. To store any remaining dough, wrap it well and refrigerate or freeze for up to 1 week.

Cutting brownies or bars

1 Lift brownies/bars from the pan
Carefully peel the aluminum foil away from the sides of the baking pan and lift the cooled bars or brownies out of the pan.

2 Cut away the foil, if needed
If the foil sticks to the brownies or bars after baking, use a small knife to cut the foil away from the sides.

3 Warm the knife
Have ready a tall pitcher or glass filled with very hot water and a long, sharp knife. Dip the knife into the water to warm it and then wipe it clean with paper towels. A long, hot knife will help to cut the bars or brownies into even slices.

4 Cut the bars or brownies
Calculate how many vertical and horizontal rows you will need and, using a chef's knife, score the bars or brownies. Then, cut the bars or brownies along the score marks to create equal-sized pieces, warming the knife and wiping it clean between cuts.

Using a cookie press

1 Fill the cookie press
Follow the manufacturer's instructions to fit the cylinder with the cutting disk of your choice (here, a flower shape). Use a spoon to firmly pack the cookie dough into the cylinder of the cookie press, following the markings to discern a maximum fill line.

2 Press out the cookies
Securely attach the handle to the cookie press. Hold the cookie press upright and position it over an ungreased cookie sheet so that it is touching lightly, then press the dough out onto the sheet.

Forming & cutting biscotti

1 Form the logs
Line a cookie sheet with parchment (baking) paper or a silicone baking mat. Moisten your fingers and use them to gently press a portion of the biscotti dough into a rectangle about 10 inches (25 cm) long and 2½ inches (6 cm) wide. Repeat with the remaining dough, leaving 4 inches (10 cm) of space between the logs.

2 Bake the logs
Bake the cookie logs according to your recipe, or until the edges are light brown and the tops feel firm when touched gently. Let the logs cool.

3 Slice the logs and bake again
Using a serrated knife, cut each log into ¾-inch (2-cm) slices, or according to your recipe. Return the slices to the prepared cookie sheet, separating them so that air can circulate. Bake according to your recipe, or until the biscotti are golden around the edges and crisp.

4 Let the biscotti cool
Let the biscotti cool on the baking sheet for about 5 minutes. Then, using a spatula, transfer the cookies to a wire rack to cool completely, about 30 minutes. The biscotti will become crisp throughout as they cool.

COOKIES & BARS

Making & using a paper cone

1 Create the cone's tip
Start with a large triangular piece of parchment (baking) paper. With the center point of the triangle facing you, place your index finger in the middle of the base, and roll one of the side points towards the center.

2 Roll the cone
Continue rolling the paper, keeping its tip as tight as possible. Use your fingers to guide and secure the tip that you created in step 1.

3 Fold the ends inside
Adjust the tightness at the tip of the cone by pulling on the ends of the paper, then fold the ends inside the cone to secure it.

4 Fill the cone
Hold the cone open with one hand and, using a teaspoon, fill the cone about three-fourths full with icing, melted chocolate, or another decorative topping.

5 Fold the top over
Once the cone is filled, fold the ends of the paper over a few times to keep the icing from leaking out. Snip a small bit off the end of the cone to begin piping.

6 Pipe the design
Use the paper cone to pipe designs like dots or lines on cookies, cakes, or other items. This method is especially useful when you don't have a pastry bag on hand, or are working with small amounts of icing.

Glazing cookies

1 Outline the edges
For a basic glaze, combine 1 cup (4 oz/ 125 g) confectioners' (icing) sugar with 3 tablespoons heavy (double) cream. To this, you can add flavorings, such as vanilla or almond extract, or food coloring, to create the desired taste and look. Fill a paper cone about one-third full with the glaze and pipe an outline around the edge of the cookie.

2 Flood the glaze
Flooding is a technique that produces a clear, shiny finish. Pipe glaze into the center of the outlined cookie. The glaze should be loose enough to flood the cookie, but you can also nudge it into the corners with the point of the paper cone.

TROUBLESHOOTING
If the glaze hardens while spreading, stir in a few more drops of heavy (double) cream to loosen it up. You can store unused glaze in the refrigerator overnight and re-moisten it with drops of cream or water before using.

3 Let the glaze set
Let the glaze set and harden for 1–3 hours before serving the cookies or before piping other designs you want to remain distinct on top of the cookies.

Creating a swirl pattern

1 Dot the cookie with icing
Glaze a cookie by piping an outline around the edges and then flooding the middle with glaze (see entry 94). While the glaze is still wet, use a paper cone filled with a contrasting color to pipe dots onto the glazed cookie.

2 Make swirls
Gently drag a toothpick or wooden skewer through the piped dots, making swirling motions to achieve the desired effect.

Puréeing liquid mixtures with a food processor

1 Add the mixture to the work bowl
Working in batches, ladle a small amount of the item to be puréed into the work bowl of a food processor, taking care not to overfill the bowl. Working in batches ensures an even consistency.

2 Process the mixture
Secure the top on the food processor and pulse the machine a few times. Turn on the motor and process the mixture until it is smooth. If the mixture is hot, such as a soup, take care not to burn yourself.

3 Scrape down the sides
During processing, stop the machine a few times and use a silicone spatula to scrape down the sides of the work bowl.

TROUBLESHOOTING
If the liquid begins to ooze from the bottom of the food processor, you have filled the bowl too full. Stop the food processor, remove some of the mixture, and continue to process.

Puréeing liquid mixtures with a blender

1 Add the mixture to the blender
Working in batches, ladle the mixture into the blender, filling it
2 inches (5 cm) short of the top. Try to include an even proportion
of liquids to solids.

2 Blend the mixture
Start blending on low speed, then gradually increase the speed.
If you are blending a hot mixture, protect your hand with a towel
on top of the blender; steam can force the lid off.

Puréeing liquid mixtures with an immersion blender

1 Insert the wand into the mixture
Push the blender's wand into the mixture. Be sure that the blade
is completely submerged in the liquid to prevent spattering.
Turn on the blender and begin to purée.

2 Blend the mixture
Move the wand to reach all areas of the pot. When the mixture
reaches the desired consistency, turn off the blender and wait until
the blade stops spinning to remove it from the pot.

Making fresh bread crumbs

1 Dry the bread, if necessary
Start with slices of slightly stale bread with
a sturdy texture. Lay the bread slices flat on
a sheet pan overnight to dry out, or use bread
about 2 days past its peak of freshness.

2 Tear the slices into pieces
Fit a food processor with the metal blade.
Then, tear the bread into small pieces and
drop into the work bowl. Alternatively, drop
the pieces into the container of a blender.

3 Pulse to create crumbs
Pulse the food processor or blender until the
bread pieces are chopped into small crumbs.
You may need to do this in batches to ensure
that the crumbs are processed evenly.

4 Pour the crumbs into a bowl
Pour the crumbs into a bowl to measure them
for a recipe. You can use the bread crumbs
plain or you can coat or brown the crumbs in
butter or oil if directed.

Making dried bread crumbs

1 Dry the bread in the oven
Preheat the oven to 200°F (95°C). Arrange slices of coarse country bread, such as French or Italian bread, on a rimmed baking sheet. Let the slices dry in the low oven heat for about 1 hour.

2 Break the slices into pieces
Fit a food processor with the metal blade. Then, tear the bread into small pieces and drop into the work bowl. Alternatively, drop the pieces into the container of a blender.

3 Pulse to create crumbs
Pulse the food processor or blender until the bread pieces are ground into fine crumbs. You may need to do this in batches to ensure that the crumbs are processed evenly.

4 Pour the crumbs into a bowl
Pour the crumbs into a bowl, then measure them. If you are not using them right away, store the crumbs in an airtight container in the refrigerator for up to 1 month.

Frying tortilla chips

1 Cut corn tortillas into triangles
Create a stack of up to 8 corn tortillas and place on a cutting board. Using a serrated knife, cut the stack into 8 even wedge-shaped sections.

2 Pour the oil into the pan
A wok 12–14 inches (30–35 cm) in diameter or a large, deep heavy pot works the best for deep-frying. Pour in corn or peanut oil to a depth of 2 inches (5 cm).

3 Heat the oil
Attach a deep-frying thermometer to your wok or pot. Turn on the burner to medium-high and heat the oil until it reaches 375°F (190°C). This may take up to 10 minutes, depending on your stove.

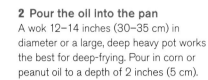

4 Fry the tortilla triangles
Carefully drop enough tortilla triangles into the oil to form a single layer on the surface. Fry, turning occasionally with a skimmer, until the tortillas are crisp and golden brown, 2–3 minutes.

5 Drain the chips
Using the skimmer, lift the tortilla chips out of the oil and place on paper towel–lined baking sheets. Blot the tops of the chips gently with additional paper towels.

6 Season the chips
Let the oil return to 375°F before frying the remaining chips. Lightly sprinkle the chips with salt before serving.

Frying potato chips

1 Heat the oil
Pour 2 inches (5 cm) of corn or peanut oil into a wok or deep, heavy pot and attach a deep-frying thermometer. Turn on the burner to medium-high and heat the oil to 325°F (165°C). This may take up to 10 minutes.

2 Prepare the potato slices
While the oil is heating, peel, thinly slice, and soak russet potatoes (see entry 322 or 323). Spin them dry in a salad spinner and drain on a paper towel–lined baking sheet. Pat the tops with additional paper towels.

3 Fry the potatoes once
Carefully slide about 1 cup (4 oz/125 g) of the potatoes into the hot oil. Fry the potatoes, using a skimmer to turn them occasionally, until they look firm and start to crisp around the edges, about 3 minutes.

4 Drain the chips
Using a skimmer, lift the potato chips out and place in a single layer on paper towel–lined baking sheets. Let the oil return to 325°F before frying the remaining chips in the same way.

5 Fry the chips a second time
Let the chips cool for at least 15 minutes. Reheat the oil over medium-high heat to 375°F (190°C). Again working in batches, fry the chips as you did before until crisp and medium-brown in color, 1–2 minutes.

6 Drain and season the chips
Transfer the chips to clean paper towel–lined baking sheets and blot the tops of the chips gently with more paper towels. Lightly sprinkle the chips with salt before serving.

Making pita chips

1 Slice the pita bread rounds
Create a stack of up to 3 pita bread rounds and place on a cutting board. Using a serrated knife or a chef's knife, cut the stack into 12 even wedge-shaped sections. Preheat the oven to 325°F (165°C).

2 Split open the wedges
Starting at the point of each triangle, carefully peel apart the layers until they lie flat, and then slice through the seam to separate the 2 layers.

3 Season the wedges
Arrange the wedges in a single layer and close together on rimmed baking sheets. Brush each wedge lightly with extra-virgin olive oil. Flavor the wedges as you like by sprinkling them with poppy, sesame, or fennel seeds and/or with paprika.

4 Bake the pita wedges
Bake the wedges until they are dry, crisp, and golden brown, 10–15 minutes.

Making toast cups

1 Shape the toast cups
Preheat the oven to 400°F (200°C). Brush the insides of miniature muffin cups with melted butter. One at a time, fit 3-inch (7.5-cm) rounds of thin white bread into each prepared cup.

2 Bake the toast cups
Bake until golden brown, about 10 minutes. Use tongs to gently remove the toast cups from the pans and transfer to wire racks to cool before serving.

Making crostini

1 Brush the bread slices with oil
Preheat the oven to 300°F (150°C). Arrange ¼-inch (6-mm) baguette slices in a single layer on a rimmed baking sheet and brush them lightly with extra-virgin olive oil.

2 Bake the bread slices
Bake the slices, turning once, until dried, crisp, and tinged with gold, about 30 minutes. Let the toasts cool completely on the baking sheets before serving.

COOKING BASICS

Clarifying butter

1 Melt the butter
Clarified butter is used to make filo-based pastries and in Indian cooking. Melt the butter in a saucepan over medium heat. After it melts, watch until the butter starts to bubble rapidly.

2 Skim off the foam
Immediately reduce the heat to medium-low and cook for 1 minute. Remove the pan from the heat, let stand for 2 minutes to let the milk solids settle to the bottom, and then use a large spoon to skim the foam off the top.

3 Pour off the butterfat
Carefully pour the clear yellow butterfat into a heatproof measuring cup. Pour very slowly, avoiding the white milk solids and liquid that have settled on the bottom of the pan.

4 Discard the milk solids
Discard the white milk solids and any liquid left behind. These are the parts of the butter that burn. Use the clarified butter as directed in your recipe.

Making a compound butter

1 Blend soft butter with flavorings
Put room temperature butter in a bowl. Using a silicone spatula, mash and fold the finely chopped flavoring ingredients (here, chopped olives and garlic) with the butter until it is smooth and uniformly mixed.

2 Spread the butter on waxed paper
Place a 12-inch (30-cm) square of waxed paper on a work surface and scrape the butter mixture onto it. Form a rough strip down the length of the paper, leaving about 1 inch (2.5 cm) uncovered along all sides.

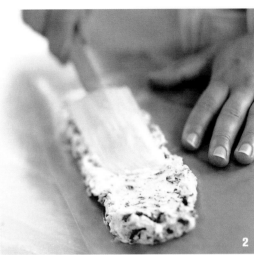

3 Roll the butter into a log
Roll the paper around the butter, applying light pressure and tucking the paper under the butter to form an evenly round log.

4 Twist the ends of the waxed paper
Twist the paper at the ends of the log in opposite directions to seal; it will look like a large piece of saltwater taffy. Refrigerate the butter log for at least 30 minutes. Use for topping grilled meat, poultry, or vegetables.

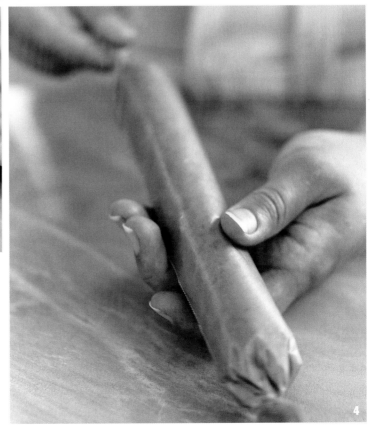

Dicing bacon

1 Slice the bacon into strips
Stack 2 or 3 bacon slices on top of one another on a cutting board and cut them lengthwise into narrow strips. Use thick-cut bacon, if possible, for the most uniform dice.

2 Dice the bacon
Cut the bacon strips crosswise at ¼-inch (6-mm) intervals to create small dice. If desired, freeze the bacon for about 20 minutes first to make it easier to cut.

Pitting olives

1 Pound the olives
Place the olives in a locking plastic bag, force out the excess air, and seal the bag. Using a meat pounder or a rolling pin, gently pound the olives to loosen the pits.

2 Remove the pits
Remove the crushed olives from the bag and separate the pits from the olive flesh with your fingers. Use a paring knife to cut the flesh from the pits of any stubborn olives.

Toasting nuts or seeds

1 Toast the nuts or seeds in a pan
Place the nuts (here, pine nuts) or seeds in a dry frying pan over medium heat. Stir them frequently to prevent burning. This process brings out the oils and flavors of the nuts or seeds.

2 Cool the nuts or seeds
As soon as the nuts or seeds are golden brown, after 2–3 minutes, transfer them to a plate so they don't continue to cook in the pan. They will become a little crisper as they cool.

Removing the skin of nuts

1 Toast the nuts
Place the nuts (here, hazelnuts/filberts) on a rimmed baking sheet and toast in a 350°F (180°C) oven until the color deepens and they become fragrant, 15–20 minutes.

2 Rub the nuts to remove the skins
After the nuts have cooled, rub them firmly with a kitchen towel and use your fingers to pull away any stubborn skins. If the skins don't come off easily, toast for another few minutes, then try again.

Boiling eggs

1 Lower the eggs into the water
Fill a saucepan with water and bring to
a full boil over high heat. Gently lower
1 or more eggs into the water and reduce
the heat to low. Simmer for 4 minutes
for soft, runny yolks; 6 minutes for eggs
with medium-firm yolks; and 8 minutes
for eggs with firm yolks.

2 Peel the eggs, if desired
Eggs with soft yolks, or soft-boiled eggs,
can be served as is in their shells. For
medium- or hard-cooked eggs, transfer
the eggs to an ice bath to stop the cooking.
After a few minutes, remove the eggs
from the water and hit them against a
counter to crack them all over, then peel
away and discard the shell.

3 Slice the eggs
To serve, cut medium-cooked eggs (top)
or hard-cooked eggs (bottom) in half or
quarters lengthwise, or into slices crosswise.

TROUBLESHOOTING
Overcooked eggs will have a gray-green
ring around the yolks and rubbery
whites. It's best to discard overcooked
eggs and start again.

Baking eggs

1 Crack the eggs into ramekins
Preheat the oven to 350°F (180°C). Crack
eggs and add them individually into buttered
ramekins, being careful to not let any shell
pieces drop into the dish.

2 Season and bake the eggs
Season the eggs with salt, pepper, and any
other spice called for in your recipe. Some
recipes call for adding a small amount of
cream for richness. Place the ramekins on
a baking sheet and bake until the egg
whites are set, but the egg yolks are still
runny, 10–15 minutes.

Poaching eggs

1 Acidulate the water
Bring a generous amount of water to a simmer in a large sauté pan. Add a teaspoon of distilled white vinegar or lemon juice. This will help the egg whites coagulate to form nicely rounded poached eggs.

2 Crack the egg into a dish
Crack one egg into a ramekin or another small dish. This will help you pour the egg into the hot liquid. Check for shells.

3 Pour the egg into the water
Gently ease the egg into the simmering water, starting near one edge of the pan. Repeat with the remaining eggs. Keep track of the order in which you added the eggs.

4 Simmer the eggs
Gently simmer the eggs, using a slotted spoon to keep them separated, for 3 minutes if you like runny yolks or 5 minutes if you prefer the yolks more set.

5 Remove the eggs from the water
Using the slotted spoon, gently scoop out the first egg you put into the water, blot it on a paper towel, and transfer it to a cutting board. Repeat with the remaining eggs.

6 Trim the eggs
Use a paring knife to trim off the ragged edges of the eggs to make a neat appearance. Serve right away.

1 Melt the butter
Place a 7- or 8-inch (18- or 20-cm) nonstick frying pan over medium heat and add about ½ tablespoon unsalted butter. Crack an egg into a small bowl and check for shells.

2 Add the eggs to the pan
When the butter is melted, carefully slide the egg into the pan. Repeat to add another egg. Reduce the heat to low and cook until the whites are firm and the yolks begin to thicken, about 3 minutes.

3 For sunny-side-up eggs:
Tilt the pan and spoon the pooled butter from the edge. Drizzle the butter over the eggs to baste them. Slide the eggs onto a plate and serve right away.

4 For over-easy or over-hard eggs:
Use a nonstick spatula to flip the eggs over gently. Cook for about 20 seconds for over-easy eggs and about 1–1½ minutes for over-hard eggs. Serve right away.

Scrambling eggs

1 Beat the eggs
Break the eggs into a bowl, check for shells, and add a pinch each of salt and pepper. Some recipes may call for other ingredients—like water or cream—to be added. Beat the eggs with a whisk or fork until well blended.

2 Pour the eggs into the pan
Place a nonstick frying pan over medium heat and add a small amount of unsalted butter. When the butter is melted, pour in the beaten eggs and reduce the heat to low.

3 Cook the eggs
Cook the eggs, stirring with a silicone spatula. As you cook, push the firmer eggs toward the center of the pan, letting the liquid eggs run to the sides. The more you stir the eggs, the smaller the curds will be.

4 Check the consistency
If you like soft-textured, moist eggs, cook them for 4–5 minutes. For firmer, drier eggs, cook them for 7–8 minutes. Serve right away.

Classic omelet

An omelet features beaten eggs cooked in a shallow pan and often filled with flavorful ingredients. Typically served for breakfast, an omelet also makes a wonderful light lunch or dinner dish. It can be filled with a variety of toppings to suit your preference.

INGREDIENTS

4 large eggs

¼ cup (2 fl oz/60 ml) water, milk, or heavy (double) cream

1 teaspoon fresh lemon juice, optional

Fine sea salt and freshly ground pepper

1 tablespoon unsalted butter

2 green (spring) onions, chopped

½ cup (1 oz/30 g) shredded aged white Cheddar cheese

MAKES 2 SERVINGS

1 Whisk the eggs
In a large bowl, combine the eggs, water, lemon juice (if using), and a pinch each of salt and pepper. Use a whisk to beat the mixture just until well blended. (Too much air will affect the omelet's texture.) A folded dish towel under the bowl will help steady it while you whisk.

2 Melt the butter
Place a 10-inch (25-cm) nonstick frying pan or omelet pan (see note) over medium-high heat and add the butter. When the butter has melted and the foam begins to subside, tilt the pan to distribute the butter evenly.

5 Add the omelet fillings
When the eggs have set in an even layer and there is no more standing liquid, after about 4 minutes, scatter the green onions and Cheddar cheese over half the omelet.

MORE OMELETS

Omelet with fine herbs

Follow the recipe to make the Classic Omelet. In step 1, add 1 tablespoon each minced fresh chervil, finely snipped fresh chives, minced fresh flat-leaf (Italian) parsley, and minced fresh tarragon to the eggs. Proceed with the recipe, omitting the cheese and onions.

Tomato and avocado omelet with cilantro

Follow the recipe to make the Classic Omelet. In step 5, replace the green onions with ¼ cup (1¾ oz/50 g) finely chopped tomato and replace the cheese with ½ cup (2½ oz/75 g) diced avocado. Proceed with the recipe. Garnish the finished omelet with 1 tablespoon minced fresh cilantro (fresh coriander).

Asparagus and Gruyère omelet

Blanch 12 oz (375 g) asparagus, cut into 1-inch (2.5-cm) lengths, and set aside. Follow the recipe to make the Classic Omelet. In step 5, replace the onions with the blanched asparagus and replace the Cheddar cheese with Gruyère cheese. Proceed with the recipe.

3 Add the egg mixture
Pour the egg mixture into the pan, using a silicone spatula to scrape all the ingredients from the bowl into the pan.

4 Distribute the eggs evenly
Let the eggs cook for 30 seconds, then use the spatula to push the cooked eggs carefully toward the center, while keeping the eggs in an even layer. Tilt the pan so that the uncooked eggs will flow toward the edges, and the omelet will cook evenly.

6 Fold the omelet
Use the spatula to fold the untopped half of the omelet over the filled half to create a half circle. Let the omelet cook for about 30 seconds longer, then slide it out onto a warmed plate and serve right away.

Vegetable frittata

A frittata is a mixture of eggs, cheese, and other ingredients cooked slowly in a frying pan until firm. It differs from an omelet, as the flavorings are blended with the beaten eggs instead of being used as a filling. Also, frittatas are typically cut into wedges for serving.

INGREDIENTS

5 large eggs

Fine sea salt and freshly ground pepper

1 tablespoon olive oil

2 medium zucchini (courgettes), cut into ½-inch (12-mm) cubes

⅓ cup (2½ oz/75 g) ricotta cheese

Leaves from 2 sprigs fresh basil, torn into small pieces, plus more for garnish, optional

MAKES 2 SERVINGS

1 Beat the eggs
In a bowl, combine the eggs and a pinch each of salt and pepper. Use a whisk to beat the mixture just until well blended. (Too much air will affect the frittata's texture.) Set aside. Preheat the oven to 350°F (180°C).

2 Heat the oil
Place an 8-inch (20-cm) nonstick, ovenproof frying pan over medium heat. Add the oil and heat until it shimmers.

5 Cook the eggs
Reduce the heat to low and cook, stirring, for 1 minute. Place the pan in the oven and bake until the frittata has gently risen and is set, 8–12 minutes.

MORE FRITTATAS

Chicken sausage & sun-dried tomato frittata

Follow the recipe to make the Vegetable Frittata. In step 3, replace the zucchini with ½ lb (250 g) cooked chicken sausage, cut into ½-inch (12-mm) slices. Sauté until warmed through, 1–2 minutes. Stir in 3 oil-packed sun-dried tomatoes, drained and cut into small pieces. Omit the ricotta cheese and basil. Proceed with the recipe.

Bacon & arugula frittata

Follow the recipe to make the Vegetable Frittata. In step 2, omit the oil and add 4 strips of thick-cut bacon to the preheated frying pan. Fry the bacon until the edges are crisp, about 8 minutes. Transfer to paper towels to drain. Cut the bacon crosswise into 1-inch (2.5-cm) pieces. In step 3, pour off all but 1 tablesoon of the bacon fat from the frying pan, and over medium heat, sauté 2 cups (2 oz/60 g) arugula (rocket) until just wilted. Sprinkle the bacon over the arugula and proceed with the recipe, omitting the ricotta and basil.

Southwestern frittata

Follow the recipe to make the Vegetable Frittata. In step 3, replace the zucchini with 1 Yukon gold potato, peeled and cut into ½-inch (12-mm) cubes. Sauté until the potatoes are tender and browned, about 8 minutes. In step 4, replace the ricotta and basil with 1 can (4 oz/125 g) diced green chiles, drained, and 1 cup (4 oz/125 g) shredded pepper jack cheese. Proceed with the recipe. Top with salsa and sour cream, if desired.

3 Sauté the zucchini
Add the zucchini, season lightly with salt and pepper, and sauté until softened and lightly browned, 1–2 minutes.

4 Add the remaining ingredients
Add the ricotta cheese and the basil to the pan with the zucchini and stir until well mixed. Pour in the beaten eggs.

6 Cut the frittata into wedges
Slide the frittata out of the pan onto a cutting board. Using a chef's knife, cut the frittata into 4 wedges. Garnish with torn basil leaves, if desired, and serve right away.

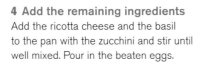

Quiche Lorraine

Quiche is a savory custard-based pie. Traditionally offered as a first course, now it is more commonly served as a main course at brunch or lunchtime. True quiche Lorraine contains bacon and onions, but some add Gruyère cheese. Other flavorings can easily be substituted.

1 Arrange the bacon on the crust
In a frying pan over medium heat, fry the bacon until the edges are crisp, about 8 minutes. Transfer to paper towels to drain. Cut the bacon crosswise into 1-inch (2.5 cm) pieces. Arrange the pieces evenly in the prebaked crust. Set aside.

2 Make the custard
Preheat the oven to 350°F (180°C). In a large bowl, whisk together the eggs, salt, pepper, and nutmeg until blended. Add the cream and milk and whisk until well blended.

INGREDIENTS

4 slices thick-cut lean bacon

1 recipe Flaky Pie Dough (see entry 240 or 241), partially blind baked (see entry 247)

3 large eggs

½ teaspoon salt

⅛ teaspoon freshly ground pepper

Pinch of freshly grated nutmeg

¾ cup (6 fl oz/180 ml) heavy (double) cream

¾ cup (6 fl oz/180 ml) whole milk

1 tablespoon unsalted butter, cut into ¼-inch (6-mm) pieces

SERVES 8

4 Pour the custard into the shell
Slowly pour the custard over the bacon in the crust. Dot the top with the butter pieces.

5 Bake the quiche
Bake the quiche until the top is lightly browned and the filling is just barely set when you give the dish a gentle shake, 40–45 minutes. Transfer the quiche to a wire rack and let cool for 5 minutes. Cut into wedges to serve.

MORE QUICHE COMBINATIONS

Bacon-Gruyère quiche

Follow the recipe to make Quiche Lorraine. In step 4, sprinkle 1 cup (4 oz/155 g) shredded Gruyère cheese on top of the custard and proceed with the recipe.

Broccoli-Cheddar quiche

Blanch 12 oz (375 g) broccoli, cut into 1-inch (2.5-cm) florets, until barely tender (see entry 341), pat dry, and set aside. Follow the recipe to make Quiche Lorraine. In step 1, replace the bacon with the blanched broccoli. In step 4, sprinkle 1 cup (4 oz/125 g) shredded Cheddar cheese on top of the custard and proceed with the recipe.

Spinach-feta quiche

Follow the recipe to make Quiche Lorraine. In step 1, replace the bacon with 1 cup (1 oz/30g) steamed spinach, or thawed, frozen spinach, drained and squeezed completely dry. In step 4, sprinkle 1 cup (5 oz/155 g) crumbled feta cheese on top of the custard and proceed with the recipe.

Asparagus-leek quiche

Blanch 1 cup (2 oz/60 g) cut-up asparagus spears (1-inch/2.5-cm pieces) until barely tender (see entry 341), pat dry, and set aside. Sauté two chopped leeks, white and light green parts only, until soft, and set aside. Follow the recipe to make Quiche Lorraine. In step 1, replace the bacon with the blanched asparagus and sautéed leeks and proceed with the recipe.

Mushroom-thyme quiche

Follow the recipe to make Quiche Lorraine. In step 1, replace the bacon with 1 cup (3 oz/90 g) sautéed mushrooms, adding 2 tablespoons fresh thyme to the mushrooms during the last minute of cooking. In step 4, sprinkle 1 cup (4 oz/155 g) shredded Swiss, Gruyère, or Cheddar cheese on top of the custard and proceed with the recipe.

Artichoke–red pepper quiche

Follow the recipe to make Quiche Lorraine. In step 1, replace the bacon with 1 can (14 oz/440 g) artichoke hearts, drained and quartered. In step 4, sprinkle 1 cup (4 oz/155 g) shredded mozzarella or fontina cheese on top of the custard. Before baking, arrange two red bell peppers (capsicums), roasted and peeled (see entry 321) and cut into ½-inch (12-mm) strips, over the custard and proceed with the recipe.

3 Strain the custard
Pour the egg mixture through a medium-mesh sieve into a measuring cup to ensure that there are no stray egg shell fragments or membranes.

Cleaning a whole fish

1 Inspect the fish
You can buy a whole fish that has been gutted and scaled, or *dressed,* by the fishmonger, but it may still need further cleaning. Look for gills, fins, stray scales, and blood or entrails inside.

2 Trim the sharp fins, if present
Lay the fish on one side. Using a boning knife or paring knife, make shallow ½-inch (12-mm) incisions next to the fins on both the upper side (dorsal fin) and the lower or belly side (anal fin).

3 Remove the fins
Using fish tweezers, needle-nose pliers, or a kitchen towel, pull the fins away along with the supporting bones. Repeat steps 2 and 3, if necessary, on the other side of the fish.

4 Remove any stray scales
Using the back of a stiff knife, scrape away any stray scales, working from the tail end toward the head. You may want to do this inside a large bag or over the sink to keep the scales from scattering.

5 Scrape away any blood inside
With the tip of the knife, slit open the membrane along the backbone inside the cavity (the kidney strip), then scrape and rinse out any traces of blood and entrails.

6 Snip off the gills
If the gills, which look like pink or red crescents, are still present, snip them out with kitchen scissors. Rinse the fish well inside and out under running cold water and pat it dry.

Filleting a whole fish

1 Make a cut below the head
Separate the flesh from the head on one side: With the head pointing away from you, and using a fillet knife, make a diagonal cut halfway through the fish just below the gill.

2 Cut along the back
Starting at the head, run the knife along the back, cutting through the skin and into the flesh about 1 inch (2.5 cm) deep until you reach the tail and can see the backbone.

3 Retrace the cut
Using long, smooth strokes, retrace the cut along the top side of the backbone with the tip of the knife to free the top part of the fillet.

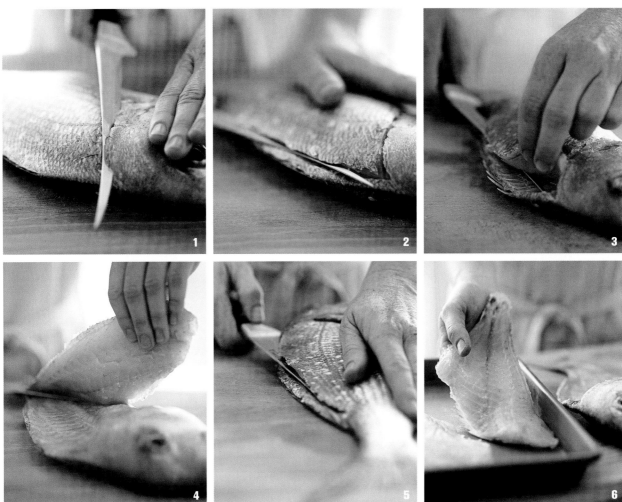

4 Remove the first fillet
Lift up the edge of the flesh to reveal the ribs. Cut the flesh away, sliding the knife as you go along the curve of the ribs to remove as much flesh as possible. Remove the first fillet.

5 Cut the second fillet
Turn the fish over and make another crosswise diagonal cut to separate the flesh from the head. Again, cut along the top side of the backbone to free the top part of the second fillet.

6 Remove the second fillet
Cut the flesh away as before, sliding the knife along the ribs. Remove the second fillet. Reserve the bones from a lean fish, if desired, for making fish stock or fumet (see entries 295 and 296).

Skinning a fish fillet

1 Hold the skin securely
Position the tail end of a fillet near the edge of a cutting board. Use a fillet knife or other long, slim-bladed knife to cut vertically down to, but not through, the skin.

2 Slide the knife under the fillet
Holding the skin taut, position the blade at a slight angle upward between the skin and the flesh. Slide the blade back and forth along the skin, as if "shaving" off the flesh. Discard the skin and rinse the fillet.

Cutting out pin bones

1 Cut along the sides of the bones
The pin bones of some fish are difficult to pull out and should be removed with a knife. Lay a fillet skin(ned) side down. Using a boning or fillet knife, cut along one side of the pin bones and then the other.

2 Pull out the strip with the bones
Using your fingers, pull out the thin strip of flesh containing the bones and discard. This method works well for flatfish or when you are cutting fish into cubes, as for ceviche.

Pulling out pin bones

1 Feel for the bones
Lay a fillet skin(ned) side down. Run a fingertip along the fillet near the center. If you feel the tips of bones sticking up, the pin bones are still in place.

2 Pull out the bones
Using fish tweezers or needle-nose pliers, pull out the bones one by one, gripping the tip of each bone and pulling up diagonally. This method will preserve the shape of the whole fillets.

Portioning fish fillets

1 Note the fillet's angle
Look at the thick end of the fillet, which will probably be cut at an angle. Lay your knife against this cut edge and note the angle of the blade. You'll want to hold the knife at this same angle as you cut.

2 Cut the fillet in half by weight
Estimate the halfway point of the fillet, bearing in mind the weight difference due to the tapering shape. Holding the knife at the same angle as the fillet end, cut the fillet into 2 pieces of about equal weight.

3 Cut the fillet into serving portions
Divide each half into serving-sized portions (typically 4–6 oz/125–185 g each) according to your recipe. The cuts may need to be farther apart as you approach the tail.

4 Weigh the portions for accuracy
Done correctly, you should have all pieces roughly equal in weight, which will cook in the same amount of time. Use a kitchen scale, if desired, for accuracy.

FISH

Cutting raw fish into cubes

1 Skin, bone, and trim the fish
Skin the fish and remove any pin bones, if necessary (see entries 122–124). Use a boning or fillet knife to remove any white tendons, connective tissue, or dark spots.

2 Cut the fish into slices
Notice the way the muscle fibers (or grain) run. Using the boning or fillet knife, cut the fish with the grain into slices as wide as you want the final cubes to be.

3 Cut the slices into strips
Lay the slices flat on the cutting board one or two at a time. Cut the slices into strips that are the same width as the slices.

4 Cut the strips into cubes
Line up the strips, a few at a time, and cut them crosswise into even cubes, or dice. Be sure to keep the fish cold until you are ready to use it.

Testing fish for doneness visually

1 Cut into the fish
Using the tip of a paring knife, slice into the flesh of the fish. Unless you are cooking fish to the rare stage, the interior should be barely opaque but still very moist.

TROUBLESHOOTING
Overcooked fish will look dry, be very firm, and will flake apart when you cut into it. To prevent overcooking, test for doneness periodically as shown at left.

Testing fish for doneness by temperature & texture

1 Test the fish by temperature
Insert an instant-read thermometer into the thickest part (usually near the head), but don't go through the meat into the cavity. Most fish are done when they reach 115°–125°F (46–52°C).

2 Test the fish by feel
Insert a wooden skewer or wire cake tester into the thickest part of the fish. It should enter easily with little resistance. Or, touch the skewer to your lower lip; it should be quite warm.

Fish steamed in parchment

Cooking fish in parchment (baking) paper pouches, or *en papillote*, combines the convenience of baking and the delicate moist heat of steaming in one cooking method. The juices from the fish, vegetables, and herb butter mingle to form a light, flavorful sauce.

INGREDIENTS

4 red snapper, or other firm, lean, mild fish fillets, 4–6 oz (125–185 g) each

4 tablespoons (2 oz/60 g) unsalted butter, at room temperature

4–6 sprigs fresh flat-leaf (Italian) parsley

3 or 4 sprigs fresh thyme

3 or 4 blades fresh chives

Kosher salt and freshly ground pepper

1 fennel bulb, about ¾ lb (375 g), cut into thin slices

1 large carrot, cut into julienne

4 teaspoons dry white wine such as Sauvignon Blanc

MAKES 4 SERVINGS

1 Create the packets
Preheat the oven to 400°F (200°C). Cut out 4 pieces of parchment (baking) paper, each 12 by 15 inches (30 by 38 cm). Lay 1 sheet on a dry work surface, with the long edge facing you, and fold it in half like a book. Crease about 1 inch (2.5 cm) on both ends of the fold, but not the middle.

2 Place the fish on the paper
Use scissors to cut about 2 inches (5 cm) off the opposite open corners to ease folding. Open the parchment and lay a fillet, skinned side down, about 1 inch (2.5 cm) to one side of the fold, leaving at least 2 inches (5 cm) of paper on the other three sides.

6 Seal the packet
When you reach the other end, twist the end of the paper to seal the packet. Repeat to press the creases again to make sure the packet is sealed. This will ensure that the steam remains inside the packet to cook the fish and vegetables. Lay the packet on a rimmed baking sheet. Repeat to seal the remaining packets.

3 Add the vegetables and butter
Mix together the butter, parsley, thyme, chives, and a pinch each of salt and pepper. Scatter one-fourth of the fennel slices and julienned carrots on top of the fish, then drizzle with 1 teaspoon of the wine. Spread one-fourth of the herb butter on the other side of the fold. Repeat to create the remaining packets.

4 Enclose the fish
Working with 1 packet at a time, fold the paper back over the fish and vegetables, matching the edges. Starting at the end of the fold nearest you, fold the corner of the parchment in toward the fish, creasing the fold and creating a new corner.

5 Make a series of folds
Fold that new corner in toward the center and crease again, creating another new corner. Continue in this way all around the packet, making a curved border around the fish.

 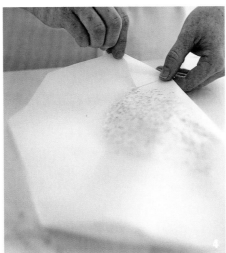 

7 Bake the fish packets
Put the baking sheet in the oven and let the fish and vegetables steam in their packets until the paper puffs up and begins to brown, 7–9 minutes. To test the fish for doneness, insert a wooden skewer through the paper into the thickest part of the fish, leave it there for a few seconds, then pull it out and immediately touch the tip to your lower lip. If it is quite warm, the fish is done.

Poached salmon

130

RECIPE

Poaching, or cooking in gently simmering liquid, is one of the best ways to preserve the delicate silky texture of salmon and other types of fish (tuna, halibut, and cod also work well). Here, a simple, but highly flavored court bouillon serves as the poaching medium.

INGREDIENTS

1 large yellow or white onion, cut into thick slices

6 cups (48 fl oz/1.5 l) water

1 cup (8 fl oz/250 ml) dry white wine such as Sauvignon Blanc

2 or 3 sprigs fresh tarragon

2 or 3 sprigs fresh flat-leaf (Italian) parsley

6 peppercorns

1 bay leaf

1 salmon fillet, about 2 lb (1 kg)

1 teaspoon kosher salt

¼ teaspoon freshly ground white pepper

Hollandaise Sauce or Béarnaise Sauce (entry 279) for serving, optional

MAKES 6 SERVINGS

1 Make the court bouillon
In a wide, nonreactive saucepan, add the onion slices, water, wine, tarragon, parsley, peppercorns, and bay leaf. Bring to a simmer over medium-high just until small bubbles break on the surface. Reduce the heat to maintain a bare simmer and cook until the liquid has a full herbal flavor, about 20 minutes.

2 Strain the court bouillon
Strain liquid through a fine-mesh sieve lined with cheesecloth (muslin) into a heatproof bowl and discard the solids. Return the court bouillon to the pan and set aside.

6 Poach the fish
Adjust the heat so the court bouillon never boils; a bubble or two breaking the surface now and then is fine. Poach the fish for about 10 minutes per inch (2.5 cm) of thickness. About 1 or 2 minutes before the estimated cooking time has elapsed, test a piece of fish with a wooden skewer. The skewer should enter the thickest part easily but encounter a little resistance when it hits uncooked meat in the center. When only a small pocket of undercooked center remains, remove the pan from the heat.

FISH

3 Cut the fillet into portions
Skin the fillet (see entry 122). Examine the fillet to determine if there are any pin bones. If present, pull out and discard the bones (see entry 124) Using a chef's knife, cut the fillet into 6 equal portions (see entry 125).

4 Weigh the portions, if desired
If desired, as you work, use a kitchen scale to weigh each piece. You're aiming for portions weighing 5–6 oz (155–185 g) each. (Alternatively, purchase six 5- to 6-oz fillets from the fishmonger.) Season the fish on both sides with the salt and white pepper.

5 Add the fish to the liquid
Place the pan with the court bouillon over high heat. While the liquid is heating, compare the depth of the liquid to the thickness of the salmon pieces and add water if necessary to match. When steam begins to rise from the liquid but before it starts bubbling, reduce the heat to low. Ease the pieces, skinned side down, into the warm liquid.

7 Drain and serve the fish
Drain each piece of fish briefly on a paper towel, then transfer to warmed plates. Serve right away with the sauce of your choice.

Deep-fried fish fillets

Deep-frying gives mild white fish fillets a light, crisp texture and deep golden color that's difficult to achieve with any other method. The flour coating helps to protect the fish from the heat, and the beer in the batter adds sweetness and airiness.

INGREDIENTS

¾ cup (4 oz/125 g) all-purpose (plain) flour, plus about ½ cup (2½ oz/75 g) for dredging

¾ teaspoon kosher salt

1 cup (8 fl oz/250 ml) brown or amber ale

1½–2 lb (750 g–1 kg) skinned firm white fish fillets such as cod, halibut, or large flounder

¼ teaspoon freshly ground pepper

Peanut, corn, or canola oil for frying

MAKES 6 SERVINGS

1 Make the batter
In a bowl, whisk together the ¾ cup flour with ¼ teaspoon of the salt. Slowly pour in the beer, whisking just until all the flour is moistened; it's fine if a few small lumps remain. Set the batter aside at room temperature.

2 Season the fish
Cut the fillets into 12 roughly equal pieces as even in thickness as possible (about 2 oz/60 g each). Fold very thin tail sections in half, or roll them up skinned side in, to more closely match the others in thickness. Sprinkle the fish evenly with the remaining ½ teaspoon salt and the pepper.

6 Batter and fry the fish
When the thermometer reads between 350°F (180°C) and 360°F (182°C), the oil is ready for frying. Slide the dredged fish into the batter. Using the tongs, lift the fish pieces one by one out of the batter, waiting a second or two for the excess batter to drip away, and gently lower them into the hot oil. If you have a splatter screen (a large screen with a handle that fits directly over the pot), put it in place immediately.

3 Set up your frying station
Choose a large, deep heavy pot. Set up the following items near the stove, in order going toward the pot: the plate of fish, a shallow dish with the remaining ½ cup flour for dredging, the bowl of batter, and tongs for adding the fish pieces to the hot oil.

4 Set up your equipment
On the other side of the pot, perhaps over a couple of unused stove burners, set a warmed baking sheet topped with a wire rack and the wire skimmer. If you like, put several layers of paper towels under the rack to absorb the cooking oil. Make sure this pan is not too close to the frying burner or the paper might catch fire.

5 Dredge the fillets in flour
Fill the pot no more than half full of oil. Clip a deep-frying thermometer to the side of the pot. Place the oil over high heat. Meanwhile, dip 3 or 4 fish pieces in the flour and turn them to coat well, then shake off the excess. This is known as *dredging,* and it helps the batter adhere to the fish.

7 Drain the fish
Fry the fish pieces until golden brown, about 3 minutes, turning the pieces over once with the skimmer. Scoop up the pieces with the skimmer, let drain for a few seconds over the pot, then transfer to the wire rack. While the first batch of fish is frying, flour and batter the next batch of 3 or 4 pieces. Keep an eye on the oil temperature and adjust the heat as needed.

Sautéing fish fillets

1 Dredge the fillets in flour
Season the fish with salt and pepper. Place a sauté pan over medium-high heat. Add a thin layer of olive oil to the warm pan and heat. Meanwhile, dredge the fillets in the flour, shaking off the excess.

2 Sauté the fillets
When the oil shimmers, add as many fillets to the pan as you can without crowding. Cook until the bottoms are golden brown, about 2 minutes. Using a wide spatula, turn the fillets. Cook until golden brown on the second side, about 1 minute longer.

Broiling fish steaks

1 Add the fish to a heated pan
Heat a heavy, ovenproof frying pan over medium-high heat. Add a thin layer of olive oil, swirling the pan to coat it lightly. Choose the best-looking side of the fish (here salmon steaks), and lay the steaks face down in the pan. Preheat the broiler (grill).

2 Sear the first side of the fish
Cook until the first side is lightly browned, about 1 minute. Then, using a sturdy offset spatula, turn the steaks and remove the pan from the heat. Searing the steaks on the stove top first begins the browning process that will continue under the broiler.

3 Brush on a glaze, if desired
Working quickly, brush any glaze called for in your recipe (here, a honey-mustard glaze), in a thick layer on top of the steaks. Put the pan under the broiler and broil until the glaze is browned and a skewer easily enters the center of the fish, or an instant-read thermometer inserted in the thickest part registers 120°F (49°C), about 4 minutes.

4 Serve the fish steaks
Use the spatula to transfer the steaks to warmed plates and serve right away.

Carving a whole fish

1 Transfer to a serving platter
Whole fish can be presented on a serving
platter or served directly from the cooking
vessel. To transfer the fish to a platter,
use a spatula and large spoon.

2 Cut through the skin
Using the edge of a metal serving spoon,
cut through the skin lengthwise along
the dorsal fin on the upper side of the
fish. Use a second spoon to steady
the fish as you cut.

3 Remove the first fillet
Slide the bottom spoon against the bones
and toward the ribs to lift away a portion
of the flesh and skin, using the other spoon
to steady it from the top.

4 Remove the backbone
Once all the flesh on the top fillet is removed,
slide a spoon under the backbone and lift
it away. This gives you access to the second
fillet underneath.

FISH

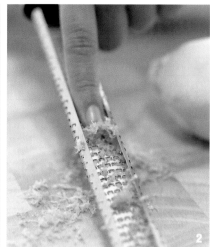

Grating citrus zest

1 Zest the fruit
Citrus fruits are easiest to zest when whole. Use a rasp grater or the small grating holes on a box grater-shredder to remove only the colored portion of the peel, not the bitter white pith underneath.

2 Clean off the grater
Don't forget to scrape all the zest from the back of a grater, where it naturally gathers. After zesting, juice the fruit, if desired.

Mincing citrus zest

1 Remove the zest from the fruit
If your recipe calls for coarser pieces of zest than you can get from grating, use a vegetable peeler to remove strips of just the colored portion of the peel, not the bitter white pith. If you mistakenly include some of the pith, scrape it off with a paring knife.

2 Mince the zest
Stack 2 or 3 zest strips, then use a chef's knife to cut them lengthwise into very thin strips. Cut the strips crosswise into very fine pieces.

Juicing citrus fruit

1 Cut the fruit in half
Press and roll the citrus fruit firmly against the work surface to break some of the membranes holding in the juice. Then, using a chef's knife, cut the fruit in half crosswise.

2 Juice the citrus
For small amounts of juice, use a citrus reamer to pierce the membranes as you turn and squeeze the fruit. Catch the juice in a bowl and strain it to remove the seeds before using. For larger amounts, you can use a citrus press or electric juicer.

Sectioning citrus

1 Cut off the ends of the fruit
Sections of citrus fruit, free of peel and pith, are sometimes called citrus *suprêmes*. Using a utility knife or a chef's knife, cut a thin slice from the top and bottom of the fruit to expose the flesh.

2 Cut away the peel and pith
Stand the fruit on the board on a flat end. Following the curve of the fruit, cut away all the peel and white pith. Continue in this fashion, working your way around the fruit.

3 Trim any remaining pith
It is hard to remove all of the pith during the first pass, so to clean up the fruit, angle it and, using a gentle sawing motion, trim away any remaining bits of white pith.

4 Release the segments
Working over a bowl, make a cut on both sides of each segment to free it from the membrane, letting the segment and juice drop into the bowl below.

Peeling & coring apples

1 Peel the apple

Using a vegetable peeler, preferably one with a swivel blade, and starting at the stem end, remove the peel from the apple flesh in a circular motion.

2 Cut the apple into quarters

Cut the peeled apple in half from stem to blossom end. Turn the halves flat side down and cut them in half again to make quarters. If desired, rub the apple flesh with a cut lemon to prevent browning.

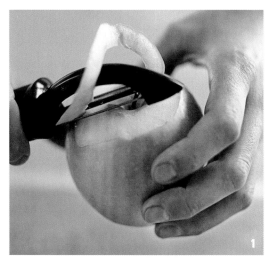

3 Cut out the core

Using a paring knife, make an angled incision into the center on one side of the core. Turn the quarter and make another incision to complete the V cut and release the core. Repeat with the remaining quarters.

4 Or, core a whole apple:

To core a whole apple, hold the apple firmly and push the corer straight down through the apple. It may take a little muscle.

Peeling & coring pears

1 Peel the pear
Holding the pear at a slight angle and starting at the stem end, use a vegetable peeler, preferably one with a swivel blade, to remove the peel from the pear. Rotate and repeat to remove the rest of the peel.

2 Cut the pear in half
A peeled pear can be slippery, so make sure you stabilize it on the cutting board with one hand. Using a utility knife or a chef's knife, halve the pear lengthwise. If desired, rub the flesh with a cut lemon to prevent browning.

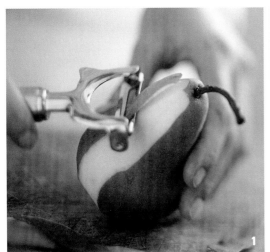

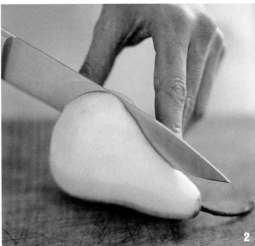

3 Scoop out the core
Use a melon baller to scoop the seeds from a pear half. Next, use the melon baller to create a shallow channel from the core to the stem. Repeat with the remaining half.

4 Or, core a whole pear:
To core a whole pear while leaving the stem end intact, use a melon baller to scoop out the seeds and tough core from the pear's blossom end.

FRUIT

Peeling stone fruit

1 Score the bottom

The best way to peel peaches, nectarines, plums, and other thin-skinned fruits is to plunge them into boiling water, or *blanch* them. First, use a paring knife to cut a shallow X on the bottom of each fruit.

2 Place in boiling water

Using a slotted spoon, lower the fruit, 1 or 2 pieces at a time, into a pot of boiling water. Let them sit until the skin loosens, 15–30 seconds, depending on ripeness.

3 Transfer to ice water to cool

Immediately transfer the fruit to a large bowl of ice water. This step, called *shocking*, will stop the cooking process.

4 Peel the fruit

When the fruit is cool enough to handle, find the X you made in step 1. Grasp a corner of loose skin between your thumb and a paring knife and pull off the skin. Repeat to remove all of the peel.

Pitting stone fruit

1 Cut the fruit in half
Using a paring knife, cut the fruit in half lengthwise, cutting carefully around the pit at the center. Rotate the halves in opposite directions to separate them.

2 Pit the fruit
Use the tip of the knife to gently dig under the pit and ease it out. You may have to try from a couple of different angles, depending on the ripeness of the fruit and whether you are using clingstone fruit.

Pitting cherries

1 Split the cherry with a paring knife
Using a paring knife, cut around the whole cherry to cut it in half. Rotate the halves in opposite directions to separate them. Use your fingers or the knife to the pry the pit from the cherry.

2 Or, use a cherry/olive pitter:
Position a stemmed cherry, stemmed side up, in the cradle of a cherry/olive pitter. Hold the pitter over a small bowl and press down, ejecting the pit into the bowl.

Hulling strawberries

1 Insert a knife near the stem
Use your thumb to push back the stem leaves. Insert a paring knife at an angle into the strawberry flesh until it reaches the middle of the top part of the berry.

2 Pull off the stem and hull
Place the thumb of the hand holding the knife on top of the stem and make a circular cut to release the hull.

Working with melon

1 Cut the melon in half
Place the melon on its side on a cutting board. Put a hand on one end of the melon to secure it in place on the board. Using a chef's knife, carefully but firmly cut the melon in half crosswise.

2 Scoop out the seeds
Use a large spoon to scoop out the seeds from the center of the melon and discard the seeds. Sometimes it is helpful to tilt the melon slightly for stability.

3 Cut the melon halves into wedges
Stand a melon half hollow side up. Using a chef's knife, cut it in half. Repeat with the other melon half to create 4 wedges.

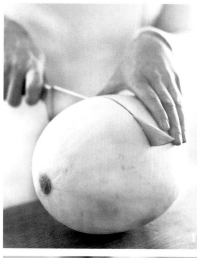

4 Remove the skin from the flesh
One at a time, stand each wedge, skin side down, on the board. Carefully cut the melon flesh from the skin, following the curve of the wedge.

5 Cut the wedges into portions
Lay each wedge on one of its sides on the board. Cut each wedge lengthwise into even semicircular pieces.

6 Cut the pieces into rough cubes
Working with 1 or 2 melon pieces at a time, stack the pieces, then cut them crosswise into rough cubes.

Working with watermelon

1 Cut the melon into wedges
Using a large chef's knife, carefully cut the watermelon in half, then cut each half in half again to make large wedges.

2 Remove the skin from the flesh
Cut the pink flesh from the green rind: One at a time, place the melon wedges on the cutting board and, using the chef's knife, gently cut the flesh from the rind following the curve of the rind.

3 Cut the wedges into strips
If the watermelon has seeds, remove the seeds by gently scooping them out with a grapefruit spoon. Lay the wedges on their sides and, using the chef's knife, cut them lengthwise into even strips.

4 Cut the strips into cubes
Line up 2 or 3 strips at a time and then cut crosswise into rough cubes. Repeat with the remaining wedges.

Working with mangoes

1 Pit the mango
Stand a mango up on its narrow side on a cutting board, with the stem end facing away from you. Using a utility knife or a chef's knife, cut down the length of the fruit, about 1 inch (2.5 cm) from the stem and just grazing the pit. Repeat on the other side of the pit.

2 Score the flesh
Place one mango half, cut side up, on the board. Using a paring knife, make cuts ½ inch (12 mm) apart in a crisscross pattern in the flesh, stopping short of the skin.

3 Peel back the skin
With both hands, hold the scored mango half from its skin side and push up to expose cubes of mango flesh.

4 Cut off the mango cubes
Using the paring knife, carefully cut across the base of the cubes to free them, letting them fall into a bowl. Repeat steps 2–4 with the remaining mango half.

Working with papayas

1 Peel off the skin
Using a vegetable peeler, preferably one with a swivel blade, peel the papaya from stem end to blossom end. Use a chef's knife to cut the papaya in half lengthwise.

2 Scoop out the seeds
Hold the papaya over a small bowl and, using a large spoon, scoop out the seeds into the bowl. Repeat with the remaining half. The seeds are edible and, if desired, can be washed and added to salads or other dishes for a peppery bite.

Working with pineapple

1 Slice off the skin
Using a serrated knife, cut off the top (crown) and bottom from the pineapple. Stand the pineapple upright on a cutting board and slice off the skin in long strips, following the curve of the pineapple and leaving the small, brown "eyes."

2 Cut out the "eyes"
Lay the pineapple on its side and, using a paring knife, cut away the brown "eyes" by inserting the knife at an angle and cutting around the eye until it comes free. Repeat to remove all the eyes.

3 Slice the fruit
Using the serrated knife, cut the pineapple crosswise through the core into slices according to your recipe.

4 Remove the core
Working with one slice at a time, use a paring knife to cut out the hard circular core at the center. Discard the core piece and repeat with the remaining slices.

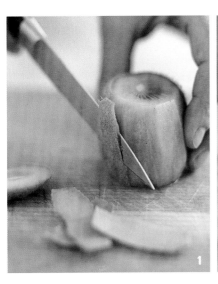

Working with kiwifruit

1 Peel off the fuzzy skin
Place a kiwi on its side on a cutting board. Using a utility or paring knife, cut off the stem and blossom ends. Turn the kiwi upright and cut off the skin in long strips, following the curve of the fruit.

2 Slice the fruit
Lay the peeled kiwi on its side and cut it crosswise into slices.

Simmering dried beans

1 Sort the beans
Place the dried beans in a colander. Sort through the beans and discard any that are wrinkled or blemished, along with any pebbles or grit. Rinse the beans well and transfer them to a large saucepan.

2 Soak the beans
Cover the beans with water by 2 inches (5 cm) and soak for at least 8 hours. (Quick-soak method: Bring the water to a boil over high heat, reduce the heat to low, and simmer for 2 minutes. Let cool in the liquid.)

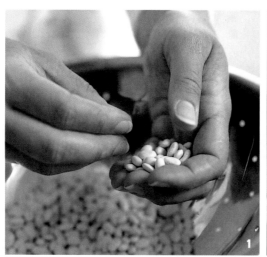

3 Cook the beans
Drain the beans and return them to the saucepan. Add water or stock to cover and bring to a gentle boil over high heat. Reduce the heat to medium-low and simmer, partially covered, until tender, 45–55 minutes.

4 Drain the beans
Drain the beans through a sieve into the sink or over a large bowl if you wish to save the cooking liquid.

Making a bean purée

1 Process the beans
Add drained cooked or canned beans to
a food processor and pulse until a coarse
purée forms. Stop the machine occasionally
to scrape down the sides of the bowl
with a silicone spatula.

2 Thin the purée
With the motor running, slowly pour stock,
water, or reserved cooking liquid through the
feed tube of the food processor until the
purée reaches the desired consistency. It
should still be thick enough to hold its shape.

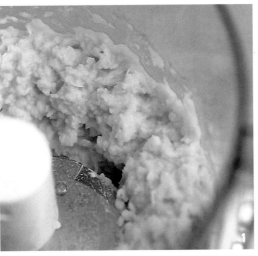

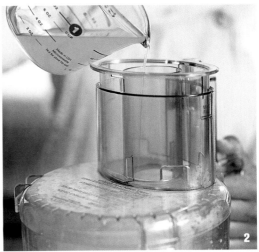

3 Add flavorings
With the motor running, add any liquid
flavorings, such as olive oil or lemon juice, so
they will be thoroughly mixed with the beans.

4 Adjust the seasonings
Transfer the finished purée to a bowl. At this
point, you can stir in any other ingredients
you'd like: reserved whole beans, fresh herbs,
spices, and salt and pepper. Refrigerate for
at least 1 hour to blend the flavors.

Cooking long-grain rice

1 Add rice to the water
In a heavy saucepan with a tight-fitting lid, combine 1¾ parts water, 1 part rice, and a small amount of salt. (Some recipes call for first rinsing the rice until the water runs clear.)

2 Cover and simmer
Bring the water a boil over high heat, then reduce the heat to low, cover, and simmer until the rice is tender and the water is absorbed, 15–20 minutes.

3 Fluff the rice
Let the rice sit in the pan, undisturbed, for 5–10 minutes, then use a fork to "fluff" the grains before serving.

4 To cook other types of rice:
To cook short or medium-grained rice (top), use 1½ parts water; to cook brown rice (right), use 2 parts water and cook for 45–60 minutes; to cook wild rice (left), use 3 parts water and cook for about 1 hour.

Making rice pilaf

1 Sauté the aromatics
In a heavy saucepan with a tight-fitting lid over medium heat, add a small amount of butter or olive oil. If the recipe calls for aromatics such as minced onion or garlic, sauté until translucent before adding the rice.

2 Stir in the rice
Add the rice to the aromatics in the pan and sauté, stirring frequently, until the grains are coated with butter or oil and heated through.

3 Pour in the hot stock
Pour in 1¾ parts hot stock for every 1 part rice and bring to a boil over high heat, stirring the grains occasionally. Reduce the heat to low, cover, and simmer until the grains are tender, 15–20 minutes.

4 Fluff the rice
Let the rice stand in the pan, undisturbed, for 5–10 minutes, then use a fork to "fluff" the grains before serving.

Making polenta

1 Add polenta to boiling liquid
In a heavy saucepan over high heat, bring 5 parts stock or water to a boil and add a large pinch of salt. Add 1 part coarse yellow cornmeal (polenta) to the boiling liquid in a very thin stream, stirring constantly with a whisk to prevent lumps.

2 Cook the polenta
Reduce the heat to low and simmer, stirring often, until the polenta pulls away from the sides of the pan but is still thin enough to fall from the whisk, 20–45 minutes.

3 Stir in the flavorings
Remove the pan from the heat and stir in butter and grated Parmesan cheese, if desired. Serve right away or follow step 4 to make firm polenta.

4 Cut firm polenta into pieces
For firm polenta, pour the soft polenta into a buttered baking pan and spread in an even layer. Cover and refrigerate until firm enough to cut into shapes, at least 2 hours. Pan-fry or grill the polenta shapes before serving.

Working with bulgur wheat

1 Soak the grains
Bulgur wheat can be soaked or cooked, depending on your recipe. For the soaking method, add 1 part bulgur wheat to a large heatproof bowl. Stir in 2 parts boiling water, cover with plastic wrap, and let stand until tender, about 1 hour.

2 Cook the grains
In a saucepan, combine 1 part bulgur wheat and 2 parts water. Bring to a boil over high heat, then reduce the heat to low and simmer, covered, for 10–12 minutes.

Making couscous

1 Cook the couscous
There are two types of couscous, regular and instant. For regular couscous, add 1 part grain to 2 parts boiling liquid and boil for 10 minutes, then let it stand, covered, for 15–20 minutes. For instant couscous, stir 1 part grain into 1 part boiling liquid, cover, remove from the heat, and let stand 5–10 minutes.

2 Fluff the couscous
After the couscous has absorbed all the water, use a fork to "fluff" the grains before serving.

Cooking lentils

1 Sort and rinse the lentils
Sort through the lentils and remove any grit. Pour the lentils into a bowl of cold water and discard any that float to the surface. Drain the lentils and rinse well.

2 Simmer the lentils
Add the lentils to a saucepan and cover with cold water by 2 inches (5 cm). Bring to a boil over high heat, then reduce the heat to low and simmer until tender. For red or yellow lentils, cook for 8–10 minutes. For green or brown lentils, cook for 30–45 minutes. Drain before serving.

Making oatmeal

1 Measure out the oats and water
If using rolled oats, you'll need 1 cup (3 oz/90 g) oats for 2 cups (16 fl oz/500 ml) water. For 1 cup (6 oz/185 g) steel-cut oats, you'll need 2½ cups (20 fl oz/625 ml) water.

2 Cook the oats
In a heavy saucepan over high heat, bring the water to a boil. Stir in the oats, reduce the heat to low, and simmer, uncovered, stirring occasionally, until tender and creamy, 5–8 minutes for rolled oats or 20–25 minutes for steel-cut oats.

Basic risotto

Risotto is an example of the Italian talent of turning the simplest ingredients into a sublime dish. There, risotto is served as a first course, or "primi," to complement a main course. It can be easily varied with vegetables, cheese, poultry, or seafood.

2 Sauté the rice
In a large, heavy saucepan, heat the oil over medium heat. Add the onion and sauté until softened, about 4 minutes. Add the rice and stir until the grains are coated with oil and translucent with a white dot in the center, about 3 minutes.

1 Heat the stock
In a saucepan over medium heat, bring the stock to a gentle simmer. Reduce the heat to very low and keep the stock warm on a nearby burner.

INGREDIENTS

6 cups (48 fl oz/1.5 l) Chicken Stock (see entry 298)

¼ cup (2 fl oz/60 ml) extra-virgin olive oil

½ cup (2½ oz/75 g) finely chopped yellow onion

2 cups (14 oz/440 g) Arborio or Carnaroli rice

1 cup (8 fl oz/250 ml) dry white wine, such as Sauvignon Blanc, at room temperature

1–2 tablespoons unsalted butter

Parmigiano-Reggiano cheese, grated, to taste, optional

Salt and freshly ground pepper

MAKES 6 SERVINGS

5 Check the consistency
After about 20 minutes of cooking, taste a small amount of risotto. When done, the rice grains will be almost tender to the bite but slightly firm at the center, and the risotto will look creamy. If it's not quite done, continue to cook, adding more stock as needed.

3 Incorporate a ladleful of stock
Add the wine and cook, stirring, until completely absorbed. Add a small ladleful of the simmering stock and cook, stirring frequently, until the stock is almost completely absorbed.

4 Add the stock in increments
Continue to add the stock in small amounts, cooking and stirring the rice until the stock is nearly all absorbed. This will take about 20 minutes. Reserve about ¼ cup (2 fl oz/60 ml) of the chicken stock.

6 Stir in the flavorings
Remove the risotto from the heat. Stir in the butter, Parmesan cheese (if using), and salt and pepper to taste. Serve right away.

MORE RISOTTOS

Asparagus risotto

Blanch 12 oz (375 g) asparagus, cut into 2-inch (5-cm) lengths until barely tender (see entry 341) and set aside. Follow the recipe to make Basic Risotto. In step 6, add the blanched asparagus with the butter and proceed with the recipe.

Mushroom risotto

In a large saucepan over medium-high heat, melt 2 tablespoons unsalted butter. Add 12 oz (375 g) mixed cleaned sliced mushrooms and sauté until softened, about 5 minutes. Stir in 1½ teaspoons minced fresh thyme and set aside. Follow the recipe to make Basic Risotto. In step 6, add the mushroom mixture with the butter and proceed with the recipe.

Four-cheese risotto

Follow the recipe to make Basic Risotto. In step 6, omit the butter and stir in ½ cup (3 oz/90 g) room-temperature mascarpone cheese, ¼ cup (1 oz/30 g) crumbled Gorgonzola cheese, ¼ cup (1 oz/30 g) finely grated Parmigiano-Reggiano cheese, and ¼ cup (1 oz/30 g) finely grated Asiago cheese and proceed with the recipe.

161

Setting up a gas or propane grill

1 Secure the fuel line
Following the manufacturer's directions for your grill, secure the grill's gas line to the fuel tank or other fuel source.

2 Light the grill
Following the manufacturer's directions for your grill, turn the gas nozzle to the "open" position. Open the grill lid, turn the burners on, and depress the ignition switch. Adjust the heat level as directed in your recipe.

162

Using wood chips with a smoker box

1 Add dry chips to a smoker box
If you have a smoker box, usually made from cast iron, remove the vented cover and add 1 handful of dry wood chips to the bottom of the box.

2 Ignite the chips
Use a gas wand or long-handled match to ignite the dry chips. When fully lit, add wet chips, a handful at a time, to the box to create a head of smoke.

163

Using wood chips with a foil packet

1 Create a foil packet
Fold a 12-by-16-inch (30-by-40-cm) piece of aluminum foil in half and place a handful of dry chips in the center. Fold over and crimp the three open sides. Tear open the top to reveal the chips.

2 Ignite the chips
Place the foil packet directly over a heat element until the dry chips ignite. Add the soaked chips, a handful at a time, on top of the dry chips to create a head of smoke.

Using a chimney starter

1 Stuff the chimney starter
A chimney starter is an easy way to start a charcoal fire, and it will not impart unwanted flavors to your food. Remove the grill grate. Turn the chimney starter upside down on the fire bed and stuff loosely with newspaper.

TROUBLESHOOTING
If the paper is packed too firmly, it will hinder the oxygen flow and prevent the paper from lighting. You should only need 2–3 full sheets of crumpled paper.

2 Add the coals
Turn the chimney starter right side up on the fire bed, keeping the newspaper secure in the bottom. Add briquettes or hardwood charcoal to the top of the canister.

3 Ignite the newspaper
Using a gas wand or long-handled match, light the newspaper. The flames will rise upward and ignite the coals.

Direct-heat charcoal grilling

1 Pour the ignited coals into the fire bed
When the coals in the chimney starter are covered with a layer of white ash, use a grill mitt to turn the chimney starter over and dump the coals into the fire bed.

2 Arrange the coals to form heat zones
Using long-handled tongs, arrange the coals 2 or 3 layers deep in one-third of the fire bed and 1 or 2 layers deep in another third, leaving the remaining third free of coals.

Indirect-heat charcoal grilling

1 Arrange the coals on two sides of the grill
After pouring the coals into the firebed (see above), use long-handled tongs to arrange the coals in 2 equal piles on 2 sides of the grill, leaving the center free of coals.

2 Position a drip pan in the center
Place an aluminum-foil pan in the area between the coals to catch the dripping fat and create a cool zone for the grill. Add enough water to fill the pan halfway up the sides.

Using wood chips with a charcoal grill

1 Soak the wood chips
Put several handfuls of hardwood chips, such as mesquite, hickory, or cherry, in a large bowl with water to cover. Let soak for at least 30 minutes.

2 Arrange the coals
Set up the grill for indirect-heat grilling (see entry 166). Position the drip pan in the center and fill it halfway with water.

3 Add the wood chips
Sprinkle a handful of soaked wood chips directly onto the hot coals. The moist wood chips will smolder, releasing their aromatic smoke slowly as you cook.

4 Replace the grill grate
Position the grill grate over the coals and cook the food according to your recipe. Add more wood chips through the grill grate as needed to keep up a head of smoke.

Oiling a grill grate

1 Dip rolled paper towels in oil
Pour a moderate amount of canola oil into a small container. Fold 4 paper towels in half, then roll them up tightly into a cylinder. Using tongs, grasp the towels and soak them in the oil.

2 Brush the grate with the oiled towels
Still using the tongs, brush the grill grate with the oiled towels. The oil keeps food, particularly fish and other delicate items, from sticking to the grill grate and makes cleanup easier.

Cleaning a grill

1 Scrub the grill with a wire brush
Before and after cooking, while the grill is hot, use a long-handled wire brush to scrape off any food particles that are stuck on the grill grate. This is an important step in grill maintenance.

2 Close the grill cover
When you're finished grilling, be sure that the burners are off on a gas grill, and close the grill cover. For a charcoal grill, close the vents on the side of the grill to inhibit the oxygen flow.

Creating crosshatch grill marks

1 Line up the food
Place the food on the preheated grill, making sure the pieces all face the same direction. Take note of the order in which you put the food on the grill, so you know which piece to turn first.

2 Rotate the food
Let the food cook undisturbed for one-fourth of the cooking time to develop good grill marks. Using tongs, rotate each piece 90 degrees and continue cooking, undisturbed, for another one-fourth of the cooking time.

3 Turn over the food
Starting with the first piece of food, turn over the pieces, again lining them up in the same direction. You'll notice the square-shaped cross-hatching you created in steps 1 and 2.

4 Crosshatch the second side
Let the food cook undisturbed for another one-fourth of the cooking time to develop good grill marks. Using tongs, again rotate each item 90 degrees and continue cooking for the remaining amount of time, as directed in your recipe.

Plank grilling

1 Soak the planks
In a pan or sink, soak the hardwood plank(s) in cold water to cover for at least 2 hours or up to overnight. Drain well. Prepare a charcoal or gas grill for indirect-heat grilling over medium heat.

2 Prepare the grill and cook
Place fish fillets on the plank, move to a cool part of the grill, and cook according to your recipe. Some recipes call for charring the planks before cooking on them.

GRILLING BASICS

Working with mint, basil, or sage

1 Select the herb
Large-leafed herbs such as basil (top left), sage (top right), and mint (bottom) can be either slivered or chopped. Choose bunches with bright green, fragrant leaves. Avoid those with wilted or discolored leaves.

2 Pull the leaves from the stems
Rinse the herbs and pat them dry. Use your fingers to pull off the large leaves one at a time from the stems. Discard the stems and any discolored leaves.

3 Stack and roll the leaves
Stack 5 or 6 herb leaves on top of one another, then roll the stack lengthwise into a tight cylinder.

4 Cut the leaves into ribbons
Using a chef's knife, cut the leaves crosswise into narrow slivers. These ribbons are known as a *chiffonade*. To chop the herbs, gather the slivers into a pile and rock the blade over them to cut into small pieces.

Working with tarragon, parsley, or cilantro

1 Select the herb
Herbs such as tarragon (top left), flat-leaf
(Italian) parsley (right), and cilantro (fresh
coriander/bottom) are delicate. Choose
bunches with bright green, fragrant leaves.
Avoid those with wilted leaves.

2 Pluck the leaves from the stems
Rinse the herbs and pat them dry. Grasp the
leaves between your thumb and index finger
and pluck them from the stems. Discard the
stems and any discolored leaves.

3 Chop the leaves
Gather the leaves on a cutting board. Rest
the fingertips of one hand on the tip of a
chef's knife and rock the blade back and forth
briefly over the leaves to chop coarsely.

4 Finely chop or mince the leaves
Continue to regather the leaves and rock
the blade over them until they are chopped
into small, even pieces (finely chopped),
or into pieces as fine as possible (minced).

HERBS & SPICES

Working with oregano, marjoram, or thyme

1 Select the herb
Small-leafed, branched herbs such as thyme (right), marjoram (left), and oregano (top) are a bit hardier than other herbs. Choose bunches with bright green, fragrant leaves. Avoid bundles with limp stems or branches.

2 Remove the leaves from the stems
Rinse the herbs and pat them dry. Remove the petal-like leaves by gently running your thumb and index finger down the stems. Discard the stems and any discolored leaves.

3 Chop the leaves
Gather the leaves on a cutting board. Rest the fingertips of one hand on the tip of a chef's knife and rock the blade back and forth briefly over the leaves to chop coarsely.

4 Finely chop or mince the leaves
Continue to regather the leaves and rock the blade over them until they are chopped into small, even pieces (finely chopped), or into pieces as fine as possible (minced).

Working with rosemary

1 Remove the leaves from the woody stem
Rinse the rosemary and pat it dry. To remove the sturdy leaves of rosemary, carefully run your thumb and index finger down the stems or pull the leaves off the stems with your fingertips.

2 Finely chop or mince the leaves
Rest the fingertips of one hand on the tip of a chef's knife and rock the blade over the leaves. You'll want to finely chop or mince rosemary since it has a strong flavor and sharp leaves.

Snipping chives

1 Gather the chives into a bundle
Discard any wilted or yellowed chives. Rinse the chives and pat them dry. Gather a small amount of the blades into a little bundle that fits comfortably in your hand.

2 Snip the chives
Using kitchen scissors, finely snip the chives into small pieces or snip them into slightly longer lengths as directed. (Alternatively, use a very sharp chef's knife to cut the chives into slices.)

Making a bouquet garni

1 Wrap the ingredients
Rinse and wring out a 10-inch (25-cm) square of cheesecloth (muslin). Spread out the damp cheesecloth on a work surface and place the herbs or spices in the middle.

2 Tie the bundle
Bring the four corners of the cheesecloth together and tie them with a length of kitchen string, forming a secure bundle with no gaps. Use the bouquet garni according to your recipe.

Working with chiles

1 Quarter the chile lengthwise
Many cooks wear a disposable latex glove on the hand that touches the chile to prevent irritation from its potent oils. Using a paring knife, cut the chile into halves lengthwise, then into quarters.

2 Remove the seeds and ribs
Using the paring knife, cut away the seeds and ribs from each chile quarter. *Capsaicin*, the compound that makes chiles hot, is concentrated in these areas; removing them lessens the heat.

3 Slice the quarters into strips
Place the quarters, cut side up, on the cutting board. Cut into narrow strips about ⅛ inch (3 mm) wide. Take care not to pierce the glove.

4 Dice and mince the strips
Line up the chile strips and cut them crosswise at ⅛-inch intervals. Rest the fingertips of one hand on the top of the knife and rock the blade back and forth over the pieces to mince them.

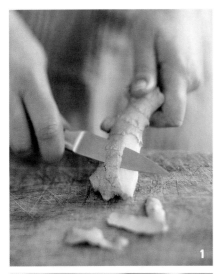

Peeling & mincing fresh ginger

1 Peel the ginger
Using a paring knife or a vegetable peeler, peel away the papery brown skin from the ginger to reveal the light flesh underneath. (If you are using smooth-skinned young ginger, you may choose not to peel it, depending on the dish.)

2 Cut the ginger into disks
Grip the ginger with one hand and, using a utility knife, paring knife, or chef's knife, cut the ginger into disks about ⅛ inch (3 mm) thick.

3 Cut the ginger into julienne
Stack the disks on top of each other, a few at a time, and cut the disks into ⅛ inch (3-mm) strips, called *julienne*.

4 Mince the ginger
Line up the ginger strips and cut them crosswise at ⅛-inch intervals. Rest the fingertips of one hand on top of the knife blade near the tip and rock the blade back and forth over the pieces to mince them.

Grating nutmeg

1 Grate the nutmeg
The flavor of freshly grated nutmeg is far superior to that of the preground spice. Run a whole nutmeg over a rasp grater or specialized nutmeg grater to grate it into very fine pieces.

2 Measure the grated nutmeg
Use a measuring spoon to measure out the amount needed in your recipe. A little nutmeg goes a long way, so start with the minimum amount when seasoning a dish.

Toasting & grinding whole spices

1 Heat the pan
Toasting whole spices before grinding brings out their natural oils and punches up the flavor. Heat a small, dry frying pan over medium heat. To test the heat level, hold your hand, palm down, over the pan.

2 Add the seeds
When you can feel the heat rising, measure the spices (here, cumin and fennel seeds) and add them to the pan.

3 Toast the spices
Toast the seeds, stirring or shaking the pan constantly, until the seeds are very fragrant and have turned a slightly deeper shade of brown, about 1 minute. Remove the pan from the heat.

4 Cool the spices
Immediately transfer the toasted seeds to a mortar or an electric spice grinder and let cool completely, about 10 minutes.

5 To grind the spices by hand:
If you are working with a mortar, use a pestle to crush the cooled seeds, pressing it firmly against the seeds and rotating it against the sides of the mortar. Continue to grind until all the seed pieces are about the same size.

6 To grind the spices by machine:
If using an electric coffee mill or spice grinder, pulse the machine on and off continually until the cooled seeds are evenly ground.

Cracking peppercorns

1 Crush the peppercorns
Spread out a small amount of peppercorns on a cutting board. Using the bottom of a heavy saucepan, press firmly on the peppercorns to crush them; you will hear the peppercorns crack.

2 Evaluate the consistency
When ready, the peppercorns will be evenly coarse in texture. Continue to crack the peppercorns, if necessary. Brush off any pepper that sticks to the pan bottom.

Working with saffron

1 Add saffron threads to liquid
You only need a small amount of saffron to flavor and color foods. Slightly crush the saffron threads and add them to a small amount of warm liquid.

2 Let the saffron steep
Let the saffron steep for a few minutes. Its warm yellow color will infuse the liquid. When possible, add saffron toward the end of the cooking process to protect its delicate flavor.

Working with dried herbs

1 Measure out the herbs
Measure the herbs called for in your recipe. In general, the amount of dried herbs used is about one-third the amount of fresh herbs. Dried herbs are typically added at the beginning of the cooking process; fresh herbs near the end.

2 Crush the herbs
To release the aromatic oils, crush the dried herbs between your fingers or in the palm of your hand before using.

Sharpening a knife with a stone

1 Push the blade over the stone
Following the manufacturer's instructions, wet the stone with water or mineral oil. Hold the knife blade against the stone at a constant 15- to 20-degree angle, then push the blade across the stone from tip to end in one smooth motion.

2 Pull the blade over the stone
Turn the knife over and maintaining the same angle, pull the knife back toward you in a long, even stroke. Repeat several times.

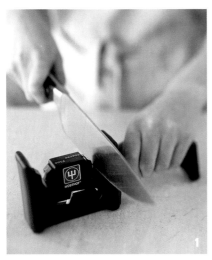

Using a manual knife sharpener

1 Grind the knife edge coarsely
Following the manufacturer's instructions, pass the knife through the slot with the coarsest grinding stone.

2 Smooth and hone the blade
Pass the knife through the slot of the finest grinding stone to smooth out the edge and hone the knife.

Honing a knife

1 Run the blade across the steel
Swipe each side of the cutting edge a few times across and along the length of the steel, alternating sides and holding the knife at a 15- to 20-degree angle.

2 Repeat the strokes
Repeat 3–10 times to realign the sharp cutting edge of the knife. To keep your knives in top form, get in the habit of honing them after each use.

Wielding a knife

1 Hold the knife comfortably
First, be sure the knife is very sharp. Cutting with a dull blade can be dangerous. The knife handle should feel comfortable and secure in your grip. If desired, extend your index finger onto the top part of the blade.

2 Adjust your hand position
Some cooks hold the knife a little higher on the handle, with the index finger and thumb of the cutting hand on the bottom part of the blade. This position might be more comfortable for cutting certain foods.

3 Curl under your fingertips
As you are cutting, curl under the fingertips of your other hand to keep them away from the edge of the knife. With experience, you can move your knuckles directly against the blade to help gauge the width of the cut.

4 Keep your palm flat
When making a horizontal cut, place your noncutting hand flat on top of the food, keeping your fingers well out of the way of the knife.

5 Use a two-part slicing motion
To create slices, cut straight down through the food, letting the tip of the knife touch the cutting board first. Then, pull the knife downward and back toward you to complete the cut.

6 Use a rocking motion
For chopping or mincing, place your non-cutting hand on top of the knife blade. Rock the blade back and forth and up and down over the food to cut it into smaller pieces.

Cutting vegetables

1 Slice the vegetables

Cutting vegetables into similar-sized pieces helps them cook evenly and contributes to a nice appearance. Using a chef's knife, cut the vegetables lengthwise into even slices. Discard or save irregular pieces for stock.

2 Cut the slices into sticks

Stack 2 or 3 slices at a time, then cut the slices lengthwise into sticks that are the same width as the thickness of the slices.

3 Cut the sticks into dice

Gather a few sticks at a time into a compact bundle, then cut the sticks crosswise into pieces that are the same length as the width of the sticks. Done properly, you will end up with evenly sized cubes, called *dice*.

4 Julienne the vegetables

Julienne are very thin rectangular cuts. Follow steps 1 and 2, but make the initial slices very thin. For round vegetables such as carrots, you can make the initial slices diagonal instead of lengthwise, if desired.

5 Mince the vegetables

Gather the julienned vegetables into small bundles, then cut them crosswise into very small pieces, or *mince*. Since the pieces are so small, you don't need to worry about being so precise when mincing.

6 Roll-cutting vegetables

Also called an oblique cut, this is used for round vegetables, especially when roasting. Hold the knife on a diagonal and cut the vegetable. Roll the item a half turn, and cut again. Repeat the roll before each cut.

Working with round vegetables or fruits

1 Trim the ends
Using a chef's knife, carefully cut a slice off the top and bottom ends of the vegetable or fruit (here, a rutabaga). Stand it on one of its flat ends on the cutting board, using your fingers to hold it steady at the top.

2 Peel away the skin
Using a paring knife and following the curve of the vegetable or fruit, cut away the peel in long strokes around the circumference of the vegetable or fruit.

3 Cut the food into small pieces
Switch back to the chef's knife and cut the item into pieces as directed in your recipe.

TROUBLESHOOTING
When exposed to the air, some pale root vegetables or fruits will discolor. Keep them in a bowl of water, with or without lemon, until ready to use.

KNIFE SKILLS

Grinding meat in a food processor

1 Cut the meat

Put the meat cubes on a cutting board (here, boneless beef round for making hamburgers). Using a chef's knife, cut the meat into ¾-inch (2-cm) cubes.

2 Freeze the meat cubes

Without crowding, spread the meat cubes in a single layer on a rimmed baking sheet lined with waxed paper. Freeze until the meat begins to form ice crystals around the edges, about 40 minutes.

3 Grind the meat

In small batches, transfer the partially frozen meat chunks to a food processor. Pulse the processor about 20 times, or until the meat is very finely chopped into little pieces less than ⅛ inch (3 mm) square.

4 Season the meat

Transfer the ground meat to a clean bowl and repeat to grind the remaining meat cubes. Season according to your recipe.

Forming hamburger patties

1 Divide the ground beef
Line a rimmed baking sheet with waxed paper. Using clean hands, divide the beef into equal portions (1 lb/500 g of ground beef usually makes 4 patties).

2 Form the patties
Moistening your hands each time, lightly pat each portion into a patty according to your recipe. Standard hamburger patties measure 4–4½ inches (10–11.5 cm) in diameter and about ¾ inch (2 cm) thick. Place the patties on the lined baking sheet.

Forming meatballs

1 Test for seasonings
Mix the meatball ingredients according to your recipe. To check the seasonings, fry a small nugget of the meatball mixture until fully cooked. Let cool slightly, then taste and adjust the seasonings accordingly in the rest of the mixture.

2 Portion the meatballs
Using an ice cream scoop, scoop up some of the meatball mixture and release the portion onto a rimmed baking sheet lined with parchment (baking) paper.

3 Roll the meatballs
Moisten your hands with cool water to prevent the mixture from sticking to them. Roll each portion between your palms to form a ball. Return the ball to the baking sheet and repeat with the remaining portions, always moistening your hands before you roll each ball.

4 Use a gentle touch
Remember to handle the meat mixture lightly. If you pack or squeeze them, the meatballs could turn tough and dry.

Trimming a beef or pork tenderloin

1 Trim the external fat
Use a boning knife or chef's knife to make long, even strokes to remove the fat from the exterior of the tenderloin. Try not to rip the meat as you trim.

2 Locate the silver skin
Look for the thin, white membrane, called *silver skin* running the length of the meat; it is very tough and needs to be trimmed before cooking. Slide the knife under the silver skin to free the tip of the skin from the flesh.

3 Pull the silver skin taut
Position the knife where the silver skin meets the flesh and begin to cut, using your fingers to pull away the skin in the direction of the cut. Angle the knife against the skin, not the meat, to avoid tearing it.

4 Remove the silver skin
As you work, turn the tenderloin on the board and continue to remove the silver skin in sections. Do not pull too hard or work too fast or you risk tearing off some of the meat with the silver skin.

Cutting a tenderloin into medallions

1 Trim the meat
Follow steps 1–4 above to remove the external fat and silver skin from the meat. Medallions should be very lean.

2 Cut the meat into portions
Using a chef's knife, cut the meat crosswise into slices ¾–1 inch (2–2.5 cm) thick, or according to your recipe.

Trimming a brisket

1 Rinse and dry the brisket
If the meat comes in a vacuum-packed plastic bag, open it and drain it in a sink. Rinse the brisket under running cold water and pat completely dry with paper towels.

2 Trim a layer of surface fat
Using a boning knife or a chef's knife, trim the surface fat from the brisket, leaving a layer ¼–½ inch (6–12 mm) thick. Leaving some of the fat helps to moisturize the meat as it cooks.

Slicing brisket or flank steak

1 Locate the meat's grain
Notice the way the meat fibers are running through the meat; this is called the *grain*. Brisket and flank steak need to be sliced across the *grain* to enhance the meat's tenderness.

2 Slice the meat
Holding a meat fork in one hand, use the fork to steady the meat. Try not to insert the tines into the flesh. Hold the knife at a 45-degree angle and cut the meat into thin slices.

Trimming a roast

1 Trim a layer of surface fat
Using a boning knife or a chef's knife, begin to cut away the external fat on the surface of the roast. Cut the fat off in long, uniform strips to ensure an even layer. Discard the fat.

2 Leave on some of the fat for flavor and moisture
Leave a layer of fat ¼–½ inch (6–12 mm) thick on the roast. This small amount will help to flavor and moisturize the meat as it cooks, particularly when slow-roasting or braising.

Carving a boneless roast

1 Slice the meat
Without inserting the tines too deeply, use a fork to hold the roast steady on a carving board. Using a carving knife or chef's knife, cut the meat across the grain into slices ¼–½ inch (6–12 mm) thick.

2 Transfer the slices to a platter
Grasp 1 or more slices of meat at a time between the knife and fork and carefully transfer them to a warmed platter. Tent the platter with aluminum foil to keep the meat warm.

Carving a standing rib roast

1 Let the meat rest
Resting allows the juices to settle and the meat to firm up, making it easier to carve. Transfer the meat to a warmed platter. Loosely cover the roast with aluminum foil and let rest for 15–20 minutes.

2 Remove the bones from the meat
Transfer the roast, with the bones upright, to a carving board. Using the tines of a carving fork to steady the roast and a long carving knife, cut the rib bones away from the large, meaty section of the roast.

3 Cut the roast into slices
Turn the meat so any crust faces up. Cut the meat across the grain (or opposite the direction of the muscle fibers) into slices ¼–½ inch (6–12 mm) thick.

4 Separate the bones
The meat attached to the bones is flavorful, too. If you wish, cut between the ribs to separate, and serve with the sliced meat.

MEAT

Trimming a steak

1 Trim the fat
Using a boning knife or a chef's knife, trim away most of the external fat around the edge of the steak. For rib-eye steaks, you can also cut out the nugget of fat often found in the center, if desired.

2 Retain a thin layer of fat
Many people like to leave a layer of fat ¼–½ inch (6–12 mm) thick around the steak. This small amount helps to flavor and moisturize the meat as it cooks. Discard the fat you remove.

TROUBLESHOOTING
Steaks can curl when cooked over high heat. To prevent this from happening, use a boning knife or a paring knife to score the steaks: Cut 2 or 3 shallow, evenly spaced slashes in the surrounding fat.

3 Ready the steaks for seasoning
As you trim the steaks, put them on a plate in a single layer. If you stack them on top of each other, they will pull juices from one another. Season the steaks according to your recipe.

Cutting beef for stew

1 Trim the meat and cut into strips
Using a chef's knife or a boning knife, trim away and discard most of the external fat on the exterior of the meat. Then, cut the beef into 2-inch (5-cm) strips, or according to your recipe.

2 Cut the meat into cubes
A few at a time, line up the meat strips and cut them crosswise to create 2-inch cubes, or according to your recipe.

Stir-frying beef

1 Heat the wok
Place the wok over high heat. Hold your hand over the pan and when you feel the heat rising upward, add a small amount of the peanut or canola oil. Carefully tilt and rotate the pan so that the oil is distributed over the pan's surface and is very hot.

2 Add the meat
Immediately add the meat to the wok, spreading it out over the surface. Let it cook undisturbed for 20–30 seconds to brown on one side, then stir vigorously with spatulas or spoons, moving the meat over the surface of the pan and up the sides, to expose it evenly to the heat. Add a little more oil if the meat seems to be sticking.

3 Keep the meat moving
Continue to cook over high heat, constantly stirring and tossing the meat in the wok, until the meat is browned on all sides; this will usually take 1–3 minutes. (If you are using a wok less than 14 inches/35 cm in diameter, cook the meat in 2 batches to avoid crowding the pan.)

4 Stir-fry the remaining ingredients
Many stir-fry recipes call for cooking the ingredients in batches. Here, the meat is transferred to a plate while the vegetables are being cooked.

Carving T-bone or porterhouse steaks

1 Remove the tenderloin portion
After the steaks have rested, use a carving knife or a boning knife to cut the smaller piece of meat (the tenderloin, which is sometimes called the *fillet*) away from the bone.

2 Remove the strip portion
Next, run the knife along the bone to remove the larger piece of meat. This is often called the *strip,* and it comes from the top loin part of the steer's short loin. Cut the portions into thin slices if desired.

Browning meat

1 Dry and season the meat
Pat the meat cubes completely dry with paper towels. Put the meat in a large bowl and add the seasonings called for in your recipe. Rub the pieces well to coat them evenly with the seasonings.

2 Add the meat to the pan
Place a large, heavy pan over medium-high heat. When it's hot, add a small amount of oil. When the oil shimmers, add the seasoned meat to the pan in a single layer with ½ inch (12 mm) of space around each piece.

3 Brown all sides
Cook until dark golden brown on all sides, using tongs to turn the meat as it browns.

TROUBLESHOOTING
A crowded pan will cause the meat to steam, rather than brown. To prevent this from happening, brown the meat in batches, transferring each batch to another pan or plate as it is ready.

Testing beef for doneness by temperature

1 Test a steak for doneness
Insert an instant-read thermometer horizontally into the center of the steak. Be sure not to touch any bone, which could skew the reading.

2 Test a roast for doneness
Insert the thermometer into the thickest part of the roast, away from any bone. Keep in mind the temperature will rise 5–10°F (3–6°C) as the meat rests.

Testing beef for doneness visually

1 Cut into the meat
Use a paring knife to make a small cut in the thickest part near the center of the meat (away from the bone, if present). Pull the meat apart and note its color. Keep in mind the meat will cook a bit more as it rests.

2 Rare beef
Steak cooked to the rare stage is deep red at the center and very juicy. A roast will be rarest at the center, with varying degrees of doneness as you near the edges.

3 Medium-rare beef
Beef cooked to the medium-rare stage is deep pink in the center. It will be firmer than rare beef but still juicy.

4 Medium beef
Beef cooked to the medium stage will be light pink in the center. The texture is firm and compact. Most cuts of meat (with the exception of braising cuts) are best if not cooked further than medium, as the meat tends to toughen and dry out the longer it is cooked.

MEAT

Trimming a pork shoulder

1 Remove the skin
Pork is sometimes sold with the skin, or rind, still intact. If present, use a boning knife or a chef's knife to trim off and discard the tough skin.

2 Trim the fat
Trim the surface fat from the pork shoulder, leaving a layer ¼–½ inch (6–12 mm) thick to help flavor and moisturize the meat as it cooks. Move the knife in slow, even strokes, pulling the fat toward you as you cut so as not to remove any of the meat.

Brining pork

1 Mix the dry ingredients
Most brines are a mixture of salt, sugar, herbs, and spices. Combine these dry ingredients in a mixing bowl large enough to hold the pork and the brine, and whisk to combine.

2 Add the water
Add the water called for in your recipe. Some recipes call for hot water at this stage to help the salt and sugar dissolve.

3 Whisk the ingredients
Whisk the ingredients well to ensure that the salt and sugar are completely dissolved. If you used cool tap water, this could take a few minutes.

4 Add the pork
Some recipes call for adding ice water to cool down and dilute the brine. When the brine is cool, add the pork and let soak according to your recipe.

Stuffing pork chops

1 Cut a pocket in the chop
Insert a sharp, thin-bladed knife into the middle of the meat
on the side away from the bone, cutting all the way to the bone.
Retrace the cut a few times to enlarge the pocket.

2 Fill the pocket with stuffing
Holding the pocket open with one hand, use a teaspoon to fill
the pocket with the stuffing of your choice. Secure the pocket
closed with a skewer.

Assembling pork skewers

1 Cut the pork into strips
Using a chef's knife, cut a trimmed boneless pork loin into slices
no more than ½ inch (12 mm) thick, then cut the slices into strips
that are the same thickness.

2 Weave the strips onto skewers
Marinate the strips, if called for in your recipe, then weave the
strips, accordion style, onto soaked bamboo or metal skewers. This
will keep the meat from spinning on the skewer.

MEAT

Making pork or veal cutlets

1 Cut the meat into medallions
Trim the pork or veal cutlets, if necessary, then cut the meat crosswise into slices about ¼ inch (6 mm) thick.

2 Pound the medallions
One at a time, place the medallions between 2 sheets of plastic wrap. Starting at the center and working outward, use a meat pounder to flatten the meat evenly.

Breading cutlets

1 Dredge the cutlet in flour
Have ready your "breading station": pour all-purpose (plain) flour onto a plate. Beat 2 or more eggs in a wide bowl. Pour dried bread crumbs onto another plate. Have ready a cooling rack set in a rimmed baking sheet. One at a time, add a cutlet to the flour, turning to coat all sides. Shake off the excess flour.

2 Dip the floured cutlet in egg
Dip the cutlet into the bowl with the eggs, coating it evenly. Let the excess egg drip back into the bowl.

3 Coat the cutlet with bread crumbs
Dip the egg-coated cutlet into the bread crumbs, turning to coat both sides completely. You may need to use your other hand to gently pat the crumbs onto the cutlet or fill in any bare patches.

4 Set aside and repeat
Set the breaded cutlet on the rack. Repeat steps 1–3 to coat the remaining cutlets with flour, egg, and bread crumbs.

Panfrying pork chops

1 Brown the pork chops
Select a heavy-bottomed sauté pan and place over medium-high heat. Add a small amount of olive or vegetable oil and heat until shimmering. Add the pork chops, leaving a ½ inch (12 mm) or more around each chop. Cook until browned on the first side, about 2 minutes.

2 Brown the second side
Using tongs, carefully turn the chops and cook until browned on the second side and cooked to your liking, about 3 minutes for medium meat.

3 Transfer to a platter
Transfer the cooked pork chops to a warmed platter and cover loosely with aluminum foil. Let them rest for about 5 minutes before serving.

4 Evaluate the pan drippings
If desired, make a pan sauce from the drippings. Ideally, the drippings will be dark brown, which corresponds to full flavor. If the drippings don't seem brown enough, place the pan on the stove top over high heat and cook them for 1–2 minutes until they are dark brown.

Testing pork for doneness

1 Test the pork by temperature
Insert an instant-read thermometer into the thickest part of the meat away from any bone. The temperature should be at least 140°F (60°C). The temperature will also rise 5°–10°F (3°–6°C) as the pork rests.

2 Test the pork by sight
Using a chef's knife, cut the meat into slices. Pork cooked to the medium stage should be light pink in the center. It will be firm but still juicy.

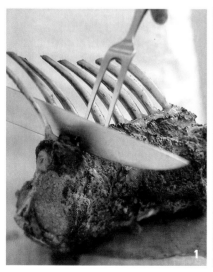

Frenching lamb

1 Cut through the fat layer
Most lamb racks these days come already
Frenched, that is, the bones trimmed and
cleaned of fat and sinew. But some artisanal
producers package their lamb unfrenched.
It's easy to clean a lamb rack yourself: Using
a boning knife, score the fat on the back of
the rack about 1 inch (2.5 cm) from where
the meaty portion starts.

2 Free the tissue between the bones
Turn over the rack and score the tissue
between the bones. Use the knife to cut
through the sinew on both sides of the
bones, loosening the rectangular pieces
of tissue formed by the cuts.

3 Pull off the fat and sinew
Turn the rack over again, grasp the fat
on the back, and pull firmly to remove the
fat and tissue that you loosened with
the knife. You may need to go over any
stubborn areas again with the knife to
ensure all the fat and sinew pulls away.

4 Clean the bones
Firmly rub a kitchen towel over each bone
to clean any remaining bits of meat or
fat from the rack.

Carving a rack of lamb

1 Hold the rack steady
Steady the rack on a carving board with
a carving fork. Insert a carving knife
between the first and second ribs. You may
need to jiggle the knife a bit to find the
meaty spot between the bones.

2 Separate the bones
Cut straight down to separate the first chop
from the rack. Repeat to separate the
remaining chops. Some recipes call for
cutting the rack into 2-chop portions.

Carving a leg of lamb

1 Grip the leg with a kitchen towel
Place the leg on a carving board that has a recessed channel around the perimeter to help catch the juices. Hold the end of the shank bone firmly with a kitchen towel, angling the leg down and away from you.

2 Prepare to carve
Turn the leg onto its side to expose the meaty part of the shank. Tilt the leg slightly upward and, using a carving knife, make a thin cut away from yourself and the bone.

3 Carve the meat off the bone
Continue carving the meat parallel to the first slice and to the bone into slices ½ inch (12 mm) thick until you reach the bone.

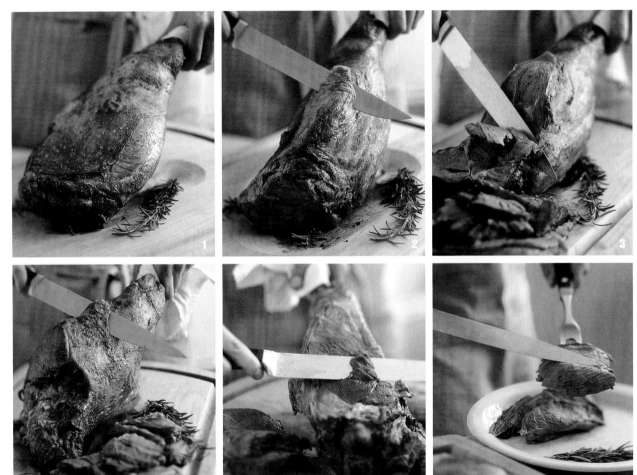

4 Carve the second side of the leg
Turn and carve the second side of the leg in the same way you carved the first, creating ½-inch slices. As you cut, arrange the meat in neat piles on the carving board.

5 Note the levels of doneness
As you reach the center of the leg of lamb, the meat will be progressively rarer. Arrange the meat in separate piles reflecting the relative doneness so your guests can choose what they like.

6 Transfer to a serving platter
Using the fork and carving knife in unison, gently lift the sliced pieces from the board and transfer to a warmed serving platter in a neat pile.

Cooking dried pasta

1 Salt the boiling water

Bring a large pot three-fourths full of water to a rolling boil. You'll need about 5 qt (5 l) of water to cook 1 pound (500 g) of pasta. Add about 2 tablespoons kosher salt to the water.

2 Add the pasta to the water

Add the dried pasta to the boiling water all at once. Use a wooden spoon to push any strands below the surface of the water, if necessary, so all the strands cook evenly.

3 Stir the pasta

Using the spoon, gently stir the pasta from time to time to prevent it from sticking together. Adjust the heat if needed to keep the water at a boil, but don't let it boil over.

4 Test the pasta for doneness

After 7 minutes, taste a piece of pasta. It should be tender but still slightly chewy, with a thin white line at the core. If not, continue to cook for 1–2 minutes and test again.

5 Reserve some cooking water

Spoon out 2 ladlefuls of the pasta-cooking water. This starchy water can later be used to adjust the consistency of the pasta and sauce after they have been tossed together.

6 Drain the pasta

Put a colander in the sink and slowly pour the pasta away from you into the colander. Shake the colander just once; the pasta should still be slightly moist.

Cooking fresh pasta

1 Salt the boiling water
Bring a large pot three-fourths full of water to a rolling boil. You'll need about 5 qt (5 l) of water to cook 1 pound (500 g) of pasta. Add about 2 tablespoons kosher salt to the water.

2 Add the pasta to the water
Add the fresh pasta to the boiling water all at once. Since fresh pasta cooks so quickly, it's important to make sure all the pasta is added at the same time.

3 Stir the pasta
Using a wooden spoon, gently stir the pasta occasionally to prevent it from sticking together. Adjust the heat if needed to keep the water at a boil, but don't let it boil over.

4 Test the pasta for doneness
After 1½ minutes, remove a strand from the pot, let it cool slightly, and taste it. It should be tender but still slightly chewy. If not, continue to cook for several seconds and test again.

5 Reserve some cooking water
Spoon out 2 ladlefuls of the pasta-cooking water. This starchy water can later be used to adjust the consistency of the pasta and sauce after they have been tossed together.

6 Drain the pasta
Put a colander in the sink and slowly pour the pasta away from you into the colander. Shake the colander to remove excess water; the pasta should still be slightly moist.

Cooking fresh filled pasta

1 Salt the boiling water
Bring a large pot three-fourths full of water to a rolling boil. You'll need about 5 qt (5 l) of water to cook 1 pound (500 g) of pasta. Add about 2 tablespoons kosher salt to the water.

2 Add the pasta to the water
Drop 2 or 3 pieces of filled pasta (here, ravioli), into the pot at a time until you have added about half of them. It's best to cook fresh filled pasta in batches so the pieces don't stick together.

3 Gently stir the pasta
Using a slotted wooden spoon, gently stir the pasta occasionally to keep it from sticking together. Adjust the heat so the water barely simmers. If the water boils too rapidly, the pasta may break open.

4 Watch for floating pasta
A reliable sign that filled pasta are finished cooking is when they begin to rise to the water's surface. This usually takes about 2 minutes.

5 Test the pasta for doneness
Scoop out 1 piece of pasta with the slotted spoon and transfer to a cutting board. Using a paring knife, cut off a corner where the dough is doubled. Taste the corner; it should be tender but still slightly chewy.

6 Drain the pasta
Use the slotted spoon to transfer the cooked pasta, a few pieces at a time, to a colander. After they have drained for a few seconds, pour them into a warmed serving bowl.

Saucing fresh pasta

1 Add the pasta to the sauce
Cook and drain the fresh pasta, reserving some of the cooking liquid. Add the drained pasta to the pan with the warmed sauce, according to your recipe.

2 Add cheese, if desired
Sprinkle freshly grated Parmesan or any other cheese over the pasta in the pan, if called for in your recipe.

3 Toss the pasta
Using 2 wooden spoons or spatulas, toss the ingredients together: bring the pasta from the bottom of the pan to the top until all the strands are evenly coated with the sauce and cheese, if using.

4 Adjust with cooking water
If the mixture looks dry as you toss, drizzle a little of the reserved cooking water over the pasta and continue to toss.

PASTA

Fresh egg pasta dough (food processor method)

Fresh pasta enriched with eggs forms a delicate foundation for a variety of dishes. A food processor makes quick work of mixing the flour, eggs, and oil into a soft dough before you knead it into a smooth, silky mass.

1 Add the flour to the work bowl
Fit a food processor with the metal blade. Add 2 cups (10 oz/315 g) of the flour to the food processor work bowl. Set the remaining ½ cup (2½ oz/75 g) flour nearby; you'll use it later to adjust the consistency of the dough.

2 Add the eggs and oil
Crack the eggs against a flat surface and drop them into a small glass measuring cup. Check for shells, then add the olive oil to the measuring cup. Pour the egg-oil mixture into the processor.

INGREDIENTS

2½ cups (12½ oz/390 g) unbleached all-purpose (plain) flour, plus extra for dusting

4 large eggs

2 teaspoons extra-virgin olive oil

MAKES ABOUT 1 LB (500 G)

5 Lightly knead the dough
Transfer the dough to a lightly floured work surface and knead lightly until it feels damp without being sticky and is an even yellow color with no streaks of flour, 1–2 minutes.

When making fresh pasta dough, keep in mind that the amount of flour the dough will absorb varies according to the flour, the freshness of the eggs, and the weather. You may need a bit more flour on a rainy day and a little less on a hot, dry day.

3 Mix the dough

Process the mixture until the flour is evenly moistened and crumbly; this will take about 10 seconds. Pinch the dough to test its consistency.

4 Adjust the consistency

If the dough seems excessively sticky, add the reserved flour 1 tablespoon at a time, processing until just incorporated. Process until the dough comes together to form a loose ball on top of the blade and feels moist but not sticky when pinched, about 30 seconds.

6 Let the dough rest

Shape the dough into a ball. It will be quite elastic at this point and would spring back on itself if you attempted to roll it out. Cover the ball with a large overturned bowl and let it rest for 30 minutes before rolling.

FLAVORING FRESH PASTA

Herb pasta dough

Add 1 tablespoon crumbled dried herbs, such as marjoram or thyme, to the work bowl with the flour in step 1 and continue with the recipe.

Black pepper pasta dough

Add 1 teaspoon finely ground black pepper (preferably freshly ground) to the work bowl with the flour in step 1 and continue with the recipe.

Spinach pasta dough

Process ½ cup (3½ oz/105 g) packed cooked spinach and 3 large eggs until smooth and well blended. Add 2 cups (10 oz/350 g) unbleached all-purpose flour and process until evenly moistened and crumbly, about 10 seconds. Add additional flour, 1 tablespoon at a time, and continue to process until the dough comes together in a loose ball and feels moist but not sticky when pinched, about 20 more seconds. Continue with steps 5 and 6 of the recipe to finish the dough.

Fresh egg pasta dough (hand method)

Fresh egg-enriched pasta forms a delicate foundation for a variety of dishes. Making the dough by hand gives you a sense of the correct flour-to-water ratio and ideal dough consistency. You may need to adjust the quantities of flour or water, depending on the weather.

INGREDIENTS

2½ cups (12½ oz/390 g) unbleached all-purpose (plain) flour, plus extra for dusting

4 large eggs

2 teaspoons extra-virgin olive oil

MAKES ABOUT 1 LB (500 G)

You can reduce the quantities of this recipe to make just enough for 1 large or 2 small servings—the perfect quantity for a weeknight meal. Use ⅔ cup (3½ oz/105 g) plus 1 tablespoon unbleached all-purpose (plain) flour and 1 large egg. (You can omit the olive oil if you like.)

1 Make a well in the flour
Pour 2 cups (10 oz/315 g) of the flour into a mound on a clean work surface. With your fingers, gently make a well large enough to hold the eggs in the center of the mound.

2 Pour the eggs into the well
Crack the eggs into a large measuring cup and check for shells. Add the oil to the measuring cup and then pour the egg-oil mixture into the well.

6 Knead the dough
Use a bench scraper to clean the work surface, and dust the clean surface with flour. Transfer the dough to the floured surface and knead it by pushing down and away from you and turning it repeatedly until the dough feels smooth and satiny, 7–10 minutes. Sprinkle on more flour if the dough becomes sticky or soft during kneading.

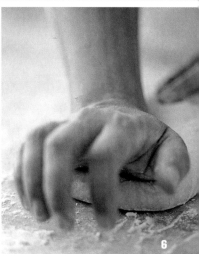

3 Whisk the eggs
Using a fork, carefully whisk the eggs in the well, without drawing in any flour, until they are just mixed together.

4 Draw in the flour
Use the fork to gradually draw the flour into the center and stir it together with the egg-oil mixture. Gently draw in more flour and mix it in this way until all of the flour is blended in and you have a shaggy mass of dough.

5 Bring the dough together
Use your hands to bring the shaggy mass of dough into a ball. When all the flour is combined, if the dough is still sticky, sprinkle more flour over the dough, a little at a time, and mix it in.

7 Let the dough rest
Clear away most of the excess flour on the work surface. Shape the dough into a ball by rolling it in a circle with both hands, applying pressure to the bottom so that the dough tucks under itself and the ball tightens up a little. Cover the ball with a large overturned bowl and let it rest for 30 minutes before rolling.

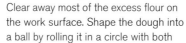

Rolling out fresh pasta by machine

1 Flour the pasta machine
Set up your pasta machine according to the manufacturer's directions, securing it to the counter firmly. Lightly dust the rollers with flour. Divide the dough into small portions.

2 Knead the dough
Flatten a dough portion into a disk ½ inch (12 mm) thick. Turn the crank to pass the disk through the rollers. Fold the dough into thirds like a letter, dust with flour, and roll again. Repeat 8–10 times until smooth.

3 Roll out the dough
Move the roller dial to the next narrowest setting and pass the dough through again, catching the thinner end with your hand and easing it onto the work surface. Dust the rollers with flour as needed.

4 Continue rolling
Continue passing the dough through progressively narrower rollers until you reach the second-to-last setting. As you work, continually adjust the dough on the work surface so it lies flat.

5 Test for thinness
Hold the dough in your hands; if you can see your hand through it, the dough is ready (it should be about 1/16 inch/2 mm thick). If it's not thin enough, pass the dough through the narrowest roller setting.

TROUBLESHOOTING
If a scrap of dough gets caught in the rollers, fold up the dough neatly, flour it well, and start the rolling process over again at step 3.

Cutting fresh pasta by machine

1 Cut the pasta into sections
Cut the dough into 10-inch (25-cm) lengths or according to your recipe. For fettuccine or lasagna, let the sections dry slightly, for 10–20 minutes, turning them once or twice. For filled pastas, use the dough right away.

2 Secure the cutting attachment
Follow the manufacturer's directions to attach the desired cutting blades and crank onto the pasta machine. Here, we're using the strand-cutting attachment for fettuccine.

3 Cut the pasta into strands
One at a time, insert the dough sections into the blades and turn the crank to create strands. Ease them onto the work surface with your free hand.

4 Let the strands dry briefly
Spread the strands out on a lightly floured baking sheet, separating them slightly, and let them dry for 10–20 minutes. They should feel a little leathery, but not brittle.

Rolling out fresh pasta by hand

1 Divide the dough
Lightly dust your work surface with flour. Using a bench scraper or a chef's knife, cut each pound (500 g) of dough into 4 equal pieces.

2 Flatten a portion into a disk
As you work with one piece of dough, keep the others under an overturned bowl. Flatten one piece of dough into a disk about ½ inch (12 mm) thick.

3 Roll out the dough
Using a lightly floured rolling pin, roll the dough away from you, applying moderate pressure. (Most pasta doughs are sturdier than pastry doughs, so you can use more strength when rolling them.)

4 Turn and roll again
Lift up the dough, flour your work surface again, if necessary, and turn the dough 90 degrees. Roll out the dough as in step 3, to desired thickness.

5 Test for thinness
Hold the dough in your hands; if you can see your hand through it, the dough is ready (it should be about 1/16 inch/2 mm thick). If it's not thin enough, continue to roll.

6 Let the dough rest
Carefully fold the dough into quarters, transfer it to a lightly floured baking sheet, and lay it flat. Let the dough rest in the refrigerator for 10–20 minutes before cutting it into sheets or strands.

Cutting fresh pasta by hand

1 Cut the pasta into sections
Place the rolled-out pasta sheet on a clean
work surface. Using a pizza cutter or a paring
knife with a ruler for guidance, cut the dough
into sections as directed in your recipe.

2 Let the sections dry
For fettuccine or lasagna, let the sections
dry for 10–20 minutes on a baking sheet
lightly dusted with flour. For filled pastas,
use the dough right away.

3 Cut the pasta into strands
On a lightly floured work surface, roll up
a pasta sheet into a loose, flat cylinder. Using
a chef's knife, cut the cylinder crosswise
to create strands. (Here, we're cutting
fettuccine into ¼-inch/6-cm strands.)

4 Let the strands dry briefly
Spread the strands out on a lightly floured
baking sheet, separating them slightly, and
let dry until a little leathery, 10–20 minutes.

PASTA

Semolina pasta dough

In this recipe, golden semolina flour, with the texture of fine sand, is combined with all-purpose (plain) flour and water, but no eggs. The result is a stiff dough that is used to make short, shaped pastas, such as orecchiette.

INGREDIENTS

2 cups (10 oz/315 g) unbleached all-purpose (plain) flour, plus extra for dusting

¾ cup (4 oz/125 g) finely ground semolina flour (do not substitute coarsely ground)

1 teaspoon kosher salt

¾ cup (6 fl oz/180 ml) warm water, or as needed

MAKES ABOUT 1 LB (500 G)

Covering the pasta with an overturned bowl is a simple and environmentally sound way of keeping the dough from drying out as it rests. The alternative is to cover the dough with plastic wrap.

1 Combine the dry ingredients
Fit a food processor with the metal blade. Add the all-purpose and semolina flours and the salt to the food processor work bowl. Pulse the machine a few times to mix the ingredients.

2 Test the water temperature
Turn on the hot water tap and let it run for a while to warm the water. Using a glass measuring cup, measure ¾ cup (6 fl oz/180 ml) of the warm tap water, then use an instant-read thermometer to check the temperature; it should register 105°F (40°C).

6 Knead the dough
Lightly knead the dough until it is smooth and feels damp without being sticky. This will take only a minute or two. Because there are no eggs or oil in this dough and it calls for harder semolina flour, it will be more difficult to work with than fresh egg pasta dough.

3 Drizzle in the water

With the food processor running, pour ½ cup (4 fl oz/125 ml) of the warm water through the feed tube in a thin, steady stream. You want to add just enough water to moisten the dough. If necessary, add the remaining water 1 tablespoon at a time; you may not need all of it.

4 Check the consistency

After about 30 seconds of processing, the dough should come together and form a loose ball on top of the blade. Remove the top of the food processor and pinch the dough to check its texture; it should feel moist but not sticky. If the dough seems too dry, add a teaspoon of water and process until blended.

5 Prepare the work surface

Dust a wood or slightly rough plastic work surface with all-purpose flour. Either surface will grip the finished dough better than a smooth surface, making kneading—and later, rolling and shaping—the dough easier. Remove the dough from the processor and place it in the center of the floured surface.

7 Let the dough rest

Shape the dough into a ball. It will be quite elastic at this point and would spring back on itself if you attempted to work with it. Cover the ball with a large overturned bowl and let it rest for 30 minutes before rolling.

Shaping cavatelli

1 Divide the dough
Lightly dust your work surface with flour. Using a chef's knife or bench scraper, cut 1 pound (500 g) Semolina Dough (see entry 229) into 4 equal pieces. Shape each piece into a short cylinder.

2 Roll the dough into logs
Place the fingers of both hands on a dough cylinder and roll it back and forth, gradually shifting your hands to the ends, to form a log about ½ inch (12 mm) in diameter. Repeat with the remaining cylinders.

3 Cut the logs into pieces
Again using the knife or bench scraper, cut each rolled-out log into ½-inch pieces. The pieces will look like tiny pillows.

4 Flatten a piece of dough
Turn a dough piece so a cut side faces up. Extend your index finger along the blade of a table knife. Hold the blade horizontally above one of the pieces and press down to flatten the dough piece.

5 Curl the dough around the knife
Drag the knife gently to one side as you press down on the dough. The dough will curl around the knife into an oblong pasta shell. Repeat steps 4 and 5 to shape the remaining pieces.

6 Let the cavatelli dry
As you work, spread the cavatelli out on a lightly floured rimmed baking sheet (don't let the pieces touch, or they might stick together). Cook them right away or let them dry for up to 2 hours.

Shaping orecchiette

1 Divide the dough
Lightly dust your work surface with flour. Using a bench scraper or chef's knife, cut 1 pound (500 g) Semolina Dough (see entry 229) into 4 equal pieces. Shape each piece into a short cylinder.

2 Roll the dough into logs
Place the fingers of both hands on a dough cylinder and roll it back and forth, gradually shifting your hands to the ends, to form a log about ½ inch (12 mm) in diameter. Repeat with the remaining cylinders.

3 Cut the logs into pieces
Again using the bench scraper or knife, cut each rolled-out log into ½-inch pieces. The pieces will look like tiny pillows.

4 Form a dough piece into a disk
Extend your index finger along the blade of a table knife. With the tip of the knife, flatten a piece of dough and drag it slightly toward you over the work surface to form a disk.

5 Press the disk over your thumb
Gently push the disk over the tip of your thumb to form a small cup. Repeat steps 4 and 5 to shape the remaining pieces.

6 Let the orecchiette dry
As you work, spread the orecchiette out on a lightly floured rimmed baking sheet (don't let the pieces touch, or they might stick together.) Cook them right away or let them dry for up to 2 hours.

Shaping ravioli

1 Mark the dough's center
Lay 1 section of pasta flat on a lightly floured work surface. Fold the dough in half lengthwise to mark the center, then unfold it so that it lies flat again.

2 Add the filling
Beginning about 1 inch (2.5 cm) from one of the short ends, place teaspoonfuls of the filling about 1 inch apart in a straight row down the center of one side of the fold.

3 Brush the dough with water
Dip a pastry brush in cool water and lightly brush around the filling; this acts as a glue that keeps the filling tightly sealed inside the pasta. Fold the dough over the filling.

4 Seal the ravioli
Using your fingers, mold the dough around the filling to eliminate any air pockets (these could cause the ravioli to burst). Press the edges of dough together firmly to seal.

5 Separate the ravioli
Using a fluted pastry wheel, cut all the way around the filled pasta strip, crimping the edges and trimming away about ⅛ inch (3 mm). Then, cut evenly between the mounds, making small pillow-shaped ravioli.

6 Set the ravioli aside
Place the ravioli in a single layer on a lightly floured rimmed baking sheet. Do not let them touch or they will stick together.

Shaping tortellini

1 Cut the pasta into squares
Place a pasta sheet on a lightly floured work surface and cut it into 2-inch (5-cm) squares. Lay the squares on a lightly floured rimmed baking sheet, spacing them apart so they don't touch.

2 Fill the pasta squares
Place about ½ teaspoon of the filling in the center of each square. Dip a pastry brush in cool water and lightly brush around the filling; this acts as a glue that keeps the filling tightly sealed inside the pasta.

3 Fold into triangles
Fold a corner of the dough over the filling to enclose it and form a triangle shape. If the edges of the pasta don't touch, remove a little of the filling.

4 Seal the triangles
Using your fingers, mold the dough around the filling to eliminate any air pockets (these could cause the tortellini to burst). Press the edges of dough together firmly to seal.

5 Bring the points together
Bring the 2 opposite points of the triangle together to form a circle and pinch the points together to seal.

6 Curl back the top point
For a decorative look, use your fingers to curl back the third point slightly so that each piece resembles a peaked cap. Place the tortellini in a single layer, not touching, on a lightly floured rimmed baking sheet.

Potato gnocchi

These light-as-air potato dumplings are a staple of Italian cuisine. Russet potatoes provide the perfect combination of starch and moisture; do not use other potato varieties, as the dumplings will lack the desired airy texture.

INGREDIENTS

5 russet potatoes, about 2½ lb (1.25 kg) total weight, baked until soft

2 large eggs

1 teaspoon kosher salt

2 cups (10 oz/315 g) unbleached all-purpose (plain) flour, plus more for dusting

MAKES 6–8 SERVINGS

To cook gnocchi, pour them, in 2 batches, into a large pot of boiling salted water and let them cook until they float, about 3 minutes. Drain and top with your favorite tomato sauce or pesto, or simply toss them with butter and grated Parmesan cheese.

1 Rice the potatoes
When the potatoes are just cool enough to handle, cut them in half lengthwise. Using a large metal spoon, scoop out the potato flesh from the skins. Fit a potato ricer with the disk with the small holes. Rice the potato onto a large, rimmed baking sheet. Spread out the potato flesh on the sheet and let it cool completely.

2 Add the egg mixture
Break the eggs into a bowl and check for shells. Add the salt and beat with a fork until blended. Drizzle the egg mixture evenly over the cooled potatoes. Then, sprinkle 1 cup (5 oz/155 g) of the flour evenly over the potatoes. Using a bench scraper, scoop, lift, and fold the potatoes to mix them with the eggs and flour until a coarse dough forms. It should look raggedy.

6 Roll the dough into a log
Using the fingers of both hands, roll the dough back and forth over the surface, gradually shifting your hands to the ends, to form it slowly into a narrow log about ½ inch (12 mm) in diameter.

3 Incorporate the flour

Sprinkle ¼ cup (1½ oz/45 g) of the remaining flour onto a work surface. Spread the potato mixture on the surface and sprinkle with another ¼ cup flour. Using the bench scraper and then your hands, scoop, lift, and fold the mixture, lightly pressing it as you work, until the flour is incorporated.

4 Shape the dough

Shape the dough into a ball, dust with flour, and cover with an overturned bowl. Dust 2 large rimmed baking sheets with flour. Using the bench scraper, scrape the work surface clean and then dust it with flour.

5 Divide the dough into 8 pieces

Using the bench scraper, cut the dough into 8 equal pieces. Slip 7 of the pieces back under the bowl. Place 1 dough piece in the center of the surface and shape it into a short cylinder.

7 Cut the log into pieces

Cut the log into ¾-inch (2-cm) pillow-shaped pieces. Place the pieces in a single layer, not touching, on the prepared baking sheets. Roll and cut the remaining dough pieces in the same way. Cover the baking sheets with aluminum foil and refrigerate for at least 1 hour or up to overnight.

Shaping turnovers

1 Cut out the dough rounds
Using thinly rolled-out pastry dough (about ⅛ inch/3 mm thick) use a pastry cutter to cut out as many rounds as possible. (Here, we're using a 3-inch/7.5-cm cutter.)

2 Fill the pastry rounds
Add a small amount of filling to the center of each round. With a finger, moisten one half of each round with water. Fold this half over and press gently to make a half-moon. Seal the edge using the tines of a fork.

3 Brush the turnovers with egg wash
When ready to bake, use a fork to mix together 1 egg and 1 teaspoon water in a small bowl; this is called an *egg wash*. Brush the egg wash evenly over the turnovers.

4 Bake the turnovers
Bake the turnovers according to your recipe until golden brown on the outside and the filling is heated through on the inside.

Making a graham-cracker crust

1 Process the graham crackers
Break the graham crackers into a food processor fitted with a metal blade. Add any other dry ingredients called for in your recipe. Here, we added nuts to the crust ingredients. Pulse until the crackers form fine crumbs.

2 Transfer the crumbs to a bowl
Transfer the crumb mixture to a mixing bowl, using a silicone spatula to scrape all of it out of the work bowl.

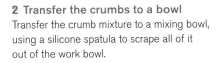

3 Stir in melted butter
Add melted butter to the crumb mixture according to your recipe, and mix well until evenly moistened.

4 Press the crumbs into the pan
Pour the crumb mixture into the pan specified in your recipe, (here, a springform pan). Using your fingertips, press the crumb mixture evenly onto the pan bottom and up the sides, if called for.

Sweet tart dough

Butter-rich tart pastry, also known as *pâte sucrée,* has a tender, cookiclikc tcxture rather than the flaky character of pie crust. Use this dough to make tarts with sweet fillings, such as Pastry Cream (entry 44) or Chocolate Ganache (entry 52).

INGREDIENTS

1¼ cups (6½ oz/200 g) all-purpose (plain) flour

½ cup (2 oz/60 g) confectioners' (icing) sugar

¼ teaspoon salt

½ cup (4 oz/125 g) cold unsalted butter

2 large egg yolks

1 tablespoon heavy (double) cream

MAKES PASTRY FOR ONE 9½-INCH (24-CM) TART

1 Combine the dry ingredients
Fit a food processor with the metal blade. Add the flour, confectioners sugar, and salt to the processor's work bowl.

2 Process the dry ingredients
Pulse the machine 1 or 2 times so that the ingredients are well mixed. Cut the butter into ¾-inch (2-cm) pieces. Add the butter pieces to the work bowl.

5 Gather the dough
Turn the dough out onto a lightly floured work surface. Using both hands, gently push the dough into a single mass. Work quickly so that the dough remains cold.

3 Mix in the butter
Process the butter-flour mixture with on-off pulses until the butter has flattened into flakes and the rest of the mixture looks like grated Parmesan cheese, about five 1-second pulses.

4 Add the egg and cream
In a small bowl, lightly beat the egg yolks, then stir in the cream. With the food processor running, pour the egg-cream mixture through the feed tube and pulse just until the mixture comes together in clumps.

6 Shape and chill the dough
Using your hands and a bench scraper, shape the dough into a flat rectangle about 6 by 3½ inches (15 by 9 cm) for a rectangular tart or a 6-inch (15-cm) disk for a round tart. Wrap well in plastic wrap and refrigerate for at least 2 hours or up to overnight.

MORE TART DOUGHS

Citrus tart dough

Follow the recipe to make Sweet Tart Dough. In step 4, add 1 teaspoon grated lemon, lime, or orange zest with the egg-cream mixture and proceed with the recipe. Use this dough for chocolate tarts or fruit tarts featuring kiwi, mango, or tropical fruits.

Vanilla tart dough

Follow the recipe to make Sweet Tart Dough. In step 4, add 1 teaspoon pure vanilla extract with the egg-cream mixture and proceed with the recipe. Use this dough for chocolate tarts or fruit tarts featuring berries.

Almond tart dough

Follow the recipe to make Sweet Tart Dough. In step 4, add 1 teaspoon pure almond extract with the egg-cream mixture and proceed with the recipe. Use this dough for fruit tarts featuring peaches, apricots, or other stone fruits.

Savory tart dough

For savory tarts or tartlets, follow the recipe for Sweet Tart Dough using the following proportions: 1 cup (5 oz/155 g) unbleached all-purpose (plain) flour, ½ cup (2 oz/60 g) cake (soft-wheat) flour, ½ teaspoon salt, and 1 large egg, omitting the sugar.

Working with tart dough

1 Roll out the dough
Lightly dust a work surface, the dough, and the rolling pin with flour. Rolling from the center toward the edges and in all directions, roll out the dough into a round 2–3 inches (5–7.5 cm) larger than your tart pan.

2 Turn the dough
Lift and turn the dough as you roll to prevent sticking. Dust the surface and the rolling pin with additional flour as needed. If the pastry sticks, use a bench scraper or an offset spatula to loosen it.

3 Line the pan with dough
Carefully roll the dough around the rolling pin and position the rolling pin over a tart pan with a removable bottom. Unroll the dough and center it in the tart pan.

4 Press the dough into the sides
Lift the edge of the dough and ease it into the outer edges of the pan, allowing the extra to flop over the sides. Lightly press the dough into the sides of the tart pan. Repeat around the entire circumference of the pan.

5 Trim off the excess dough
Using the rolling pin, roll over the top of the dough along the rim of the tart pan to cut off any excess dough. Gather up the trimmed dough and set it aside; you may need it to repair rips in the pastry.

TROUBLESHOOTING
Repair any tears in the dough by pressing scraps of dough over them. The dough scraps will bake into the crust and prevent any filling from leaking out.

Shaping & blind baking tartlets

1 Roll out the dough
Arrange the tartlet molds as close together as possible on a flat work surface. Roll out the dough between 2 sheets of waxed paper, then pull off the top sheet.

2 Line the molds with dough
Carefully flip the dough over the molds, bottom paper side up. Make sure all the molds are covered by the pastry. Press the dough onto the molds through the paper, then peel off the paper.

3 Trim the dough
Using the rolling pin, roll over the tops of the tartlet molds to cut off the excess dough. Reroll the dough trimmings and pat into any remaining shells.

4 Press the dough into the molds
Place the dough-lined molds on a large rimmed baking sheet. Using your fingers, gently press the dough into the bottom and sides of the molds.

5 Dock the dough
Dock the dough by pricking it all over with the tines of a fork; this prevents the dough from puff up during baking. Cover the molds loosely with waxed paper and chill until very firm, about 1 hour.

6 Blind bake the shells
Preheat the oven according to your recipe. Cut out generous rectangles of aluminum foil to cover the tartlet molds. Fold the foil down around the molds and fill with pie weights or dried beans. Bake as directed.

Flaky pie dough (food processor method)

The rich flavor and flake-making quality of of butter produce a pie pastry that is both versatile and delicious. The butter should be very cold so that it will form layers in the crust that will contribute to overall flakiness. Do not overwork the dough or it will be tough.

1 Process the dry ingredients
Fit a food processor with the metal blade. Add the flour, sugar, and salt to the processor's work bowl. Pulse the machine 2 or 3 times to mix the ingredients evenly.

2 Add the butter
Using a sharp knife, cut the butter into ¾-inch (2-cm) cubes and add them to the work bowl.

INGREDIENTS

1⅓ cups (7 oz/220 g) all-purpose (plain) flour

1 tablespoon granulated sugar

¼ teaspoon salt

½ cup (4 oz/125 g) cold unsalted butter

4 tablespoons (2 fl oz/60 ml) ice water or more as needed

MAKES PASTRY FOR ONE 9-INCH (23-CM) PIE

To bake a fruit-filled pie, preheat the oven to 400°F (200°C). Bake the pie for 15 minutes, then reduce the heat to 350°F (180°C). Bake for 40–45 minutes, until the crust is golden brown and the fruit is tender. Let cool slightly or completely, then cut into wedges to serve.

5 Check the consistency
When the dough is done, it should come together in a rough mass in the food processor bowl but not form a ball. Do not overmix or the crust will be tough.

3 Pulse to create coarse crumbs
Pulse the food processor 8–10 times. At this point, some of the butter pieces should be blended into the flour, but bits the size of peas should still be visible.

4 Add the ice water
Add the ice water and pulse the machine 10–12 times. To test the pie dough, stop the food processor and squeeze a piece of dough. If the dough crumbles, add more ice water, a tablespoon at a time, and pulse just until the dough holds together when pinched.

6 Shape and chill the dough
Transfer the dough to a floured work surface. Shape the dough into a 6-inch (15-cm) disk. Wrap well in plastic wrap and refrigerate for at least 1 hour or up to overnight.

MORE PIE DOUGHS

Savory pie dough

If you are making a savory pie, such as a quiche or savory galette, omit the sugar in step 1 and proceed with the recipe.

Lattice-topped pie dough

Follow the recipe for Flaky Pie Dough using the following proportions: 2 cups (10 oz/315 g) all-purpose flour; 4 teaspoons granulated sugar, optional; ¼ teaspoon salt; ¾ cup (6 oz/185 g) cold unsalted butter; and 6 tablespoons (3 fl oz/90 ml) ice water. Divide the dough into 2 portions, one twice as large as the other. Shape the larger portion into a 6-inch (15-cm) disk and the smaller one into a 3-inch (7.5-cm) disk. See entry 245 for directions for making a lattice-topped pie.

Double-crust pie dough

Follow the recipe for Flaky Pie Dough using the following proportions: 2 ⅔ cups (13½ oz/425 g) all-purpose flour; 2 tablespoons granulated sugar, optional; ½ teaspoon salt; 1 cup (8 oz/250 g) cold unsalted butter; and 8 tablespoons (4 fl oz/125 ml) ice water. Divide the dough in half and form each half into a 6-inch (15-cm) disk. See entry 244 for directions for making a double-crust pie.

Turn to entry 241 for a variety of pie fillings.

Flaky pie dough (hand method)

When making pie dough by hand, the butter does not warm up as fast as it does when using a food processor, which ensures a flaky result. Follow the proportions in entry 240 to make dough for a savory, lattice-topped, or double-crust pie.

1 Combine the dry ingredients
In a large mixing bowl, combine the flour, sugar, and salt and stir with a fork to mix the ingredients evenly.

2 Add the butter
Cut the cold butter into ¾-inch (2-cm) cubes. Scatter the cubes over the flour mixture and toss with a fork to coat evenly with the flour.

INGREDIENTS

1⅓ cups (7 oz/220 g) all-purpose (plain) flour

1 tablespoon granulated sugar

¼ teaspoon salt

½ cup (4 oz/125 g) cold unsalted butter

4 tablespoons (2 fl oz/60 ml) ice water or more as needed

MAKES PASTRY FOR ONE 9-INCH (23-CM) PIE

5 Gather the dough
When the dough is done, it should come together in a rough mass. Do not overmix or the crust will be tough. Gather the dough together gently.

3 Cut the fat into the flour
Using a pastry blender or 2 knives, cut in the butter until the mixture forms large, coarse crumbs.

4 Add the ice water
Drizzle the ice water over the flour-butter mixture and toss with a fork until the dough is evenly moist. If the dough seems too crumbly, add more ice water, a tablespoon at a time, and toss to mix.

6 Shape and chill the dough
Transfer the dough to a big piece of plastic wrap. Grab the edges of the plastic wrap and use the back of your hand through the plastic to press the dough into a disk. Wrap well in plastic wrap and refrigerate for at least 1 hour or up to overnight.

FRUIT PIE FILLINGS

Apple-spice filling

In a large bowl, combine 6 peeled, cored, and thinly sliced apples; 1 tablespoon fresh lemon juice, strained; 2 tablespoons unsalted butter, melted; ¼ cup (2 oz/60 g) firmly packed golden brown sugar; 1½ teaspoons ground cinnamon; and ⅛ teaspoon freshly ground nutmeg and mix until blended.

Peach-raspberry filling

In a large bowl, combine 6 peeled, thinly sliced peaches; ¼ cup (1½ oz/45 g) all-purpose (plain) flour; 3 tablespoons granulated sugar; 1 tablespoon fresh lemon juice, strained; and 1 teaspoon pure vanilla extract and mix until blended. Fold in 1 cup (4 oz/125 g) fresh raspberries.

Three-berry filling

In a large bowl, combine 3 cups (12 oz/375 g) blueberries; 1 cup (4 oz/125 g) *each* blackberries and raspberries; ¼ cup (1½ oz/45 g) all-purpose (plain) flour; ¼ cup (2 oz/60 g) granulated sugar; and 1 tablespoon fresh lemon juice, strained, and mix until blended.

Sour cherry filling

In a large bowl, combine 5 cups (2 lb/1 kg) pitted sour cherries; ½ cup (4 oz/125 g) granulated sugar; 1½ tablespoons cornstarch (cornflour); 1 tablespoon fresh lemon juice, strained; and ¼ teaspoon pure almond extract and mix until blended.

Each recipe makes filling for one 9-inch (23-cm) pie.

Working with pie dough

1 Roll out the dough
Lightly dust a work surface, the dough, and the rolling pin with flour. Rolling from the center toward the edges and in all directions, roll the dough into a round 2–3 inches (5–7.5 cm) larger than your pie dish or pan.

2 Turn and lift the dough
Using a bench scraper or an offset spatula, lift and turn the dough several times as you roll to prevent sticking. Dust the surface and the rolling pin with flour as needed.

3 Brush off the excess flour
Carefully roll the dough around the rolling pin, brushing off the excess flour with a pastry brush. Excess flour can make the dough tough.

4 Line the pan with dough
Position the rolling pin over a pie dish or pan. Unroll the dough and center it in the dish. Gently press the dough into the bottom and up the sides of the dish, taking care not to pull or stretch it.

5 Trim the dough
If making a single-crust pie (shown here), use a small paring knife or a pair of kitchen scissors to trim the dough, leaving a ¾-inch (2-cm) overhang.

6 Create the pie edge
Roll the overhang under itself to create a high edge on the dish's rim. Using your index finger and thumb, pinch the dough around the rim to form a fluted edge or create another decorative edge of your choice (see entry 246).

Shaping a galette

1 Arrange the fruit on the pastry
Place a thinly rolled pastry dough round on a cookie sheet lined with parchment (baking) paper. Spoon the galette filling in the center of the pastry, leaving a 2-inch (5-cm) border.

2 Fold the border over the filling
Carefully fold the border up over the filling, forming loose pleats all around the edges and leaving the center open.

3 Brush the dough with egg wash
Use a pastry brush to lightly coat the pleated dough with an *egg wash* (here, 1 egg beaten with 1 teaspoon water).

4 Sprinkle the edge with sugar
While the egg wash is still wet, sprinkle sugar over the pleated edge (here, demerara sugar). Bake in a 400°F (200°C) oven until the crust is golden brown and the fruit is soft, 8–12 minutes, or according to your recipe.

PIES & TARTS

Making a double-crust pie

1 Fill the pie
Line a pie dish or pan with pastry dough (see entry 242), then pour in the filling. Because most fruits shrink as they cook, don't be surprised if the filling is a few inches above the pie dish rim.

2 Cover with the top crust
Carefully slide the top crust over the filling, making sure to center it. Alternatively, if your dough is soft enough, you can fold it in half or quarters, center it on the filling, and unfold. You should have a slight overhang.

3 Seal and make a decorative edge
Using a sharp knife or kitchen scissors, trim the pastry, leaving a ¾-inch (2-cm) overhang. Roll the overhang over itself to create an edge. Embellish the dough (see entry 246) and sprinkle with sugar, if desired.

4 Create steam vents
Using a paring knife, cut 3 or 4 slits in the center of the top crust. This allows the steam to escape while the pie is baking.

Making a lattice-topped pie

Making a lattice-topped pie

1 Cut the dough strips
Roll out the dough into a rectangle that is 2 inches (5 cm) longer than the diameter of your pie pan and ⅛ inch (3 mm) thick. Using a pizza wheel or paring knife, trim the edges and cut the rectangle into 10 equal strips.

2 Lay a row of the strips on the filling
Starting 1 inch (2.5 cm) from the edge of the pie pan, lay 4–6 strips about 1 inch apart over the filling. Use a thin metal spatula to pick up the dough strips gently if they stick to the work surface.

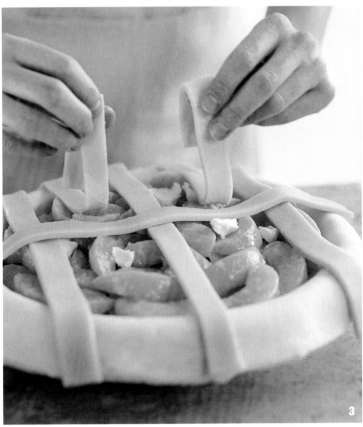

3 Fold back alternating strips
Fold back every other dough strip halfway over itself. Place a strip at a sharp angle across the unfolded strips, then return the folded strips to their flat position.

4 Weave the dough
Fold back the remaining 3 strips, place a dough strip about 1 inch away from the first one, and return the folded strips to their flat position. Repeat to complete the lattice.

PIES & TARTS

Embellishing pies

1 Flute the edge
Hold your thumb and index finger about 1 inch (2.5 cm) apart. Press them against the outer edge of the pastry while pressing your other thumb from the inside to make an indent. Repeat around the pastry edge.

2 Crimp the edge
Dust the tines of a fork with flour. Gently press down along the edge of the dough with the fork to make decorative crimp marks around the pastry edge.

3 Form a rope edge
Lightly dust the handle of a wooden spoon with flour. Hold the handle at an angle and press down on the dough along the rim in ½- to 1½-inch (12-mm to 4-cm) intervals.

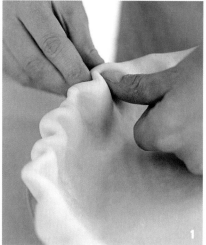

4 Create a braided edge
Prepare an egg wash (see entry 243) and lightly brush it on the rim of the pie dough. On a work surface, braid long strips of dough, about ¼ inch (6 mm) wide. Carefully transfer the braids to the rim and press gently to seal.

5 Press dough cutouts on the edge
Using a small cookie cutter, cut out small shapes from the rolled-out dough scraps. Brush one side of each cutout with egg wash (see entry 243) and press lightly on the edge of the crust to adhere.

6 Make detailed dough cutouts
Using a small cookie cutter, cut out shapes from the rolled-out dough scraps. Use the back of a paring knife to add details. Affix the shapes to the top of a double-crust pie with egg wash (see entry 243) before baking.

Blind baking a tart or pie

1 Line the dough with foil
Preheat the oven to 400°F (200°C) or according to your recipe. Line the dough with a large piece of heavy-duty aluminum foil, making sure to press the foil into the fluted edges of the dough.

2 Add weights
Fill the foil-lined crust with pie weights, dried beans, or uncooked rice. Make sure the weights cover the entire bottom of the crust. Bake the lined crust until dry, about 15 minutes or according to your recipe.

3 Check the crust
Check to see if the crust is ready by pulling up one corner of the foil. If the foil sticks, the crust is not fully dried. Return it to the oven, checking again every 2 minutes.

4 Remove the weights
Carefully remove the weights and foil. Most recipes call for the crust to be baked again until partially baked, about 5 minutes longer, or fully baked, about 10 minutes longer.

5 Let the crust cool
If filling a fully baked crust with an egg-based filling or for a tart that's served cold, let the pastry crust cool for at least 30 minutes in the pan on a wire rack.

6 Unmold the crust, if needed
Pies are usually served right from the pan, while tarts are typically unmolded. To unmold a tart crust or a filled tart, carefully press the removable bottom up through the tart ring. Use an offset spatula to release the crust from the bottom of the tart pan.

Trussing poultry

1 Trim the fat
Trussing poultry is an optional step, but some believe it gives the bird a more pleasing, uniform appearance when cooked. Place the bird breast side up on a clean cutting board. Using poultry shears, cut off any excess fat.

2 Secure the wings
Holding a wing, bend the wing tip and tuck it behind the shoulder area of the bird. Repeat with the other wing. This will keep the wings secure during cooking and prevent them from burning.

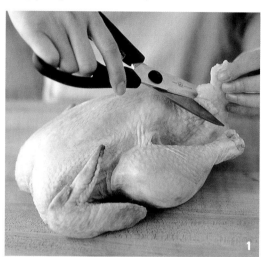

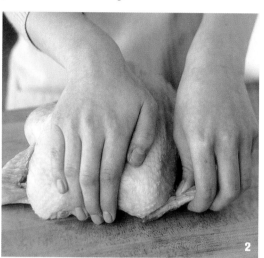

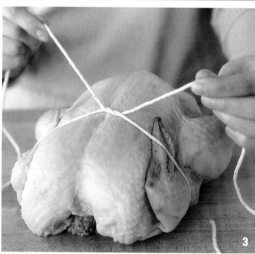

3 Or, tie the wings to the body
You can also secure the wings to the body with a length of kitchen string. Don't tie the string too tightly or it could mar the skin.

4 Tie the drumsticks
Cut a length of kitchen string, loop it around the ends of the drumsticks, and tie the string to hold them in place. This will help give the bird a compact shape.

Stuffing poultry

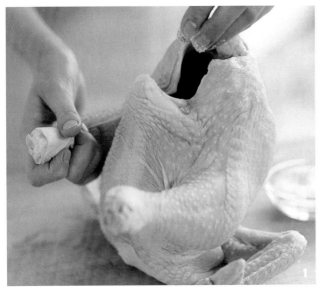

1 Season the cavity
Remove the giblets, if present, and reserve for another use.
Pat the bird completely dry with paper towels. Hold the bird
upright and season the cavity with salt and pepper.

2 Spoon the stuffing into the cavity
Hold the cavity open with one hand and, using a silicone spatula
or large spoon, fill the cavity loosely with room-temperature
stuffing. Don't overstuff the bird, which could hinder cooking.

Rubbing butter under poultry skin

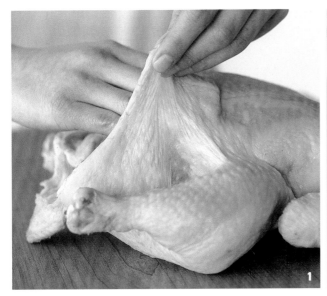

1 Separate the poultry skin from the flesh
With the bird breast side up, slide your fingers under the skin and
gently separate the skin from the breast meat on both sides, being
careful not to tear the skin. Repeat under the leg and thigh skin.

2 Rub the butter under the skin
Using a large spoon, scoop up a portion of flavored butter, slide
it under the breast, leg, and thigh skin, and push it off with your
fingers. Massage the butter through the skin to distribute it evenly.

Skinning, boning & pounding chicken breasts

1 Remove the skin
If necessary, cut whole boneless chicken breasts into halves. Working from the thick end of a breast half, grasp the skin and firmly pull it off the meat. Discard the skin.

2 Cut away the bones
Turn the chicken breast over. Starting from the thin end of the breast, and using a boning knife with a thin blade, cut the flesh away from the bone, using your other hand to pull the bone away as you cut.

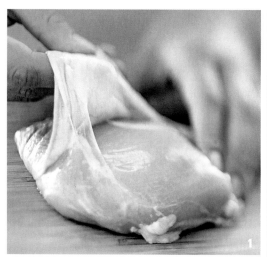

3 Remove the tenderloin
Then, still using the knife, cut away the long tenderloin and its white tendon from the breast. Reserve for another use.

4 Pound the breast half
Place 1 breast half in a plastic bag or between 2 sheets of waxed paper. Using a flat meat pounder, and working from the center outward, lightly pound the breast until it is a uniform ½ inch (12 mm) thick.

Skewering boneless chicken breast meat

1 Pound the breast
One at a time, place the chicken breast halves between 2 sheets of waxed paper or in a plastic bag. Using a meat pounder, gently pound the breast until the meat is equally thick throughout.

2 Cut the meat into cubes
Slice each breast half lengthwise into strips about 1 inch (2.5 cm) wide. Then, cut the strips crosswise into 1-inch square pieces.

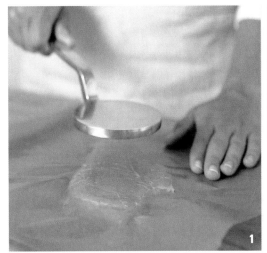

3 Soak the skewers
Meanwhile, place the wooden skewers in a long, shallow dish and cover with water. Let them soak for at least 1 hour to prevent the skewers from scorching during cooking.

4 Skewer the chicken
Drain the skewers. Thread 1 or more pieces of chicken onto each skewer, poking the skewer lengthwise through the center of each piece so the pieces lie flat.

Brining a whole chicken

1 Dissolve the salt and sugar
Brining poultry before cooking enhances flavor and moistness. In a large saucepan, combine the brine ingredients. Bring to a boil over high heat, stirring often to dissolve the salt and sugar.

2 Transfer the brine to a large vessel
Pour the brine into a large nonreactive pot or heatproof bowl large enough to hold the ingredients. Choose a vessel made from glass, ceramic, stainless steel, or plastic. Do not use uncoated aluminum.

3 Cool the brine
It is important for the brine to be cool before adding the chicken. Some recipes will call for a minimum of liquid in step 1 so that the solution can be diluted with ice water to cool it quickly.

4 Add the chicken to the brine
Add the chicken to the brining container and submerge it in the chilled brine. Place a plate on top of the chicken to keep it under the level of the brine. Refrigerate, turning occasionally, for 4–6 hours, or according to your recipe.

5 Rinse the chicken
Remove the chicken from the brine. Place the chicken in a large bowl, with the body cavity opening facing down, and let the chicken drain well for about 5 minutes.

6 Pat the chicken dry
Some recipes call for rinsing the chicken before cooking to remove some of the salty flavor left by the brine. Pat the chicken dry with paper towels and bring it to room temperature before cooking.

Brining a whole turkey

1 Combine the brine ingredients
In a stockpot large enough to hold the turkey, combine the brine ingredients. Bring to a boil over high heat, stirring often to dissolve the salt and sugar. Remove from the heat.

2 Add ice water, if using
It is important for the brine to be cool before adding the turkey. Some recipes will call for a minimum of liquid in step 1 so that the solution can be diluted with ice water to help it cool more quickly.

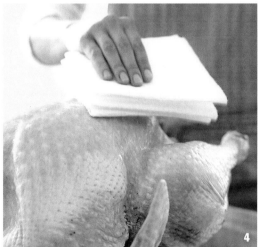

3 Add the turkey to the brine
Immerse the turkey in the brine breast side down, making sure it is completely submerged. Refrigerate for 1–3 days, or according to your recipe.

4 Pat the turkey dry
Remove the turkey from the brine, rinse well, and pat dry. Bring the turkey to room temperature before roasting.

Cutting up a whole chicken

1 Remove the legs
Place the chicken breast side up. Pull a leg away from the body. Using poultry shears, cut through the skin to expose the hip joint. Locate the joint and cut through it to remove the leg. Repeat with the second leg.

2 Separate the thighs
Locate the joint between the thigh and drumstick. Holding a leg securely, use the poultry shears to cut through the joint to separate the thigh from the drumstick. Repeat with the second leg.

3 Remove the wings
Grasp a wing and pull it away from the body. Use the shears to cut through the skin to expose the shoulder joint. Then cut through the joint to remove the wing. Repeat with the second wing.

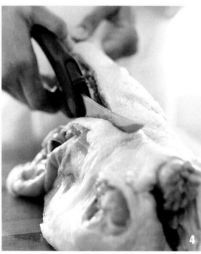

4 Remove the back
Turn the chicken over. Cut along one side of the backbone, from the body cavity to the neck cavity. Then cut along the other side and remove the back. Discard the back or save it for making stock.

5 Pull out the breastbone
Run the tip of closed poultry shears through the membrane covering the breastbone. Bend the breast upward at the center to pop out the breastbone, then pull or cut it free and discard.

6 Cut the breast into halves
Using the poultry shears, cut the breast lengthwise into halves. After cutting up the chicken, you will have a total of 8 pieces plus the back.

Butterflying chicken

1 Cut along the backbone
Place the chicken, breast side down, on a cutting board. Using poultry shears or a chef's knife, cut along one side of the backbone. Pull open chicken, taking care not to rip or tear the skin.

2 Remove the backbone
Cut down along the other side of the backbone and remove the back. Discard the back or save it for making stock.

3 Flatten the chicken
Turn the chicken breast side up, opening the cavity so that it is lying as flat as possible. Placing one hand over the other, press firmly on the breast area to break the breastbone and completely flatten the bird. You should hear and feel the breastbone crack.

4 Secure the wings
Bend each wing out from the body and secure the tip underneath the neck area.

Grilling a butterflied chicken

1 Place the chicken on the grill
Set up a gas or charcoal grill for direct-heat grilling with one area of high heat and one with low heat (see entry 165). Place a butterflied chicken (see entry 256), skin side down, on the low-heat part of the grill.

2 Weigh down the chicken
Place a cast-iron frying pan or two aluminum foil–covered bricks on top of the chicken. Cover the grill and cook the bird until the skin is golden brown, about 30 minutes for a 4 lb (2 kg) chicken.

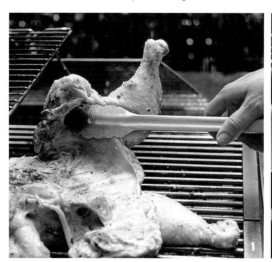

3 Cook the second side
Turn over the chicken, replace the pan or bricks, and cover the grill. Cook for about 15 minutes longer. Remove the pan or bricks.

4 Test for doneness
Insert an instant-read thermometer into the thickest part of the breast, not touching a bone. It should read 170°F (77°C). If the bird is not done, replace the pan or bricks, cook for another 5 minutes, and test again.

Sautéing boneless chicken breasts

1 Heat the butter and oil
Choose a frying pan large enough to hold the chicken breasts without crowding. Place the frying pan over medium-high heat and add a mixture of butter and canola oil to form a thin layer in the pan.

2 Coat the breasts with flour
Spread flour in a shallow dish. One at a time, lightly coat seasoned, pounded boneless chicken breasts (see entry 251) in the flour, shaking off any excess, and place the coated breasts in the pan.

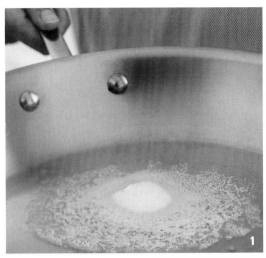

3 Sauté the chicken breasts
Cook the breasts until the bottoms are golden brown, about 3 minutes. Using tongs, turn over the breasts.

4 Test for doneness
Reduce the heat to medium and sauté until the second sides are golden brown and the breasts feel firm when pressed in the center with a fingertip, about 3 minutes longer. Transfer the breasts to a warmed platter.

POULTRY

Pan-roasting duck breasts

1 Score the skin
Using a sharp knife, make a series of parallel cuts through the skin, but not into the flesh. Make a second set of cuts at right angles to the first. This scoring will help the fat render so the skin becomes crisp.

2 Sear the breasts, skin side down
Season the breasts with salt and pepper. Heat a large, heavy ovenproof frying pan over high heat until very hot. Place the breasts, skin side down, in the pan and use a spatula to press them firmly into the hot pan.

3 Spoon off the fat
Sear for 2 minutes, tilting the pan and spooning out the accumulated fat.

4 Pan-roast the breasts
Place the pan in a preheated 400°F (200°C) oven and roast for 6 minutes. Using tongs, turn the breasts and roast until a meat thermometer inserted in the middle of each breast reads 150°F (65°C).

Testing boneless poultry pieces for doneness

1 Test by sight
For small pieces of poultry, such as thighs or boneless breasts, make small cuts into the meat. The flesh should show no sign of pink.

2 Test by touch
Press the center of the poultry piece with a fingertip. It should feel firm, but bounce back, indicating the poultry is cooked but not overdone.

Testing poultry for doneness by temperature

1 Test a whole bird
Insert an instant-read thermometer into the thickest part of the thigh away from the bone. When the poultry is done, the thermometer should read 170°F (77°C).

2 Test a bone-in cut
For an individual cut such as a turkey breast, insert the thermometer into the center of the thickest part, away from the bone.

Carving a bone-in turkey breast

1 Cut the breast from the bone
Hold a carving fork in one hand and steady the breast. Using a thin, flexible carving knife, cut the breast meat away from the rib cage in a single piece.

2 Slice the breast
Working across the length of the breast, cut the breast against the grain into slices ½ inch (12 mm) thick.

Buttermilk-fried chicken

A soak in a buttermilk brine is what makes this fried chicken, with its spicy, crunchy crust, such a crowd pleaser. The meat is tenderized by the acids in the buttermilk and seasoned throughout by the salt in the brine. The brining also keeps the chicken moist as it cooks.

INGREDIENTS

4 cups (32 fl oz/1 l) buttermilk

¼ cup (1½ oz/75 g) table salt

1 tablespoon red hot-pepper sauce

4 lb (2 kg) chicken pieces (breasts, thighs, and drumsticks)

1 cup (5 oz/155 g) all-purpose (plain) flour

¾ teaspoon baking powder

½ teaspoon freshly ground black pepper

¼ teaspoon cayenne pepper

½ teaspoon dried marjoram

½ teaspoon dried thyme

½ teaspoon dried sage

Canola oil for frying

MAKES 4 SERVINGS

1 Make the buttermilk brine
Choose a nonreactive bowl (glass, ceramic, or stainless steel) large enough to hold the chicken pieces and the brine comfortably. Pour the buttermilk into the bowl and add the salt and the hot-pepper sauce. Using a whisk, stir until the salt dissolves.

2 Brine the chicken pieces
Add the chicken to the brine, making sure that it is completely submerged. Cover the bowl and refrigerate for 6–12 hours. About 1 hour before you plan to begin frying the chicken, remove the bowl from the refrigerator and leave it on the countertop.

6 Fry the legs
Using tongs, add the drumsticks and thighs to the hot oil. The oil temperature will drop, so keep the heat on high to bring it back to 350°F. Adjust the heat as needed throughout the frying to maintain this temperature. Fry the chicken until golden brown, about 4 minutes on each side. Transfer to a rimmed baking sheet and place in the oven for 10 minutes.

3 Flour the chicken pieces

In a shallow dish, combine the flour, baking powder, black pepper, cayenne pepper, and dried herbs. Use one hand to retrieve a piece of chicken from the brine, shaking off the excess, and place the chicken in the seasoned flour. Use your other hand to coat the chicken with the flour and transfer to a baking sheet. Repeat with the remaining chicken.

4 Add the oil to a heavy pan

Use a large, heavy, deep frying pan, preferably one made of cast iron, which retains heat well. Place the pan on the stove top and pour oil to a depth of 1 inch (2.5 cm) into the pan. Insert the probe of a digital oil or candy thermometer into the oil.

5 Heat the oil

Preheat the oven to 350°F (180°C). Heat the oil over high heat until the thermometer reads 350°F (180°C). You can also test the temperature of the oil by dropping in a small bit of the flour coating. If it immediately bubbles and begins to brown, the oil is ready.

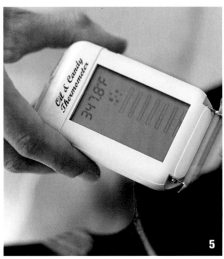

7 Fry the breasts

Meanwhile, fry the breasts in the same manner, making sure to bring the oil back to 350°F before frying. Add the breasts to the baking pan and bake the breasts with the drumsticks and thighs for 10 more minutes. Remove the chicken from the oven. Using the tip of a paring knife, make a small incision near the bone of a thigh. The meat should look opaque; there should be no sign of pink in the meat or at the bone.

Table salt has small crystals that are always the same weight per cup. Kosher salt has large flakes, which differ in weight and could impact the saltiness of a brine. As the type of salt doesn't affect the flavor of the brine, it's a good idea to use noniodized table salt for consistency.

Basic roast chicken

The perfect roast chicken, with its crisp buttered skin and tender, juicy flesh, eludes many cooks. Here's a blueprint for a simply seasoned bird that allows its natural poultry flavor to shine through. It's easy to vary the recipe based on the season or your mood.

1 Season the chicken
Preheat the oven to 450°F (230°C). Remove the giblets and neck from the body cavity; discard or save for another use. Remove any excess fat. Pat the chicken dry with paper towels. Rub the outside of the bird evenly with the room-temperature butter. Sprinkle the salt and pepper evenly over the inside and outside of the chicken.

2 Secure the wings
Bend each wing tip and tuck it under the shoulder area of the bird. Alternatively, tie the wings to the side of the chicken with a loop of kitchen string (see entry 248). Put a V-shaped roasting rack in a heavy roasting pan and brush the rack with canola oil.

INGREDIENTS

1 chicken, about 4 lb (2 kg)

4 tablespoons (2 oz/60 g) unsalted butter, 2 tablespoons at room temperature and 2 tablespoons cold

¾ teaspoon salt

½ teaspoon freshly ground pepper

Canola oil for coating the roasting rack

MAKES 4 SERVINGS

Here, the drumsticks are left untied so that the oven heat will more readily penetrate the thigh joints and the chicken will roast more evenly. If you prefer a more compact, finished look, tie the ends of the drumsticks together with kitchen string.

5 Transfer the chicken to a board
Remove the chicken from the oven. Insert a wooden spoon into the body cavity and tilt the chicken so that the juices in the cavity flow into the roasting pan. With the spoon still in the cavity, transfer the chicken, breast side up, to a carving board.

3 Roast the chicken

Place the chicken breast side up on the rack. Roast the chicken for 15 minutes. Turn the chicken onto one of its sides and return it to the oven. Turning the chicken at intervals during roasting exposes all of the skin to the oven heat to increase browning. Reduce the oven temperature to 375°F (190°C) and roast the chicken for 30 minutes. Turn the chicken onto its other side.

4 Test for doneness

Continue roasting until an instant-read thermometer inserted into the thickest part of the thigh (where it meets the drumstick), but not touching the bone, reads 170°F (77°C), about 30 minutes longer. If the chicken isn't done, return it to the oven and roast for another 5 minutes, then check again.

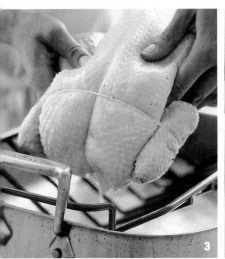

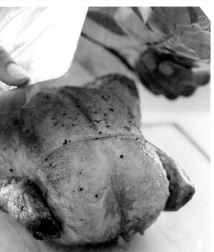

6 Let the chicken rest

Let the chicken rest for 10–20 minutes. It won't get cold, but you can tent the bird with aluminum foil, if you wish. Just keep in mind that the foil can cause the skin to steam slightly, which makes it less crisp. Carve into serving pieces (see entry 266) and serve warm.

ROAST CHICKEN VARIATIONS

Herb-roast chicken

Follow the recipe for Basic Roast Chicken. Before you start, in a small bowl, mix together 2 tablespoons room-temperature unsalted butter, 1 teaspoon chopped fresh thyme, and 1 teaspoon chopped fresh rosemary. Carefully slip your fingers under the skin and work them all around the breast and thigh areas, loosening the skin. Using your fingers, evenly distribute the butter under the loosened skin (see entry 250). Proceed with the recipe.

Spice-crusted roast chicken

Follow the recipe for Basic Roast Chicken. Before you start, in a small, dry frying pan, toast 1 teaspoon yellow mustard seeds, 1 teaspoon coriander seeds, ½ teaspoon peppercorns, and ½ teaspoon fennel seeds (see entry 110). Transfer the toasted spices to a spice grinder or a mortar and coarsely grind them with the machine or a pestle. Transfer the mixture to a small bowl. Stir in ½ teaspoon celery seeds and ⅛ teaspoon cayenne pepper. Proceed with the recipe, starting at step 1, sprinkling the spice mixture over the buttered chicken along with the salt and pepper.

Classic roast turkey

A whole turkey, roasted until beautifully browned, is the centerpiece for many special-occasion dinners. If possible, purchase a fresh turkey. If you can find only a frozen bird, allow about 4 days for it to thaw slowly, and safely, in the refrigerator.

INGREDIENTS

1 fresh turkey with neck and giblets, about 18 lb (9 kg)

½ cup (4 oz/125 g) unsalted butter, at room temperature

Canola oil for coating the roasting rack

2 cups (16 fl oz/500 ml) Brown Turkey Stock (see entry 299)

MAKES ABOUT 12 SERVINGS

1 Butter the turkey
Remove the neck and giblets and brine the turkey, if desired (see entry 254). Rinse and dry the turkey and bring to room temperature. Using your hands, spread the butter all over the skin.

2 Secure the wings
Bend each wing tip and tuck it under the shoulder area of the bird. Alternatively, tie the wings to the sides of the turkey with a loop of kitchen string (see entry 248).

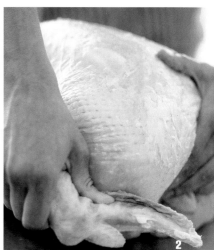

5 Roast the turkey
Roast the turkey, using a bulb baster to baste the turkey with the stock about every 45 minutes. When basting, lift up the foil to baste the breast and work quickly to keep the oven from cooling. If the liquid cooks away completely, add a little water to the pan. Continue roasting until an instant-read thermometer inserted into the thickest part of the thigh (where it meets the drumstick), but not touching the bone, reads 180°–185°F (82°–85°C), about 4 hours. During the last hour of roasting time, remove the foil from the breast.

3 Tie the drumsticks, if desired
You can leave the legs as they are, which will help the heat more readily penetrate the thigh joints. Or, for a more compact look, tie the ends of the drumsticks together with kitchen string.

4 Place the turkey in the pan
Select a roasting pan just large enough to hold the turkey. Brush a flat roasting rack with oil and place it in the pan. Position the turkey on the rack. To keep the lean breast meat moist, cover it tightly with aluminum foil.

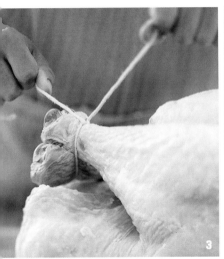

6 Let the turkey rest
Remove the turkey from the oven. Insert a sturdy, large metal spoon into the body cavity, and, supporting the turkey at the neck cavity with a carving fork, tilt it so that the juices in the cavity flow into the roasting pan. Transfer the turkey, breast side up, to a carving board. Let the bird rest for at least 20 minutes or up to 45 minutes. If the kitchen is cold, you can tent the turkey with foil. This brief rest before serving allows the juices to redistribute throughout the meat and is the key to a juicy bird.

FLAVORING TURKEY

White wine brine

To ensure a juicy and flavorful turkey, brine it first: In a nonreactive stockpot large enough to hold the turkey, combine 2 bottles (3 cups/24 fl oz/ 750 ml each) dry white wine; 1 cup (10 oz/315 g) table salt; 1 cup (7 oz/ 220 g) firmly packed light brown sugar; 2 tablespoons each dried rosemary, dried thyme, and dried sage; 1 tablespoon each dried marjoram and black peppercorns; and 4 bay leaves. Bring to a boil over high heat, stirring to dissolve the salt and sugar. Remove from the heat and stir in 6½ qt (6.5 l) ice water until melted. Carefully lower the bird into the cooled brine, cover, and refrigerate for 12–24 hours.

Herb gravy

After roasting the turkey, degrease the pan drippings (see entry 270). Measure the fat: you should have ½ cup (4 fl oz/125 ml). If not, add melted butter to supplement. Measure the juices, then add enough Brown Turkey Stock (see entry 299) to measure 6 cups (48 fl oz/1.5 l). Place the roasting pan over 2 burners and turn the heat to medium-high. Add the fat to the pan and sprinkle in ⅔ cup (3½ oz/105 g) all-purpose (plain) flour. Stir with a flat whisk to make a roux, then let the roux bubble for 1 minute. Whisk in the stock mixture and 4 teaspoons minced fresh sage. Bring to a boil. Reduce the heat to low and simmer, whisking occasionally to prevent lumps from forming, until the gravy is thick enough to coat the back of a spoon and no trace of raw flour taste remains, about 10 minutes. Adjust the seasonings.

Carving a whole chicken

1 Expose the thigh joints
Remove the trussing string, if present. Steadying the bird with a carving fork, use a carving knife or chef's knife to cut through the skin between the breast and the thigh.

2 Remove the legs
Move a leg downward to locate the thigh joint. Cut through the joint to sever the leg. Repeat on the other side of the bird to remove the second leg.

3 Separate the thighs
Holding a leg securely, cut through the joint between the drumstick and thigh to separate them. Repeat with the second leg.

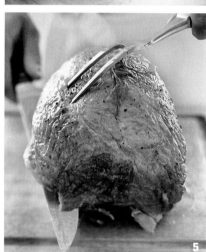

4 Remove the wings
Cut through the skin between a wing and the breast. Locate the shoulder joint and cut through it to remove the wing. Repeat on the other side to remove the second wing.

5 Make a base cut at the breast
The breast meat can be difficult to slice, or the slices can fall apart. Before carving, make a deep horizontal cut through the breast toward the bone, creating a base cut. This way, each slice will end neatly at the base cut.

6 Carve the breasts
Beginning at the breastbone, make a series of cuts downward and parallel to the rib cage, carving the meat from one side of the breast in long, thin slices. Repeat on the other side.

Carving a whole turkey

1 Remove the legs
Place the turkey breast side up on a carving board with the legs facing you. Using a carving knife, cut through the skin between the breast and thigh. Locate the thigh joint and cut through it to remove the drumstick.

2 Carve the breasts
Leave the thighs and wings on the bird to stabilize it. Just above the thigh and wing, carve a deep horizontal cut through the breast to the bone to create a base cut.

3 Carve the breast from the bone
Beginning at the breastbone, make a series of cuts downward and parallel to the rib cage, carving the meat from one side of the breast in long, thin slices. Repeat steps 1–3 on the other side.

4 Or, slice the breast into medallions
You can also remove the breast from the bone by cutting down along the breastbone to meet the horizontal cut. Place the breast flat on a cutting surface and slice it crosswise to cut into medallions.

5 Remove the thighs and wings
Pry each thigh from the joint; then, use the knife to remove the thighs. Locate the joint between each wing and the breastbone and cut through the joints to remove the wings.

6 Transfer the meat to a platter
Arrange the turkey on a platter, placing the dark meat on one side and the sliced white breast meat on the other. Garnish with sprigs of fresh herbs or as you'd like.

Making crème fraîche

1 Warm the ingredients
In a small saucepan over medium-low heat, combine 1 cup (8 fl oz/250 ml) heavy (double) cream and 1 tablespoon buttermilk. Heat to lukewarm (do not allow the mixture to simmer).

2 Cover and let the mixture thicken
Transfer the mixture to a bowl, cover, and let stand at warm room temperature until thickened, 8–48 hours, depending on your taste and recipe needs. Refrigerate until well chilled before using.

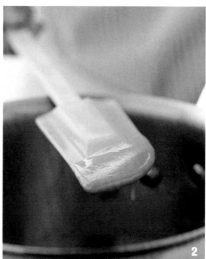

Making a roux

1 Combine the fat and flour
A roux is a combination of fat, usually butter, and flour used for thickening sauces and soups. Different recipes will call for different proportions of ingredients. In a heavy-bottomed pan over medium heat, melt the butter or heat the oil. Then, whisk in the flour until smooth.

2 Make a white roux
For a white roux, cook the mixture over low heat for 2–3 minutes, stirring constantly. The *roux* should be a pale straw color and have a lightly toasted taste.

3 Make a brown roux
For a brown roux (common in Cajun and Creole recipes), cook the mixture over medium heat for about 20 minutes, stirring constantly. The roux will be a deep, reddish brown and have a nutty taste.

TROUBLESHOOTING
Remember to adjust the heat and keep a close watch on the heat level of the burner. You want the roux to bubble very gently. If the roux cooks too quickly, it will burn and become gritty.

Degreasing pan drippings

1 Spoon the fat from the surface
Let the drippings stand for about 5 minutes to allow the fat to rise to the top. Then, use a large metal spoon to skim the fat from the surface; discard the fat.

2 Or, use a fat separator
Pour the pan drippings into a degreasing cup and let stand for a few minutes so that the fat separates from the juices. Once the drippings have settled, pour the juices into a clean measuring cup, leaving the fat behind.

Deglazing a pan

1 Add liquid to a hot pan
Place a pan containing the browned drippings left by a sauté or roast—called the *fond*—over medium-high heat until the drippings sizzle. Add stock or another liquid called for in the recipe.

2 Scrape up the browned bits
As the liquid comes to a boil, stir and scrape the bottom and sides of the pan with a wooden spatula to loosen the brown *fond*. It will be absorbed into the liquid, providing rich flavor and deep color.

Mounting a sauce with butter

1 Cut the butter into cubes
Keep the butter cold until you're ready to use it. Cut the butter in half lengthwise, then turn the butter 90 degrees and cut in half lengthwise again. Cut the butter crosswise into small cubes.

2 Gradually whisk in the butter
Remove the sauce from the heat. Add one or a few cubes of butter at a time while whisking constantly. The sauce will gain rich flavor and a nice sheen.

SAUCES

Thickening with a roux

1 Heat the fat
A *roux* is a blend of fat and flour that thickens a sauce. The fat can be oil, butter, or rendered fat from a roast. If the fat is not already hot, heat it over medium to medium-high heat.

2 Add the flour
Sprinkle flour into the hot fat following the proportions in your recipe and distribute it evenly over the bottom of the pan.

3 Whisk the flour with the fat
Using a whisk—preferably a flat roux whisk— stir together the flour and fat until well combined. The flour will absorb the fat and may darken slightly.

4 Cook the roux
Let the roux bubble for 2–3 minutes, or longer, depending on whether you need a white or brown roux for your recipe (see entry 269). As the roux cooks, it will become darker, but will lose some thickening power.

5 Add the liquid
After the roux has cooked to the stage specified in your recipe, stir in the liquid that will be thickened. Many chefs believe that the liquid should also be hot to prevent the hot fat in the roux from spattering.

6 Check the consistency and flavor
A sauce thickened with roux has an opaque appearance. Taste it to make sure the starchy flour flavor has been cooked away. If not, simmer the sauce briefly to remove the starchiness.

Thickening with a slurry

1 Combine cornstarch and water
To make what chefs call a "slurry" for thickening pan sauces or reduction sauces, combine equal parts cornstarch (cornflour) and cold water or another liquid called for in your recipe in a small bowl.

2 Blend the ingredients
Using a fork, stir together the cornstarch and water until blended. The mixture should be the consistency of heavy (double) cream.

3 Bring the sauce base to a simmer
If needed, heat the sauce base until small bubbles appear. The slurry must be added to a simmering liquid in order for it to thicken the sauce properly.

4 Add the slurry
If the slurry separates before you're ready to use it, stir it again to combine. Drizzle a small amount of the slurry into the simmering sauce base. You may not need to use all of it.

5 Boil the mixture while whisking
Whisk the slurry and liquid, letting the liquid come just to a boil to activate its thickening power. If needed, whisk in more slurry a little at a time and cook until the sauce is thickened as desired.

6 Check the consistency and flavor
A sauce thickened with a slurry has a glossy sheen. Taste it to make sure the chalky cornstarch flavor has been cooked away. If not, simmer the sauce briefly to remove the chalkiness.

All-purpose pan sauce

This all-purpose sauce owes its light consistency to a simple technique: adding stock to the drippings in a frying or roasting pan and then simmering until full flavored and slightly thickened. A few spoonfuls will dramatically enhance a dish.

INGREDIENTS

1½ cups (12 fl oz/375 ml) Brown Beef Stock (see entry 301) or Brown Chicken Stock (see entry 299)

3 tablespoons cold unsalted butter

½ shallot, finely chopped

1½ teaspoons cornstarch (cornflour), optional

2 tablespoons water, optional

¼ teaspoon salt

¼ teaspoon freshly ground pepper

1 tablespoon chopped fresh sage, optional

MAKES ABOUT 1 CUP
(8 FL OZ/250 ML)

1 Degrease the pan drippings
Evaluate the pan drippings and darken them if necesary by cooking over high heat for a minute or two. Pour the drippings from the pan into a fat separator and let stand for a few minutes until the fat rises to the top. Pour the juices into a large glass measuring cup, leaving the fat behind.

2 Replenish the pan juices
Choose beef or chicken stock to match the food you cooked, or follow your recipe. Add enough stock to the degreased pan juices in the measuring cup to make a total of 1½ cups (12 fl oz/375 ml).

6 Thicken the sauce, if desired
If you'd like the sauce to be thicker, or if your recipe calls for it, use a cornstarch slurry. Combine the cornstarch and water in a small bowl and stir to blend. Whisk a little of it into the simmering sauce, then bring to a boil just until the sauce thickens; this should take a minute or less.

3 Sauté the shallots

Return the pan with the browned bits in the bottom to the stove and place over high heat, using 2 burners if you used a roasting pan. Add 2 tablespoons of the butter and heat until the butter melts and the browned bits are sizzling. Add the shallot and cook, stirring, until the shallot softens and becomes translucent, about 1 minute.

4 Deglaze the pan

Pour the stock-juice mixture into the pan and bring to a boil, scraping up the browned bits on the bottom and sides of the pan with a wooden spoon. These browned bits, or *fond*, will add a rich flavor to the final sauce.

5 Reduce the sauce

Once the liquid has absorbed the *fond*, let the sauce boil until it has reduced to about 1 cup (8 fl oz/250 ml); this should take about 3 minutes, depending on the size of the pan. Tilt the pan occasionally to estimate the amount of liquid remaining in the bottom.

7 Finish the sauce with butter

Remove the pan from the heat. Cut the remaining 1 tablespoon butter into small cubes. While whisking constantly, drop the butter cubes, 1 or 2 at a time, into the sauce. This technique gives the sauce a slightly thicker body and nice sheen. Stir in the salt, pepper, and sage, if using, and then taste the sauce, adjusting the seasonings to your liking.

If you don't have a fat separator, you can pour the pan drippings into a heat-proof measuring cup instead. Let the drippings stand until the fat rises to the top. Then, use a soup spoon to skim off and discard the clear fat that rises to the top. Proceed with step 2 of the recipe.

All-purpose pan gravy

A pan gravy accompanies roasted or pan-fried meats or poultry and is prepared with the meat's own drippings and juices. Traditional gravies, such as this one, call for briefly cooking flour in the drippings to make a light roux.

INGREDIENTS

Melted unsalted butter, optional

3 tablespoons all-purpose (plain) flour

About 1½ cups (12 fl oz/375 ml) Brown Chicken Stock (see entry 299) or Brown Beef Stock (see entry 301)

¼ teaspoon salt

¼ teaspoon freshly ground pepper

MAKES ABOUT 2 CUPS
(16 FL OZ/500 ML)

You can alter the yield of this recipe using this formula: For every 1 cup (8 oz/250 ml) liquid, use 1½ tablespoons each fat and flour to make the roux. Using these proportions, you can make just the amount of gravy you need. Plan on about ½ cup (4 fl oz/125 ml) gravy for each serving.

1 Pour off the pan drippings
Evaluate the pan drippings and darken them if necessary by cooking them over high heat for a minute or two. Pour the drippings from the pan into a fat separator and let stand for a few minutes until the fat rises to the top.

2 Degrease the pan juices
Pour the light brown pan juices into a large glass measuring cup; reserve the fat in the separator. You should have about 2 cups (16 fl oz/500 ml) of juices. If you're short, add stock to the pan juices to make up the amount.

6 Evaluate the consistency
The gravy should be thick enough to coat the back of a wooden spoon. If the gravy is too thick, thin it with more heated stock or water. If it's too thin, continue to simmer until the desired consistency is reached.

3 Make a roux

Place the roasting pan on 2 burners over medium heat. Meausure out 3 tablespoons of the reserved fat and add it to the pan. If you're short, add melted butter to the pan to make up the amount. When the fat is hot, sprinkle in the flour.

4 Cook the roux

Using a flat whisk (sometimes called a roux whisk), whisk the flour into the hot drippings until smooth. Let the mixture bubble until the raw flour smell is gone, about 1 minute.

5 Deglaze the pan

Increase the heat to medium-high. Pour the stock mixture into the pan and bring to a boil, scraping up the browned bits on the bottom and sides of the pan. Reduce the heat to medium-low and simmer the gravy, whisking often, until it has thickened to the consistency of heavy (double) cream, about 10 minutes.

7 Adjust the seasonings

Stir in the salt and pepper and taste the gravy. If it tastes a little dull, stir in more salt or pepper until it tastes nicely balanced. If desired, pour the gravy into a saucepan through a fine-mesh sieve to remove any undissolved pan drippings. Keep warm over very low heat until ready to serve.

Béchamel sauce (white sauce)

Béchamel is the most basic white sauce of all. Classically trained cooks are taught to make béchamel in three thicknesses. The medium-thick version has the most use in the kitchen and is the sauce shown here.

1 Steep the onion in the milk
In a small saucepan, combine the milk, onion slice, and bay leaf. Place over medium heat and heat just until tiny bubbles appear around the edges of the pan, about 5 minutes. Do not boil. Remove the saucepan from the heat, cover, and let stand for 10 minutes. Remove and discard the onion and bay leaf. Re-cover to keep warm.

2 Make a roux
In a 2½- to 3-qt (2.5- to 3-l) heavy-bottomed saucepan, melt 3 tablespoons of the butter over medium-low heat. When the butter has melted and the foam subsides, stir in the flour. Reduce the heat to low. Let the mixture bubble for 2 minutes, then remove from the heat and let cool for 1 minute.

INGREDIENTS

2 cups (16 fl oz/500 ml) whole milk

One ¼-inch (6-mm) slice yellow onion

½ bay leaf

3–4 tablespoons (1½–2 oz/ 45–60 g) cold unsalted butter

3 tablespoons all-purpose (plain) flour

¼ teaspoon salt

⅛ teaspoon freshly ground pepper, preferably white pepper

MAKES ABOUT 2 CUPS
(16 FL OZ/500 ML)

5 Evaluate and strain the sauce
Taste the sauce; it should taste creamy with no trace of raw flour flavor. If lumps are still visible, pour the sauce through a fine-mesh sieve into a heatproof bowl.

3 Whisk in the infused milk

Slowly and evenly whisk the warm milk into the roux. Retun the pan to medium heat and bring the mixture to a boil, whisking often and making sure you reach the bottom and sides of the pan. Reduce the heat to medium-low and simmer gently, whisking often, until the sauce thickens, about 5 minutes.

4 Test the consistency

Dip a wooden spoon into the sauce to coat it. Draw your finger through the sauce on the back of the spoon: it should leave a clean track. If you are using the sauce in a recipe such as lasagna, stir in the salt and pepper. If you are making a cheese sauce, do not add the seasonings until after you add the cheese and taste the sauce, as the cheese itself will be salty.

Mornay sauce

Strain the unseasoned sauce into a clean saucepan. Whisk in ½ cup (2 oz/60 g) shredded Gruyère cheese and 3 tablespoons freshly grated Parmesan cheese. Cook over low heat, whisking constantly, until the cheese has melted and the sauce is smooth. Adjust the seasonings. Use to top cooked broccoli, cauliflower, or other vegetables.

Cheddar sauce

Strain the unseasoned sauce into a clean saucepan. Whisk in 2 cups (8 oz/250 g) shredded extra-sharp Cheddar cheese. Cook over low heat, whisking constantly, until the cheese has melted and the sauce is smooth. Adjust the seasonings. Use as a sauce for steamed vegetables, baked potatoes, or to make macaroni and cheese.

Gorgonzola sauce

Strain the unseasoned sauce into a clean saucepan. Whisk in ⅔ cup (4 oz/125 g) crumbled Gorgonzola cheese. Cook over low heat, whisking constantly, until the cheese has melted and the sauce is smooth. Adjust the seasonings. This sauce goes well with grilled steaks and roasted beef tenderloin.

6 Use or store the sauce

If you are not using the sauce right away, cut up the remaining 1 tablespoon butter into cubes and dot the sauce with the butter. Cover it with a piece of plastic wrap, pressing the wrap directly onto the surface of the sauce to prevent a skin from forming. Let the sauce cool, then store it in the refrigerator for up to 2 days. Reheat it in a saucepan over low heat, stirring constantly with a wooden spoon or whisk, adding a little hot water or milk to thin it, if necessary.

Beurre blanc

Rich with butter, beurre blanc is similar to hollandaise, but with more punch. The base of this sauce is a blend of dry white wine, vinegar, and shallot—all that acid helps hold the pale yellow sauce together and gives it a distinctive flavor.

INGREDIENTS

1 shallot

1 cup (8 fl oz/250 ml) dry white wine, such as Sauvignon Blanc or Pinot Grigio

2 tablespoons white wine vinegar

1 cup (8 oz/250 g) cold unsalted butter

¼ teaspoon salt

⅛ teaspoon freshly ground pepper, preferably white pepper

Leaves from 2 sprigs fresh tarragon, chopped, optional

MAKES ABOUT ⅔ CUP
(5 FL OZ/160 ML)

1 Make the sauce base
Peel and dice the shallot. In a small nonreactive saucepan over high heat, combine the wine, vinegar, and diced shallot. Bring the mixture to a boil and cook until the liquid has reduced to 2 tablespoons, about 5 minutes. Remove from the heat and let cool for about 30 seconds.

2 Cut the butter into cubes
While the wine mixture is cooling, cut each stick of butter in half lengthwise. Turn the slices 90 degrees and cut in half legthwise again. Then, cut the butter crosswise into ½-inch (12-mm) cubes.

4 Season the sauce
Stir in the salt and pepper and then taste the sauce. It should taste both tangy and creamy, with a nice acidity from the wine. If you think it tastes a little dull, stir in a bit more salt and pepper until the flavors are nicely balanced and to your liking.

5 Finish the sauce
If desired, strain the sauce through a fine-mesh sieve into a serving bowl. Stir in the tarragon, if using.

FLAVORING AND USING BEURRE BLANC

3 Blend in the butter

Place the sauce base over medium-low heat. Add a few cold butter cubes to the saucepan and whisk until the cubes are almost completely incorporated. Continue adding the butter, a few cubes at a time, whisking until the mixture transforms into an ivory-colored sauce with the consistency of thick, heavy (double) cream.

Beurre rouge

Follow the recipe to make Beurre Blanc, but in step 1, replace the white wine with dry red wine, preferably a wine that's not heavily oaked, and the white wine vinegar with red wine vinegar. Use to top grilled or sautéed veal chops or beef steaks.

Orange beurre blanc

Follow the recipe to make Beurre Blanc. In step 5, add the grated zest of 1 orange in place of the tarragon. Use on grilled or sautéed fish fillets.

Lemon beurre blanc

Follow the recipe to make Beurre Blanc, but in step 1, replace the wine vinegar with lemon juice. In step 5, add the grated zest of 1 lemon in place of the tarragon. Use on steamed or boiled artichokes or to complement shellfish.

Lime beurre blanc

Follow the recipe to make Beurre Blanc. In step 5, add the grated zest of 1 lime in place of the tarragon. Use for grilled or sautéed chicken.

Balsamic beurre blanc

Follow the recipe to make Beurre Blanc, but in step 1, replace the wine vinegar with balsamic vinegar. In step 5, add the minced leaves from 1 sprig fresh rosemary in place of the tarragon. Use to enhance lamb dishes.

Using leftover beurre blanc

Leftover Beurre Blanc can be chilled for up to 1 day and then used like a compound butter (see entry 107). Put small pieces of the cold sauce on top of hot food, and it will melt and liquefy to form a flavorful accompanying sauce.

Hollandaise sauce

Delicate hollandaise sauce should taste primarily of butter, with only a hint of lemon; so, it is important that you use the best butter you can find. A European-style butter is suggested here because of its high butterfat content and rich, tangy flavor.

INGREDIENTS

4 cold large egg yolks

2 tablespoons water

1 cup (8 oz/250 g) unsalted, European-style butter, clarified (see entry 106)

2–3 teaspoons fresh lemon juice

¼ teaspoon salt

⅛ teaspoon freshly ground pepper, preferably white pepper

MAKES ABOUT 1 CUP
(8 FL OZ/250 ML)

As you become more proficient, you can try making hollandaise in a saucepan alone, rather than over simmering water. Be careful to keep the heat extremely low. A heat diffuser—a piece of equipment that sits directly on the burner to dissipate the heat—is especially helpful.

1 Set up a double boiler
Bring 1 inch (2.5 cm) of water to a simmer in a saucepan or the bottom part of a double boiler over medium heat. Place a metal bowl or the top part of a double boiler on top of the saucepan, making sure that its bottom does not touch the simmering water. Reduce the heat to maintain a bare simmer and put the egg yolks in the bowl.

2 Add the water to the eggs
Add the water to the egg yolks and, using a handheld mixer on high speed or a whisk, beat until the yolks are slightly thickened and pale yellow, about 30 seconds. Aerating the yolks helps with the emulsification process.

5 Strain the hollandaise
Strain the sauce through a fine-mesh sieve set over a bowl. This removes any bits of cooked egg white or *chalazae*, thin white cords attached to the egg yolk.

SAUCES

3 Slowly add the butter

Check to make sure the water is still just barely at a simmer. If the heat is too high, the egg yolks can curdle. With the mixer on low speed, mix constantly while gradually drizzling the clarified butter into the yolks. Take your time adding the butter at the beginning so that the sauce doesn't separate. Once half of the butter has been added, you can mix in the remainder at a slightly faster pace.

4 Check the consistency

The finished sauce should be smooth, glossy, and barely warm. If the sauce appears to be separated into semisolid and liquid parts, you have added the butter too quickly. If you detect this problem early on, try whisking 1 table-spoon cold water into the sauce to bring it back together. For a more serious case, you may still be able to save it (see entry 280).

Béarnaise sauce

In a small nonreactive saucepan over medium heat, combine ¼ cup (1½ oz/45 g) minced shallots, 3 tablespoons white wine vinegar, 2 tablespoons chopped fresh tarragon, and ¼ teaspoon coarsely ground pepper. Bring to a boil and cook until the mixture is reduced and syrupy, about 2 minutes. Set aside. Follow the recipe to make Hollandaise Sauce. In step 6, whisk in the shallot mixture instead of the seasonings. Pair with grilled meats and fish.

Blood orange hollandaise

In a small nonreactive saucepan over medium heat, cook ¼ cup (2 fl oz/60 ml) blood orange juice until reduced by half, about 2 minutes. Set aside. Follow the recipe to make Hollandaise Sauce. In step 6, whisk in the reduced blood orange juice and the grated zest of ½ blood orange instead of the lemon juice. Pair with fish or shellfish.

Blender hollandaise

For a thicker hollandaise, make it in a blender: Place the yolks and water in a blender and pulse to combine. With the machine running, slowly add the clarified butter in a steady stream through the hole in the lid, until blended and thickened. Strain, if desired, and adjust the seasonings.

6 Adjust the seasonings

Whisk in 2 teaspoons of the lemon juice and the salt and pepper, and then taste the sauce. If it tastes a little dull, add more salt, pepper, or lemon juice a little at a time until the flavor is to your liking.

Fixing broken hollandaise

TROUBLESHOOTING
If you mix the butter and egg too fast (see entry 279), the hollandaise may "break," or separate into liquid and semisolid parts.

1 Pour the sauce into a cup
To repair the broken hollandaise, it needs to be slowly blended with fresh egg yolks. Start by pouring the sauce and any remaining butter into a liquid measuring cup.

2 Clean the bowl
Thoroughly wash and dry the bowl that the broken hollandaise was in so you can make a fresh start.

3 Start with new egg yolks
Put 2 egg yolks into the clean bowl. Using an electric mixer or a whisk, beat the yolks with 1 tablespoon water until thickened, about 30 seconds. Place the bowl over barely simmering water in a saucepan.

4 Drizzle in the broken sauce
Mixing constantly, slowly drizzle in the broken hollandaise. (You can also blend the egg yolks in a blender and drizzle in the broken sauce from the hole in the top.) This should re-emulsify your separated hollandaise.

5 Check the consistency
If the hollandaise is thick and emulsified but has small bits of egg in it, strain the sauce through a fine-mesh sieve. Since you added 2 fresh egg yolks, you may need to adjust the seasonings to acheive the desired flavor.

Fixing broken mayonnaise

TROUBLESHOOTING

If you mix the oil and egg too fast while making mayonnaise, the sauce may "break," or separate, developing a curdled appearance.

1 Pour the sauce into a cup

To repair the broken mayonnaise, it needs to be slowly blended with a fresh egg yolk. Start by pouring the sauce and any remaining oil into a liquid measuring cup.

2 Clean the bowl

Thoroughly wash and dry the bowl that the mayonnaise was in so you can make a fresh start.

3 Start with a new egg yolk

Put an egg yolk into the clean bowl and add 1 tablespoon of the broken sauce. Using an electric mixer, beat until the two are just combined.

4 Slowly add the broken sauce

Mxing constantly, gradually drizzle in the broken mayonnaise, adding it more slowly than you added the oil the first time.

5 Check the consistency

By carefully controlling the rate at which you combine the broken sauce and thefresh yolk, you can re-emulsify a separated mayonnaise. Taste and adjust the seasonings to your liking.

Mayonnaise

Homemade mayonnaise is much richer and creamier than its commercial counterpart. Here, we use an electric hand mixer to blend the ingredients, but mayonnaise can also be easily whipped up in a blender or food processor.

INGREDIENTS

2 large eggs

1 tablespoon fresh lemon juice

1 teaspoon Dijon mustard

¾ cup (6 fl oz/180 ml) canola or soybean oil, at room temperature

¾ cup (6 fl oz/180 ml) pure olive oil, at room temperature

¼ teaspoon salt, preferably fine sea salt

⅛ teaspoon freshly ground pepper, preferably white pepper

1 tablespoon water, optional

MAKES 1¾ CUPS (14 FL OZ/430 ML)

1 Warm the egg yolks
Put the egg yolks in a medium glass bowl placed on top of a larger bowl filled with warm tap water. Stir the egg yolks with a silicone spatula just until they lose their chill; use your finger to test the temperature. Cold ingredients do not emulsify as well as room-temperature ones. Remove the larger bowl.

2 Add the flavorings
Stir the lemon juice and mustard into the yolks with the spatula. Place a folded damp kitchen towel under the bowl to keep it from moving.

5 Mix in the rest of the oil
After the first half of the oil has been added, you can add the second half slightly faster. If the sauce breaks into semisolid and liquid parts and looks curdled, you have added the oils too quickly. See entry 281 to fix the broken mayonnaise.

3 Mix the oils together

Mix the canola and olive oils together in a liquid measuring cup. This combination of olive oil (not extra-virgin) and light-flavored vegetable oil makes a stable and clean-tasting mayonnaise.

4 Begin to slowly add the oil

Using a handheld mixer on high speed, start beating the egg-yolk mixture. While beating constantly, add the oils in a very slow, steady drizzle. As you beat, the sauce will emulsify, thicken, and change from bright yellow to an opaque cream.

6 Adjust the seasonings

Transfer the mayonnaise to a serving dish or a storage container. Stir in salt and pepper to taste. If desired, you can add a little water for a creamier mayonnaise.

FLAVORING MAYONNAISE

Lemon-herb mayonnaise

Stir the grated zest of 1 lemon, 1 tablespoon minced fresh flat-leaf (Italian) parsley, 1 tablespoon minced fresh chives, and 1 tablespoon minced fresh dill into the finished mayonnaise. Use as a dip or sauce for chilled seafood.

Aioli (garlic mayonnaise)

Replace the pure olive oil with extra-virgin olive oil. Then, stir 2 or 3 minced garlic cloves into the finished mayonnaise. Use as a dip for fried foods or cooked vegetables.

Pesto mayonnaise

Stir 2 tablespoons Basil Pesto (see entry 284) or store-bought pesto into the finished mayonnaise. Use as a spread on Italian-style sandwiches.

Tartar sauce

Stir 3 tablespoons chopped gherkin pickles, 3 tablespoons rinsed and drained capers, 1 tablespoon chopped fresh flat-leaf parsley, and a dash of hot-pepper sauce into the finished mayonnaise. Serve with fish or shellfish.

Basic vinaigrette

Oil, vinegar, salt, and pepper—that's all there is to a traditional vinaigrette sauce. Oil and vinegar don't easily blend, but when properly mixed, they emulsify to form a tangy, vibrant sauce that is perfect on fresh salad greens, steamed vegetables, or grilled fish.

1 Whisk the vinegar and salt
Place a medium bowl on a folded damp kitchen towel to steady it. Whisk together the vinegar and salt until the salt begins to dissolve. The salt is added before the oil because it dissolves more easily in vinegar alone.

2 Whisk in the mustard
If using, whisk the mustard into the vinegar-salt mixture. Besides adding flavor, mustard acts as an emulsifier which helps stabilize and bind together the oil and vinegar.

INGREDIENTS

3 tablespoons vinegar (such as red or white wine, cider, or balsamic)

¼ teaspoon salt

½ teaspoon Dijon mustard, optional

¾ cup (6 fl oz/180 ml) extra-virgin olive oil

⅛ teaspoon freshly ground pepper

MAKES ABOUT 1 CUP
(8 FL OZ/250 ML)

Although a whisk is the classic tool for emulsifying ingredients, it is not the only option when making a vinaigrette. You can also use a fork, a handheld mixer, or a mini prep (see entry 25b), or even vigorously shake the ingredients in a tightly covered jar or bottle.

4 Adjust the seasonings
Whisk in the pepper. Taste the finished vinaigrette and add more salt and pepper, if desired. If using the vinaigrette to dress greens, dip a piece of the greens into the dressing to see how they taste together. Some greens are bitter or spicy and may require an adjustment in the vinaigrette seasonings.

5 Use or store the vinaigrette
Use the vinaigrette right away, or store it for up to 5 days. The olive oil will solidify when chilled but will melt if left at room temperature for about 30 minutes.

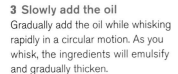

3 Slowly add the oil
Gradually add the oil while whisking rapidly in a circular motion. As you whisk, the ingredients will emulsify and gradually thicken.

ASSORTED VINAIGRETTES

Blender vinaigrette

The blender's blades break up the oil into smaller droplets than a whisk does, giving the vinaigrette a smoother and thicker consistency. Put the vinegar, salt, and mustard, if using, in a blender. Process to combine. With the blender running, gradually add the oil in a steady stream through the hole in the lid. Season with the pepper.

Raspberry-walnut vinaigrette

Follow the recipe to make Basic Vinaigrette but replace the red wine vinegar with raspberry vinegar and the olive oil with walnut oil. Use to dress a green salad with toasted walnuts.

Lemon-shallot vinaigrette

Follow the recipe to make Basic Vinaigrette but replace the red wine vinegar with lemon juice. Whisk the grated zest from 1 lemon and 1 tablespoon minced shallot into the finished vinaigrette. Use to dress seafood salads.

Orange-tarragon vinaigrette

In a small, nonreactive saucepan, cook 1 cup (8 fl oz/250 ml) fresh orange juice over high heat until reduced by half. In a bowl, whisk together the reduced juice, 3 tablespoons balsamic vinegar, ½ teaspoon Dijon mustard, and ¼ teaspoon salt. Gradually whisk in ¼ cup (2 fl oz/60 ml) extra-virgin olive oil. Stir in 2 teaspoons finely chopped fresh tarragon and adjust the seasonings. This vinaigrette pairs well with chicken, shrimp (prawns), steamed asparagus, or artichokes.

Roquefort & walnut vinaigrette

In a bowl, whisk together 3 tablespoons sherry vinegar and ¼ teaspoon salt. Gradually whisk in ¾ cup (6 fl oz/ 180 ml) walnut oil. Stir in 3 oz (90 g) crumbled Roquefort cheese and ½ minced shallot. Adjust the seasonings. This vinaigrette is delicious on salads featuring roasted beets.

Asian vinaigrette

Peel 1 large piece fresh ginger. Use the large shredding holes on a box grater-shredder to shred ¼ cup (1 oz/30 g) ginger into a small bowl. Squeeze the ginger in your hand over the bowl to extract the juice. You should have about 1 tablespoon ginger juice. (Discard the shredded ginger.) In a bowl, whisk together the ginger juice, 3 tablespoons unseasoned rice vinegar, and 1 tablespoon soy sauce. Gradually whisk in ⅔ cup (5 fl oz/160 ml) canola or soybean oil and 1 tablespoon Asian sesame oil. Adjust the seasonings. Use this vinaigrette for mildly bitter greens or napa cabbage slaw.

Basil pesto

In Italian, *pesto* means "pounded." Purists make pesto by hand with a mortar and pestle, but this method takes a lot of time and patience. Here, we turn to a food processor for the fastest and most convenient way to make this favorite green sauce.

INGREDIENTS

2 cloves garlic

½ cup (2 oz/60 g) finely grated *pecorino romano* or Parmigiano-Reggiano cheese

¼ cup (1 oz/30 g) pine nuts, toasted, if desired

2 cups (2 oz/60 g) packed fresh basil leaves, washed, and well dried

½ cup (4 fl oz/125 ml) extra-virgin olive oil

¼ teaspoon salt

⅛ teaspoon freshly ground pepper

MAKES ABOUT 1 CUP (8 OZ/250 G)

1 Process the chunky ingredients
Fit a food processor with the metal blade. With the machine running, drop the garlic cloves through the feed tube. Turn off the machine, add the cheese and pine nuts, and pulse briefly.

2 Add the basil
Use a silicone spatula to scrape down the sides of the work bowl. Add the basil leaves and pulse a few times to chop the leaves coarsely. Scrape down the sides again.

4 Scrape down the sides
As you work, stop the machine occasionally and scrape down the sides of the work bowl. Stir in the salt and pepper and taste the pesto. If it tastes flat, add more cheese, salt, or pepper until the flavors are nicely balanced.

5 Use or store the pesto
Use the pesto right away, or store in the refrigerator with a thin layer of olive oil on top to slow discoloration for up to 1 week. Before using, bring the pesto to room temperature and stir well.

3 Slowly add the oil
Turn on the machine and pour the oil in a thin, steady stream through the feed tube. You're aiming for a moderately thick paste.

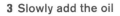

MORE PESTOS

Pesto with walnuts & pecorino

Follow the recipe to make Basil Pesto, replacing the pine nuts with chopped walnuts and using only *pecorino romano* cheese in place of any Parmigiano-Reggiano. Use this pesto when you prefer a slightly sharper sauce.

Mint pesto

Follow the recipe to make Basil Pesto, replacing the fresh basil with fresh mint leaves. Spread this pesto on lamb during the last 10 minutes of roasting or grilling, or use as a zesty condiment.

Rosemary-walnut pesto

Follow the recipe to make Basil Pesto, replacing the pine nuts with chopped walnuts, and the basil with 1¾ cups (1¾ oz/50 g) packed fresh flat-leaf (Italian) parsley leaves and ¼ cup (⅓ oz/10 g) chopped fresh rosemary. Use this version to accompany grilled chops and steaks.

Arugula pesto

Follow the recipe to make Basil Pesto, replacing the basil with stemmed arugula (rocket) leaves. Use this peppery sauce on pasta or grilled shrimp (prawns).

Pistou (Provençal-style pesto)

Follow the recipe to make Basil Pesto, replacing the pine nuts with sliced (flaked) natural or blanched almonds and the *pecorino romano* and Parmigiano-Reggiano cheeses with finely shredded Gruyère cheese. Use this sauce as a condiment for soup or grilled fish.

Cilantro pesto

With the motor of the food processor engaged, drop 2 cloves garlic and 1 seeded and chopped jalapeño chile through the feed tube. Stop the machine, add ¼ cup (1 oz/30 g) shelled pumpkin seeds and ½ cup (2 oz/60 g) grated *cotija* cheese, and pulse briefly. Add 2 cups (2 oz/ 60 g) packed fresh cilantro (fresh coriander) leaves and pulse to chop. Turn on the machine and slowly pour ½ cup (4 fl oz/125 ml) extra-virgin olive oil through the feed tube to form a moderately thick paste. Stir in the grated zest of 1 lime, 1 tablespoon fresh lime juice, and salt and pepper to taste. Use this pesto to accompany roasted pork or grilled chicken.

All-purpose tomato sauce

Keep good-quality canned tomatoes in your pantry to make an easy but tasty tomato sauce in about 20 minutes. This basic sauce is infused with red wine and spiked with red pepper flakes. For a bolder sauce, use more garlic.

INGREDIENTS

1 tablespoon olive oil

1 yellow onion, diced

3 or 4 cloves garlic, minced

2 tablespoons tomato paste

1 teaspoon dried oregano

1 teaspoon dried thyme

¼ cup (2 fl oz/60 ml) dry red wine, such as Zinfandel

1 can (28 oz/875 g) whole tomatoes

1 teaspoon granulated sugar

½ teaspoon red pepper flakes

1 teaspoon salt

⅛ teaspoon freshly ground black pepper

MAKES ABOUT 3 CUPS
(24 FL OZ/750 ML)

1 Heat the oil
Place a saucepan over medium heat and add the olive oil. Heat the oil until it just appears to shimmer.

2 Add the onion and garlic
Add the onion and cook, stirring often, until translucent, about 5 minutes. Add the garlic and cook until golden, 2–3 minutes longer. Be careful not to burn the garlic or it will taste bitter.

6 Simmer the sauce
Stirring often, bring the sauce to a boil over medium-high heat. Reduce the heat until only small bubbles occasionally break the surface of the sauce. Simmer, uncovered, until the sauce nicely coats the spoon, about 10 minutes.

3 Stir in the flavorings

Stir in the tomato paste, oregano, and thyme and cook, stirring often, until the paste is evenly distributed and the onion is a uniform light red, about 3 minutes. The tomato paste deepens the flavor and color of the the finished sauce.

4 Deglaze the pan

Raise the heat to medium-high, pour in the wine, and stir vigorously with a wooden spoon to scrape up any browned bits that may have cooked onto the bottom of the pan.

5 Add the tomatoes

Add the tomatoes and their juice, the sugar, and the red pepper flakes. The sugar balances the slight acidity in the tomatoes and gives the finished sauce a well-rounded flavor. Use the wooden spoon to crush the tomatoes slightly, if desired, or leave them whole for a chunkier sauce.

7 Adjust the seasonings

Add the salt and black pepper to the sauce and stir for about 3 minutes to distribute the seasonings evenly. Taste the sauce. If it tastes acidic, stir in a pinch more sugar. If it tastes dull, add a little more salt, black pepper, or red pepper flakes until the flavors are nicely balanced and to your liking.

Italian cooks aren't shy about using canned tomatoes for sauce when fresh tomatoes are not in season. You can find the same Italian peeled tomatoes, imported, at specialty-food stores and well-stocked markets labeled "Italian peeled tomatoes."

Cleaning clams or mussels

1 Soak the clams or mussels

Place the clams or mussels in a bowl of salt water for 10 minutes to purge any sand caught in the shells. A good ratio is ¾ cup (6 oz/185 g) of salt per gallon (4 qt/4 l) of tap water.

2 Scrub the shells, if needed

If the mussel or clam shells still feel gritty after the initial soaking, using a stiff brush, scrub them well under running cold water.

3 Wipe the shells

If the mussel or clam shells do not feel gritty after the initial soaking, they do not need to be scrubbed. Using a damp kitchen towel, wipe all of the shells clean.

4 Debeard the mussels, if needed

Remove the *beard* (the little fibrous tufts the mussel uses to connect to rocks or pilings) from each mussel by cutting or scraping it away with a knife or scissors. Some cultivated mussels do not have beards.

5 Rinse the clams and mussels

Gently place the clams or mussels in a colander and give them a final rinsing before using them in your recipe. If you are not cooking them right away, keep them in the refrigerator until needed.

Shucking clams

1 Scrub the clams
Using a stiff brush, scrub the clams well under running cold water. Discard any open clams that do not close to the touch.

2 Insert the knife
Lay a clam flat on a cutting board. Position the edge of a clam knife against the seam between the shells. Stabilize the clam with the heel of your hand (you can use a towel, if you wish, for stability). Grasp the knife handle with your other hand and lightly push until the blade slips into the seam.

3 Cut the first adductor muscle
Once you've penetrated the shell with the side of the blade, pull it almost all the way out, then work the tip up against the upper shell and move the knife around to cut the adductor muscle that's attached to the shell. (Clams have two adductor muscles on opposite ends.)

4 Cut the second adductor muscle
Keep the tip of the knife in the shell and slide the blade around toward the other side, loosening the meat and cutting the second adductor muscle.

Preparing scallops

1 Locate the dense muscle strip
Look on the shorter side of the scallop to locate the strip of smaller, denser, more opaque muscle. The strip is tough and rubbery, so you'll want to remove it.

2 Remove the dense muscle strip
Using your fingers, pull the small muscle away. The trimmings can be saved for fish fumet (see entry 296), fish stock (see entry 295), shellfish stock (see entry 297), or discarded.

Cleaning & cracking cooked lobster

1 Insert the knife
Place the cooked lobster on a grooved cutting board to catch any liquid. Holding the shell with a kitchen towel, insert the tip of a large chef's knife where the body and head sections come together.

2 Halve the lobster
Holding the lobster securely, cut through the shell to halve the head lengthwise. Turn the knife and repeat on the other side to cut the body and tail in half lengthwise.

3 Remove the claws and legs
Remove the rubber bands holding the claws closed. Using your hands, twist the claws and legs from the body. If the legs are large, they will contain a good amount of meat; discard very small legs.

4 Remove the tomalley & roe
If desired, scoop out and reserve the greenish liver, or *tomalley*. If your lobster is female, you can also reserve the coral-colored roe. Both can be added to recipes for extra flavor.

5 Remove the tail meat
Discard any remaining visceral matter in the cavity, then remove any white meat from the shell. Pull out the tail meat.

6 Crack the claws
Using a lobster cracker, nutcracker, or mallet, gently crack the hard shell of each claw in several places. Crack any large legs, as well. Use a lobster pick or your fingers to extract the meat.

Shucking oysters

1 Scrub the oysters
Using a stiff brush, scrub the oysters well under running cold water. Rinse away any mud, sand, or shell grit. Discard any open oysters that do not close to the touch.

2 Grasp an oyster
Place an oyster on a work surface and identify the flat side. Fold a kitchen towel and use it to pick up the oyster so the flat side is facing up. The towel will protect your hand.

3 Insert the oyster knife
Locate the hinge at the pointed end of the oyster. Insert the tip of the oyster knife about ½ inch (12 mm) deep into the hinge. Twist and pry the knife to loosen the top shell and break the hinge.

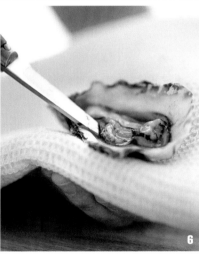

4 Detach the muscle
If the tip of the knife is muddy, rinse and wipe it clean. Slide the knife along the inside surface of the top shell to detach the adductor muscle that connects the oyster.

5 Remove the top shell
Now that you have cut the adductor muscle, the top shell should be free. Lift it away and discard. Be careful not to spill any of the juice, or oyster liquor, because this briny water adds to the oyster-eating experience.

6 Loosen the oyster
Run the knife along the inside surface of the bottom shell to loosen the oyster. If serving on the half shell, leave the oyster in the shell with its juice.

Boiled fresh crab

There's nothing like freshly cooked crab that yields sweet white meat after only briefly boiling them. If you are not using the crab for a recipe, you can add fresh herbs to clarified butter (see entry 106) for an easy dipping sauce.

INGREDIENTS

8 qt (8 l) cool water

¼ cup (1¼ oz/37 g) kosher salt

2 live Dungeness crabs, about 2 lb (1 kg) each, or 12 hard-shelled blue crabs

MAKES ABOUT 4 CUPS (1 LB/500 G) CRABMEAT

This method also works for cooking live lobsters: Start with enough cool water to cover the lobsters by 2 inches (5 cm) and add 1½ teaspoons salt per quart (litre) of water. Let the small crustaceans (lobsters under 1½ lb/750 g) steep for 10 minutes and larger ones for 15 minutes.

1 Boil the crabs
Fill a stockpot with the water and stir in the salt. Pick up the crabs from behind to avoid their claws and add them to the pot, making sure they are well covered with water. Cover the pot, turn the heat to medium-high, and bring just to a boil. When the water reaches a full boil, turn off the heat, leaving the lid on the pot.

2 Let the crabs steep
Let blue crabs steep in the hot water for about 10 minutes. Larger Dungeness crabs need about 15 minutes. Their shells will turn bright red. Using long tongs, lift the crabs from the water, turning them this way and that over the pot to drain away any water, and then transfer to a cutting board.

6 Twist off the claws and legs
Rinse the body well. Using your hands, twist the claws and legs from the body. Using a large chef's knife or your hands, cut or break the body into halves lengthwise along its center and then into quarters.

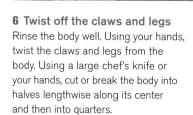

3 Remove the apron

For a Dungeness crab, place it shell side down and lift off and discard the triangular tail flap, or *apron*. Watch out for the spines on the bottom side of the crab, which are sharp.

4 Remove the top shell

Turn over the crab and, holding it by the legs, lift off and discard the hard top shell. If desired, scoop out and reserve the pale yellow crab fat in the shell. (This fat has a savory, slightly briny flavor and can be used to flavor butter or sauces.) Blue crabs, while smaller, have the same basic structure as Dungeness crabs and can be cleaned in the same way.

5 Remove the gills and intestines

Next, pull off and discard the grayish, feathery gills along both sides of the body, the jaw section at the front, and the intestines in the middle.

7 Extract the meat

Using your fingers or a lobster pick, tiny fork, or paring knife, remove the meat from all the body cavities. Switch to a nutcracker, lobster cracker, or mallet and gently crack the claws and any large legs in several places. Break away the shell pieces and remove the meat.

Peeling & deveining shrimp

1 Pull off the head and legs
Working with one shrimp (prawn) at a time, grasp the head (if still on the shrimp) in one hand and the tail in the the other and twist them apart. Pull off the small legs on the underside.

2 Pull off the shell from the meat
Starting with the section of shell closest to the head, pull it up and lift it away. As you pull away the first section of shell, it will bring the other overlapping sections with it.

3 Remove the final shell section
In some recipes, you can choose whether or not to pull off the final shell section, or "tail feathers." To do so, give the tip of the tail a squeeze as you pull so the meat remains.

4 Make a shallow groove
Using a paring knife, make a shallow cut along the outer curve almost to the tail of each shrimp. You may see a dark, veinlike intestinal tract running through the meat.

5 Remove the vein
With the tip of the knife, lift out the vein and pull it away, gently scraping it if necessary. Once you've deveined all the shrimp, place them in a colander and rinse with cold water to remove any residual grit.

TROUBLESHOOTING
Salting thawed frozen shrimp improves their flavor and texture. Sprinkle the whole, unpeeled shrimp generously with salt, let stand for up to 1 minute, and then rinse well.

1 Cut off the tentacles

Using a chef's knife, cut off the tentacles just below the eyes of the squid. Be careful not to cut too far away from the eyes or the tentacles will fall apart.

2 Remove the beak

Squeeze the cut end of the tentacles to expose the hard, round "beak" at the base. Pull out and discard the beak. Set the tentacles aside.

3 Remove the head and innards

Gently squeeze the *mantle*, or tubelike body, and pull away the head. The entrails, including the ink sac, should come away with the head. Discard the head and entrails.

4 Remove the quill

Reach into the mantle and pull out the long, transparent, plasticlike quill along with any remaining entrails and discard them. Rinse the mantle and tentacles under running cold water.

5 Remove the skin, if desired

If desired, pull off the skin from the mantle, using a paring knife to help scrape it away if necessary. If left in place, the skin will give the cooked squid a pinkish cast.

6 Cut the body into rings

Some recipes call for the squid body to be cut into rings, usually about ½ inch (12 mm) wide. Put the rings in a large bowl of cold water, swish them around to rinse away any loose bits, and then drain.

Vegetable stock

A successful vegetable stock is full flavored, but with no single vegetable dominating the finished product. Caramelizing the vegetables first deepens the stock's color and flavor. Use vegetable stock to make vegetarian soups and stews and for sauces.

INGREDIENTS

2 or 3 yellow onions, peeled

3 or 4 carrots, peeled

6 oz (185 g) fresh white mushrooms, cleaned

1 red bell pepper (capsicum), seeded

1 small leek, white and pale green parts

2 tomatoes, cored

2 or 3 stalks celery with leaves

1 small turnip, peeled

1 small parsnip, peeled

4 cloves garlic, peeled and chopped

2 cups (4 oz/125 g) torn spinach leaves

2 tablespoons extra-virgin olive oil

2 sprigs fresh flat-leaf (Italian) parsley

8–10 peppercorns

MAKES ABOUT 2 QT (2 L)

1 Heat the oil
Cut all of the vegetables into ¼-inch (6-mm) pieces. Place an 8-qt (8-l) heavy-bottomed pot over medium-high heat. When the pot is hot, add the olive oil and heat until the surface appears to shimmer.

2 Caramelize the vegetables
Add the onions, carrots, mushrooms, bell pepper, and leek and cook, stirring, until the vegetables are golden brown, about 15 minutes. Browning the vegetables before adding the liquid helps to caramelize their natural sugars, and will impart a deep flavor and golden color to the finished stock.

6 Cool the stock, if desired
If you are not using the stock right away, cool it for storage. Fill a large bowl partway with ice and water and set the bowl of stock in the ice bath to cool it to room temperature, stirring occasionally.

3 Add water to the vegetables

Add the tomatoes, celery, turnip, parsnip, garlic, spinach, parsley, and peppercorns to the pot and stir to mix the ingredients. Add water just to cover the ingredients by 1 inch (2.5 cm); more water could dilute the flavor of the stock. Bring the liquid to a boil over medium-high heat.

4 Simmer the stock

Once the stock boils, lower the heat to medium-low and simmer, uncovered, until the liquid is reduced by about one-third, 1–1½ hours. Vegetables don't release the collagen that meat bones do when they simmer, so there's no need to skim the surface of a vegetable stock.

5 Strain the stock

Place a fine-mesh sieve over a large heatproof bowl. Ladle or carefully pour the stock through the sieve and discard the solids that are left behind. You can use the stock right away, or cool and store it.

7 Use or store the stock

Cover and refrigerate the stock if you plan to use it within 3 days, or pour it into airtight containers, filling them to within about ½ inch (12 mm) of the rim (the stock expands as it freezes), and freeze for up to 3 months. To thaw frozen stock, refrigerate it for 24 hours, or transfer the frozen block of stock to a saucepan and melt slowly over low heat, covered, until liquefied.

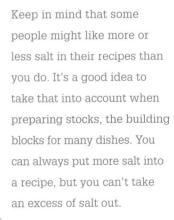

Keep in mind that some people might like more or less salt in their recipes than you do. It's a good idea to take that into account when preparing stocks, the building blocks for many dishes. You can always put more salt into a recipe, but you can't take an excess of salt out.

Fish stock

You need at least one fish head and a couple of fish *frames*, or skeletons, all carefully cleaned, to impart the desired flavor to fish stock. This step will ensure a clean-tasting stock, which is used to make fish soups and sauces.

INGREDIENTS

4 lb (2 kg) fish head(s) and frames from nonoily fish such as flounder, cod, sea bass, or snapper, cleaned

¼ cup (2 oz/60 g) plus 1 tablespoon kosher salt

½ cup (4 fl oz/125 ml) dry white wine, such as Sauvignon Blanc or Pinot Grigio

1 yellow onion, thinly sliced

1 stalk celery, thinly sliced

2 sprigs fresh flat-leaf (Italian) parsley

1 sprig fresh thyme

1 bay leaf

8–10 peppercorns

MAKES ABOUT 2 QT (2 L)

1 Rinse the fish parts
Rinse the cleaned fish parts thoroughly under cold water. With kitchen scissors, break the spine of each frame into 2 or more pieces. Gelatin that will help flavor the stock is in the spine, and this step will encourage its release.

2 Soak the fish parts
Place the head(s) and frames in a large bowl and add the salt and cool water to cover. Refrigerate for 1 hour, covered. Drain off the salted water, rinse the fish pieces, and repeat the 1-hour soak. This two-part soak ensures the fish frames are free of blood and impurities.

6 Strain and cool the stock
Ladle or carefully pour the stock through the sieve and discard the solids that are left behind. You can use the stock right away or cool and store it. To store, fill a large bowl partway with ice and water and set the bowl of stock in the ice bath to cool it to room temperature, stirring occasionally.

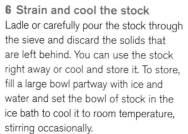

3 Bring the stock just to a boil
Drain the fish pieces, place them in an 8-qt (8-l) heavy-bottomed pot, and add water just to cover by 1 inch (2.5 cm); more water could dilute the flavor of the stock. Place the pot over medium-high heat. Without stirring, slowly bring the liquid to a boil, then reduce the heat to medium-low and simmer.

4 Skim the impurities
Use a large slotted spoon or a skimmer to skim off the grayish foam that rises to the surface. Continue skimming until the foam no longer forms. Add the wine, onion, celery, parsley, thyme, bay leaf, and peppercorns and gently simmer, uncovered, until the liquid has a nice fish flavor, about 30 minutes.

5 Line a sieve with cheesecloth
Cut a piece of cheesecloth (muslin) large enough to line the inside of a fine-mesh sieve when it is triple layered. Fold the cheesecloth, dampen it with cool water, squeeze it dry, then use it to line the sieve. Place the sieve over a large heatproof bowl.

7 Thaw the stock, then measure
Cover and refrigerate the stock if you plan to use it within 2 days, or pour it into airtight containers, filling them to within about ½ inch (12 mm) of the rim (the stock expands as it freezes), and freeze for up to 2 months. To thaw frozen stock, refrigerate for 24 hours, or transfer the frozen block of stock to a saucepan and melt slowly over low heat, covered, until liquefied.

When making fish stock, always use the bones and heads from firm, white-fleshed, nonoily fish. Parts from oily, fatty fish, such as salmon, mackerel, or tuna, would give the stock an overly strong "fishy" flavor.

Fish fumet

This quick-cooking version of fish stock is called a *fumet*, from the French for "aroma." Fish fumet is used to heighten the flavor of sauces that are served with fish. It's especially convenient when you need a flavorful base for a pan sauce.

INGREDIENTS

1½ lb (24 oz/750 g) fish heads and/or bones from white-fleshed, nonoily fish such as snapper, flounder, or halibut, cleaned

1 tablespoon canola oil

1 large leek, white and pale green part only, cut into ½-inch (12-mm) dice

1 stalk celery, cut into ½-inch (12-mm) dice

3 sprigs fresh flat-leaf (Italian) parsley

8 peppercorns

2 sprigs fresh thyme

¼ teaspoon fennel seeds

½ bay leaf

¾ cup (6 fl oz/180 ml) dry white wine, such as Sauvignon Blanc or Pinot Grigio

MAKES ABOUT 1½ QT (1.5 L)

1 Soak the fish parts
Put the heads and bones in a large bowl and cover them with cold water. Let the fish parts soak for 15 minutes, then drain and rinse them again. Soaking the fish parts removes any remaining blood and impurities and makes a clearer, fresher-tasting stock.

2 Sweat the vegetables
Place a Dutch oven or other large pot over medium-low heat, add the oil, and heat until the surface appears to shimmer. Add the leek and celery and cover. Cook, stirring occasionally, until the vegetables soften without browning, about 5 minutes. This process of slowly cooking vegetables without browning is called *sweating*.

6 Strain the fumet
Carefully pour the fumet through a sieve lined with damp cheesecloth (muslin) into a large heatproof bowl and discard the solids that are left behind. Use the fumet at once, or cool and store it.

3 Add the remaining ingredients
Tie the parsley, peppercorns, thyme, fennel seeds, and bay leaf in a small square of cheesecloth (muslin) to make a bouquet garni (see entry 177). Add it to the pot with the fish heads and/or bones and the wine. Add water to cover the ingredients by about 1 inch (2.5 cm); more water could dilute the flavor of the finished fumet.

4 Simmer the fumet
Raise the heat to high. Without stirring, slowly bring the liquid to a boil. As soon as you see bubbles start to form, reduce the heat to low.

5 Skim the impurities
Use a large slotted spoon or a skimmer to skim off the grayish foam that rises to the surface. Let the fumet simmer, skimming any foam on the surface, until the fumet is full flavored, 30–40 minutes. Add additional water, if necessary, to keep the ingredients just submerged. Make sure the fumet doesn't come to a boil, or it will become cloudy.

7 Cool and store the fumet
To cool the fumet, fill a large bowl partway with ice and water and set the bowl of fumet in the ice bath to cool it to room temperature, stirring occasionally. Cover and refrigerate for up to 2 days. Fumet is not a good candidate for freezing, as it easily picks up unwanted flavors. It's best to make it in small batches for use within a couple of days.

Fish markets, especially in Asian neighborhoods, are good sources for bones for making fumet or stock. Many customers buy whole fish and then ask the fishmongers to fillet them, so the markets often have a ready supply of fish heads and bones.

Shellfish stock

The most economical way to make a good shellfish stock is to save the shells from cooked shrimp, lobster, and crab in the freezer until you have accumulated about 4 cups (1½ lb/750 g) of shells. Use this stock as a base for seafood bisques or gumbo.

1 Chop the shrimp shells
Using a large, heavy knife, chop the shrimp shells into small pieces. Don't chop the shells too finely or they will be harder to strain.

2 Break up the tougher shells
Put the lobster or crab shells, if using, in a heavy-duty locking plastic bag and, using a rolling pin or a meat pounder, break the shells into small pieces.

INGREDIENTS

4 cups (1½ lb/750 g) mixed shells from shrimp (prawns), preferably with the heads intact, lobster, or crab

2 sprigs fresh flat-leaf (Italian) parsley

1 sprig fresh thyme

1 bay leaf

1 large yellow onion, peeled and roughly sliced

1 carrot, peeled and cut on the diagonal into ½-inch (12-mm) pieces

1 stalk celery, cut into ½-inch (12-mm) pieces

2 tablespoons tomato paste

1 teaspoon peppercorns

½ cup (4 fl oz/125 ml) dry white wine, such as Sauvignon Blanc or Pinot Grigio

1 tablespoon kosher salt

MAKES ABOUT 2 QT (2 L)

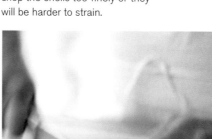

6 Strain the stock
Cut a piece of cheesecloth (muslin) large enough to line the inside of a fine-mesh sieve when it is triple layered. Fold the cheesecloth, dampen it with cool water, squeeze it dry, then use it to line the sieve. Place the sieve over a large heatproof bowl. Ladle or carefully pour the stock through the sieve and discard the solids that are left behind. You can use the stock right away or cool and store it.

3 Simmer the stock

Place all the shells in an 8-qt (8-l) heavy-bottomed pot. Add water just to cover the shells by 1 inch (2.5 cm); more water could dilute the flavor of the stock. Place the pot over medium-high heat. Without stirring, slowly bring the liquid to a boil, then reduce the heat so that the stock simmers.

4 Skim the impurities

Use a large slotted spoon or a skimmer to skim off the grayish foam that rises to the surface. The foam is made up of impurities that are released when the shells heat, and it can cloud the finished stock unless it is removed. Continue skimming until the foam no longer forms. Never stir the stock.

5 Add the aromatic ingredients

Tie the parsley, thyme, and bay leaf in a small square of cheesecloth (muslin) to make a bouquet garni (see entry 177). Add the onion, carrot, celery, tomato paste, bouquet garni, peppercorns, and wine to the pot. Simmer gently, uncovered, until the liquid has a full shellfish flavor, about 30 minutes. Stir in the salt and remove the pot from the heat.

7 Cool and store the stock

If you are not using the stock right away, cool it for storage. Fill a large bowl partway with ice and water and set the bowl of stock in the ice bath to cool it to room temperature, stirring occasionally. Cover and refrigerate the stock if you plan to use it within 2 days, or ladle or pour it into airtight containers, filling them to within about ½ inch (12 mm) of the rim (the stock expands as it freezes), and freeze for up to 2 months. To thaw frozen stock, refrigerate for 24 hours, or transfer the frozen block of stock to a saucepan and melt slowly over low heat, covered, until liquefied.

Chicken stock

Chicken stock is a staple for many soups, stews, and sauces and is an essential ingredient for risotto. Although making a homemade stock takes time, you can double or triple a recipe and freeze it in serving-size containers for later use.

INGREDIENTS

6 lb (3 kg) chicken backs and necks

1 large carrot, peeled and cut into 1-inch (2.5-cm) pieces

1 large stalk celery with leaves, cut into 1-inch (2.5-cm) pieces

1 clove garlic, peeled

1 large or 2 medium yellow onions, peeled and quartered

3 or 4 sprigs fresh flat-leaf (Italian) parsley

1 bay leaf

8–10 peppercorns

MAKES ABOUT 4 QT (4 L)

1 Combine the ingredients
Place the chicken, carrot, celery, garlic clove, onion quarters, parsley, bay leaf, and peppercorns in an 8-qt (8-l) heavy-bottomed pot and add water just to cover the ingredients by 1 inch (2.5 cm); more water could dilute the flavor of the stock. Place the pot over medium-high heat. Without stirring, slowly bring the liquid to a boil.

2 Simmer the stock
As soon as you see large bubbles begin to form on the surface of the liquid, reduce the heat until only small bubbles occasionally break the surface of the liquid, called a *simmer*.

6 Degrease the stock
Before you use the stock, carefully remove all of the fat, or the recipes made from the stock will have a greasy flavor and texture. Use a large metal spoon to skim the clear yellow fat from the surface of the strained stock.

3 Skim the impurities

Use a skimmer or a large slotted spoon to skim off the grayish foam that rises to the surface during the first 10 minutes of cooking. The foam is the result of collagen and gelatin being released from the bones and meat; if it's not removed, it will cloud the stock.

4 Develop the flavors

Continue to simmer the stock, uncovered, adjusting the heat from time to time to keep it at a gentle simmer, for 2–2½ hours. Do not stir, but continue to skim the surface every 30 minutes or so. Add more water, if necessary, to keep the ingredients just covered.

5 Strain the stock

Cut a piece of cheesecloth (muslin) large enough to line the inside of a fine-mesh sieve when it is triple layered. Fold the cheesecloth, dampen it with cool water, squeeze it dry, then use it to line the sieve. Place the sieve over a large heatproof bowl. Remove the larger solids with the skimmer or slotted spoon and then ladle or carefully pour the stock through the sieve. Discard the solids that are left behind.

7 Or, cool the stock

Or, if time allows, chill the stock before degreasing it. Fill a large bowl partway with ice and water and set the bowl of stock in the ice bath to cool it to room temperature, stirring occasionally. Cover and refrigerate the stock overnight. The fat will rise to the top and solidify, making it easy to lift it off the surface.

Chicken stock can be made in large batches and then refrigerated or frozen for later use. Make use of refrigerated stock within 3 days. Or, pour the stock into airtight containers, filling them to within about ½ inch (12 mm) of the rim (the stock expands as it freezes).

Brown chicken stock

This stock is a kitchen workhorse, good for sauces, gravies, and more. Browning the chicken pieces in the oven before simmering them with an array of vegetables creates a more robust flavor and deeper color than regular chicken stock.

INGREDIENTS

3 lb (1.5 kg) chicken backs and/or wings, chopped with a heavy cleaver into 2–3 inch (5–7.5 cm) pieces

2 tablespoons canola oil

1 small yellow onion, coarsely chopped

1 small carrot, coarsely chopped

1 small stalk celery with leaves, coarsely chopped

1 cup (8 fl oz/250 ml) water

4 sprigs fresh thyme or ½ teaspoon dried thyme

6 peppercorns

1 small bay leaf

MAKES ABOUT 2 QT (2 L)

1 Roast the chicken pieces
Preheat the oven to 425°F (220°C). Spread the chicken pieces, overlapping slightly if necessary, in a large roasting pan. Roast for 30 minutes. Turn over the pieces and continue roasting until the chicken pieces are deeply browned, about 20 minutes longer.

2 Cook the vegetables
Place a 6- to 8-qt (6- to 8-l) stockpot or Dutch oven over medium heat and add the oil. When the oil appears to shimmer, add the onion, carrot, and celery and cook, stirring occasionally, until the vegetables are beginning to brown, about 6 minutes. Remove from the heat. Remove the roasting pan from the oven. Using tongs, transfer the browned chicken pieces to the pot.

5 Simmer the stock
Add water just to cover the ingredients and place over high heat. Add the thyme, peppercorns, and bay leaves and bring just to a boil. As soon as you see bubbles forming, reduce the heat to low. Using a large slotted metal spoon or a skimmer, skim off the grayish foam that rises to the surface. Simmer the stock uncovered, regularly skimming off any new foam, until it is full flavored, at least 3 hours or up to 6 hours.

3 Deglaze the roasting pan
Protecting your hand with an oven mitt, tip the roasting pan to gather the fat at one corner. Use a spoon to remove and discard the clear fat. Place the roasting pan on the stove top over 2 burners and turn on the heat to high. When the pan drippings begin to sizzle, carefully pour the 1 cup water into the pan, stirring with a wooden spatula or spoon.

4 Transfer the liquid to the pot
Bring the water to a boil, scraping up the browned bits stuck to the bottom and sides of the pan with the wooden spatula. Protecting your hands with pot holders, pour the flavorful brown liquid that is created into the pot.

6 Strain the stock
Remove the larger solids, then strain the stock through a fine-mesh sieve lined with a triple layer of damp cheesecloth (muslin) into a large heatproof bowl. Discard the solids that are left behind. Use a large metal spoon to skim off the clear yellow fat from the surface of the strained stock. Use the stock right away, or cool and store it for up to 3 days in the refrigerator or 3 months in the freezer.

MORE POULTRY STOCKS

Brown turkey stock

Follow the recipe for Brown Chicken Stock, but replace the chicken parts with turkey wings, cut into 2–3 inch (5–7.5 cm) pieces. For additional flavor, add the giblets from 1 turkey, including the neck, heart, and gizzard, but not the liver, to the roasting pan with the wings.

Brown duck stock

Follow the recipe for Brown Chicken Stock, but replace the chicken parts with duck wings, cut into 2–3 inch (5–7.5 cm) pieces. For additional flavor, add the giblets from 1 duck, including the neck, heart, and gizzard, but not the liver, to the roasting pan with the wings.

Quick brown stock

If you don't have time to make this stock recipe from scratch, follow the recipe for Brown Chicken Stock to roast the chicken parts. Add them to a stockpot, then deglaze with 2½ qt (2.5 l) purchased low-sodium chicken broth. Bring to a boil over high heat, skim off any foam, and add a pinch of dried thyme. Reduce the heat to low and simmer, uncovered, for an hour or so. Strain the stock as directed in step 6, then use the stock as desired.

Beef stock

A generous mix of marrowbones and beef shins, two cuts good butchers traditionally carry, gives this stock a distinctive and aromatic, yet mild flavor and light body. Use it to make soups, stews, and sauces that use or accompany beef.

1 Combine the ingredients

Place the marrowbones, beef shin slices, carrots, celery, onion, parsley, bay leaf, and peppercorns in an 8-qt (8-l) heavy-bottomed pot and add water just to cover the ingredients by 1 inch (2.5 cm); more water could dilute the flavor of the stock. Place the pot over medium-high heat. Without stirring, slowly bring the liquid to a boil.

2 Skim the impurities

As soon as you see large bubbles begin to form, reduce the heat until only small bubbles break on the liquid's surface, or a *simmer*. Use a large slotted spoon or a skimmer to skim off the grayish foam that rises to the surface during the first 10 minutes of cooking.

INGREDIENTS

3 lb (1.5 kg) beef marrowbones, cracked by the butcher

2 thick slices meaty beef shin, about 2 lb (1 kg) total weight

2 large carrots, peeled and cut on the diagonal into ½-inch (12-mm) pieces

2 stalks celery with leaves, cut into ½-inch (12-mm) pieces

1 large yellow onion, peeled and cut into 1-inch (2.5-cm) cubes

3 or 4 sprigs fresh flat-leaf (Italian) parsley

1 bay leaf

8–10 peppercorns

MAKES ABOUT 2 QT (2 L)

6 Degrease the stock

Before you use the stock, carefully remove all of the fat, or the recipes made from the stock will have a greasy flavor and texture. Use a large metal spoon to skim the clear yellow fat from the surface of the strained stock.

3 Develop the flavors

Continue to simmer the stock, uncovered, adjusting the heat from time to time to keep it at a gentle simmer, for 3–4 hours. Do not stir, but continue to skim the surface every 30 minutes or so. Add more water, if necessary, to keep the ingredients just covered.

4 Remove the larger solids

To help ease straining, and make the straining process safer, remove the larger solids with the slotted spoon or a sieve and set aside.

5 Strain the stock

Cut a piece of cheesecloth (muslin) large enough to line the inside of a fine-mesh sieve when it is triple layered. Fold the cheesecloth, dampen it with cool water, squeeze it dry, then use it to line the sieve. Place the sieve over a large heatproof bowl and then ladle or pour the stock through the sieve. Discard the solids that are left behind.

7 Or, cool the stock

Or, if time allows, chill the stock before degreasing it. Fill a large bowl partway with ice and water and set the bowl of stock in the ice bath to cool it to room temperature, stirring occasionally. Cover and refrigerate the stock overnight. The fat will rise to the top and solidify, making it easy to lift off the surface.

Brown beef stock

This especially deep, rich stock is achieved by initially browning the bones and vegetables in the oven, which darkens the meat juices and caramelizes the natural sugars in the vegetables. Use it when you want an especially deep color and flavor in a soup or sauce.

INGREDIENTS

3 lb (1.5 kg) beef marrowbones, cracked by the butcher

2 thick slices meaty beef shin, about 2 lb (1 kg) total weight

2 large carrots, peeled and cut on the diagonal into ½-inch (12-mm) pieces

2 stalks celery with leaves, cut into ½-inch (12-mm) pieces

1 large yellow onion, peeled and cut into 1-inch (2.5-cm) cubes

Canola oil for oiling the pan

2 cups (16 fl oz/500 ml) water, plus extra to cover the ingredients

3 or 4 sprigs fresh flat-leaf (Italian) parsley

1 bay leaf

8–10 peppercorns

MAKES ABOUT 2 QT (2 L)

1 Roast the bones
Position a rack in the upper third of the oven and preheat to 400°F (200°C). Spread the marrowbones, beef shin, carrots, celery, and onion in a lightly oiled roasting pan. Roast, turning the ingredients once or twice, until they are a deep brown, about 45 minutes. Transfer the meat and vegetables to an 8-qt (8-l) heavy-bottomed pot.

2 Deglaze the roasting pan
Protecting your hand with an oven mitt, tip the roasting pan to gather the fat at one corner. Use a spoon to remove and discard the clear fat. Place the roasting pan on the stove top over 2 burners, turn on the heat to low, and add the 2 cups water. Using a wide wooden spatula, scrape up the browned bits stuck to the bottom and sides of the pan.

5 Develop the flavors
Continue to simmer the stock, uncovered, adjusting the heat from time to time to keep it at a gentle simmer, for 3–4 hours. Do not stir, but continue to skim the surface every 30 minutes or so. Add more water, if necessary, to keep the ingredients just covered.

3 Bring the stock to a boil
Pour the contents of the roasting pan into the pot holding the browned ingredients. Add the parsley, bay leaf, and peppercorns to the pot. Add water just to cover the ingredients by 1 inch (2.5 cm); more water could dilute the flavor of the stock. Place the pot over medium-high heat. Without stirring, slowly bring the liquid to a boil.

4 Skim the impurities
As soon as you see large bubbles begin to form, reduce the heat until only small bubbles occasionally break the surface of the liquid. Use a large slotted spoon or a skimmer to skim the grayish foam that rises to the surface during the first 10 minutes of cooking.

MORE MEAT STOCKS

Brown meat stock

Follow the recipe to make Brown Beef Stock, but replace the beef shin with veal shank. The resulting stock, made from a combination of beef and veal bones, will be subtler in flavor than a stock using all beef bones.

Brown veal stock

Follow the recipe to make Brown Beef Stock, but replace the beef marrowbones with veal marrowbones or soup bones and replace the beef shin with veal shank. The resulting stock will be mild in flavor and can be used to make refined sauces in which a more delicate flavor is desired.

Quick brown beef stock

If you don't have time to make this stock recipe from scratch, follow the recipe for Brown Beef Stock to roast the beef bones. Add them to a stockpot, then deglaze with 2½ qt (2.5 l) purchased low-sodium beef broth. Bring to a boil over high heat, skim off any foam, and add a pinch of dried thyme. Reduce the heat to low and simmer, uncovered, for an hour or so. Strain the stock as directed in step 6, then use the stock as desired.

6 Strain and degrease the stock
Remove the larger solids, then strain the stock through a fine-mesh sieve lined with a triple layer of damp cheesecloth (muslin) into a large heatproof bowl. Discard the solids that are left behind. Use a large metal spoon to skim off the clear yellow fat from the surface of the strained stock. Use the stock right away, or cool and store it for up to 3 days in the refrigerator or for up to 3 months in the freezer.

Dicing onions

1 Halve the onion
Using a chef's knife, cut the onion in half lengthwise through the root end. This makes it easier to peel and gives each half a flat side for stability.

2 Peel the onion
Using a paring knife, pick up the edge of the papery skin at the stem end of each half and pull it away. If the first layer of flesh has rough or papery patches, remove it, too.

3 Trim the onion
Trim each end neatly, leaving some of the root end intact to help hold the onion half together. Place an onion half, flat side down and with the root end facing away from you, on the cutting board.

4 Cut the onion half lengthwise
Hold the onion half securely on either side. Using a chef's knife, make a series of lengthwise cuts, as thick as you want the final dice to be. Do not cut all the way through the root end.

5 Cut the onion half horizontally
Spread your fingers across the onion half to help keep it together. Turn the knife blade parallel to the cutting board and make a series of horizontal cuts as thick as you want the final dice to be.

6 Cut the onion half crosswise
Still holding the half together with your fingers, cut it crosswise into dice. To mince the pieces, rest the fingertips of one hand on the tip of the knife, and rock the blade back and forth over the pieces.

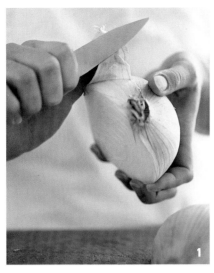

Slicing onions

1 Peel the onion
Using a chef's knife, cut the onion in half lengthwise through the root end. Peel off and discard the skin. You may also need to remove the first layer of onion if it has rough or papery patches.

2 Slice the onion
Place an onion half, cut side down, on the cutting board. Depending on your recipe, you can cut the onion half crosswise, shown here, or lengthwise. Use a chef's knife to slice downward, creating slices that are the desired thickness.

Caramelizing onions

1 Heat the butter and add the onions
Place a large, heavy-bottomed pot over medium-low heat and add a moderate amount of butter and canola oil to the pan. When the butter has melted, add the onions and coat them evenly with the fat.

2 Add the sugar
Reduce the heat to low, cover, and cook, stirring occasionally, for 15 minutes. Uncover the pan, sprinkle the onions with a small amount of sugar, and stir thoroughly to blend. The sugar enhances the naturally occurring sugar in the onions, which helps the browning process.

3 Cook the onions until golden
Continue cooking, stirring often, until the onions are a rich golden brown, about 25 minutes longer. When the onions cook at this slow pace, the sugars caramelize, causing the flavors of the onions to intensify and become more complex.

4 Deglaze the pan, if desired
If using the onions for a soup or sauce, add the liquid called for in the recipe and stir well to loosen any browned bits.

Dicing shallots

1 Separate the cloves
Sometimes you'll find plump, individual bronze-skinned shallots; other times they resemble garlic heads, with 2 or more cloves attached to one another. Separate the cloves, if necessary.

2 Halve the shallot
When you are first learning to dice shallots, you may want to use a paring knife. As you gain skill, you can switch to a larger knife. Cut the shallot in half lengthwise through the root end.

3 Peel and trim the shallot
Using the knife, pick up the edge of the shallot's papery skin and pull it away. Trim each end neatly, but leave some of the root intact to help hold the shallot half together.

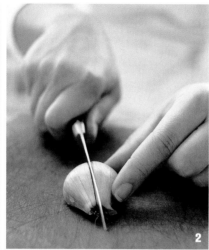
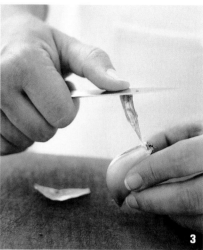

4 Cut the shallot half lengthwise
Put the flat side of the shallot half on the cutting board and make a series of thin lengthwise cuts. Do not cut all the way through the root end; it will hold the shallot layers together.

5 Cut the shallot half horizontally
Turn the knife blade parallel to the cutting board and make a series of thin horizontal cuts through the shallot half, stopping just short of the root end.

6 Cut the shallot half crosswise
Now, cut the shallot half crosswise to make dice. Dicing a shallot in this methodical way yields pieces that will cook evenly.

Chopping & mincing garlic

1 Loosen the garlic peel
Using the flat side of a chef's knife, firmly press against the clove. If you plan to mince the garlic, it's fine to smash it. If you are slicing it, use light pressure to keep the garlic clove intact.

2 Peel and halve the clove
The pressure from the knife will cause the garlic peel to split. Grasp the peel with your fingers, pull it off, and discard. Using the chef's knife, cut the garlic clove in half lengthwise through the root end.

TROUBLESHOOTING
If desired, use the tip of a paring knife to pop out the green sprout in the middle of the clove and discard it. Some cooks believe it is bitter.

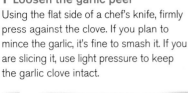

3 Cut the garlic half into slices
One at a time, use the knife to cut the garlic clove halves into very thin slices crosswise (shown here) or lengthwise. Use the slices as is or chop them.

4 Chop the garlic
Hold the knife handle with one hand; rest the fingertips of your other hand on the knife tip. Rock the knife blade back and forth over the sliced garlic until evenly chopped. Use as is or mince the garlic.

5 Mince the garlic
Gather the chopped garlic in a compact pile on the board. Clean the garlic bits off the knife and add them to the pile. Continue to chop, rocking the blade back and forth, until the garlic pieces are very fine, or *minced*.

VEGETABLES

Working with green onions

1 Trim the roots
Green (spring) onions are the young, immature shoots of the bulb onion. Recipes will specify whether to use only the white base, the green tops, or both. Using a chef's knife, trim off the roots from the onions.

TROUBLESHOOTING
When preparing green onions, be sure to feel the outer layer; if it's slimy, remove it as you would the papery skin of other onion varieties.

2 Trim the tops
Remove any wilted or browned leaves, then trim off all or part of the green tops from the long, flat leaves; these can be tough.

3 Slice, chop, or mince the onions
For thinly sliced green onions, line up the trimmed root ends and cut the onions crosswise into slices. To chop or mince the onions, rock the blade of the knife back and forth over the onion slices.

Working with leeks

1 Trim the leeks
Using a chef's knife, trim off the roots
and tough dark green tops of the leeks,
leaving only the white and pale green parts.
If the outer layer is wilted or discolored,
peel it away and discard.

2 Halve and quarter the leeks
Cut each leek in half lengthwise. Place
each half, cut side down, and cut it in half
again to create quarters.

3 Rinse the leeks well
Holding the root end of the leek, and separating
the layers to expose any sand or dirt, swish the
leeks in a bowl of cold water. Alternatively, rinse
the leeks thoroughly under running cold water.

4 Slice the leeks
Pat the leeks dry. Using a chef's knife, and
holding the layers of the leek quarter together,
cut the leek crosswise into slices according
to your recipe.

VEGETABLES

Dicing carrots

1 Peel and trim the carrots
Start with good quality, unblemished carrots. Use a vegetable peeler to remove the rough skin. Switch to a chef's knife and trim off the leafy tops, if present, and rootlike ends.

2 Cut the carrots into lengths
Cut the carrots into even lengths no longer than about 3 inches (7.5 cm). Shorter pieces are simpler to handle, making cutting and then dicing easier.

3 Create a flat edge
Before cutting each length of carrot, cut a thin slice from one side to create a flat edge. Turn the carrot onto this flat side to keep it stable while you cut.

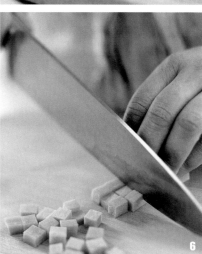

4 Cut the carrots into slices
Cut the carrot pieces lengthwise into slices as thick as you want the final dice to be. Here, we're cutting the carrots into ¼-inch (6-mm) slices.

5 Cut the carrots into sticks
Stack 2 or 3 carrot slices and turn them 90 degrees. Cut the slices lengthwise into sticks that are as thick as the first slices.

6 Cut the carrot into dice
Cut the carrot sticks crosswise to make dice. Dicing carrots methodically creates evenly sized pieces that cook at the same rate. Repeat with the remaining lengths.

Cutting carrots into sticks

1 Peel and trim the carrots
Start with good-quality, unblemished carrots. Use a vegetable peeler to remove the rough skin. Using a paring knife, trim off the leafy tops, if present, and rootlike ends.

2 Cut the carrots into lengths
Cut the carrots crosswise into 2 or 3 uniform lengths. They should be as long as you would like the final sticks to be; 3 inches (7.5 cm) is about right for crudités.

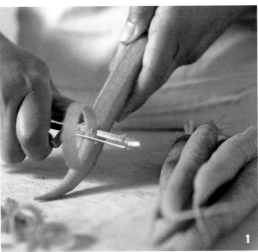

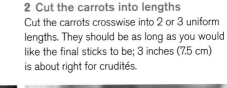

3 Cut the carrots into thirds
Switch to a chef's knife and create a flat edge to stabilize the carrot piece. Cut each carrot piece lengthwise into thirds. Each piece should be about ½ inch (12 mm) wide.

4 Cut the carrots into sticks
Cut each piece lengthwise into sticks. Space your cuts about ½ inch apart.

1 Trim the root end
Start with firm, unblemished celery with fresh-looking leaves. Using a chef's knife, trim the stalks where they meet the root end of the head of celery. Rinse the stalks.

2 Chop the leaves
The leaves are used in some dishes to provide extra celery flavor. Cut the leaves from the stalks and chop as directed in your recipe, usually coarsely.

TROUBLESHOOTING
You may encounter some celery stalks that are fibrous. Run a peeler or paring knife over the stalk to remove the strings.

3 Cut the celery into lengths
Cut the celery stalks into even lengths no longer than about 3 inches (7.5 cm). Shorter pieces are simpler to handle, making slicing and then dicing easier.

4 Cut the celery into sticks
Cut the celery pieces lengthwise into sticks that are as thick as you want the final dice to be. Here, we're cutting them into ¼-inch (6-mm) slices.

5 Cut the celery into dice
Cut the celery sticks crosswise to make dice. Dicing celery methodically creates evenly sized pieces that cook at the same rate. Repeat with the remaining lengths.

Cutting celery into sticks

1 Cut the celery into lengths
Cut trimmed celery stalks crosswise into 2 or 3 uniform lengths. They should be as long as you would like the final sticks to be; 3 inches (7.5 cm) is about right for crudités.

2 Cut the celery into sticks
Cut each celery piece lengthwise into sticks. Space your cuts about ½ inch (12 mm) apart.

Preparing mushrooms

1 Brush away the dirt
Using a mushroom brush, gently brush away any dirt from the mushrooms. Use a damp cloth or paper towel to wipe away any stubborn dirt. (Button mushrooms may be briefly rinsed.)

2 Trim the stems
Using a paring knife, trim a thin slice from the base of the stem of each mushroom. If desired, save the stems for stock, or discard.

TROUBLESHOOTING

If the whole stem is tough, trim it away entirely. Some varieties, such as shiitake, always have tough, woody stems. Be sure to remove the stems on these mushrooms to avoid tough bits in your final dish.

3 Remove the gills, if necessary
If using portobello mushrooms, remove the dark gills, which will discolor other ingredients during cooking. Use a metal spoon to scrape out the gills, then cut the caps as directed in your recipe.

Peeling tomatoes

1 Score the tomatoes
Use a paring knife to cut a small, shallow X in the bottom of a plum (Roma) or globe tomato. This process, known as *scoring,* will help you remove the skin quickly later.

2 Blanch the tomatoes
Bring a pot of water to a boil. Using a slotted spoon, plunge the tomatoes in the boiling water for 15–30 seconds, depending on ripeness, until the skins are just loosened.

3 Shock the tomatoes
Use the slotted spoon to transfer the blanched tomatoes to a bowl of ice water. This process is known as *shocking,* and it will stop the tomatoes from cooking too much.

4 Peel off the tomato skins
As soon as the tomatoes are cool, remove them from the ice water. Use a paring knife to pull off the skin, starting at the X. The skin should now peel off quickly and easily.

Seeding tomatoes

1 Halve the tomato
To seed globe tomatoes, use a chef's knife or a serrated tomato knife to cut the tomatoes in half through their "equator." Cut plum (Roma) tomatoes in half lengthwise.

2 Squeeze or scoop out the seeds
Holding a tomato half over a bowl, use a finger to scoop out the seed sacs and any excess liquid. Alternatively, squeeze the tomato half gently to push out the seeds.

Dicing tomatoes

1 Cut vertical slices
Use a chef's knife to make a shallow circular cut to remove the tomato cores, if necessary. Place each half cut side down and make a series of slices, 1/8–1/4 inch (3–6 mm) apart.

2 Cut the slices into strips
Stack 2 or 3 of the tomato slices at a time on their sides. Make a second series of slices, 1/8–1/4 inch apart, perpendicular to the first. You will end up with strips.

3 Cut the strips into dice
Line up the strips and cut crosswise into 1/8- to 1/4-inch dice. Push the diced tomatoes aside to keep them separate from your work area. Repeat steps 1–3 with the remaining tomato halves.

4 Transfer the dice
To transfer the diced tomatoes from the board to a prep bowl, use the flat side of the chef's knife to scoop up the pieces.

1 Sort through the leaves
Carefully sort through the leaves, examining each leaf separately and discarding any leaves that are yellow (or otherwise discolored), wilted, or have holes.

2 Tear the stems from the greens
If working with tender greens such as spinach (shown here), fold each leaf in half along the stem, vein side facing out. Grasp the stem with your other hand and quickly tear it away.

3 Cut the stems away
If working with tougher greens such as Swiss chard, kale, or collard greens (shown here), make a V-shaped cut on either side of the thick stem to remove it from the leaf.

4 Rinse the leaves
Fill the bowl of a salad spinner with water. Insert the spinner basket, add the leaves, and swish to loosen any sand or grit. Lift the basket, change the water, and repeat the rinsing process until no grit is visible.

5 Dry the leaves
Depending on the recipe, dry the leaves or let some of the rinsing water remain. For dry leaves, spin them in the salad spinner in batches until dry. For moist leaves, briefly drain them.

TROUBLESHOOTING
For bulky greens such as collards, which retain a lot of grit, stack a few leaves, roll them up lengthwise, and cut crosswise into narrow ribbons before rinsing.

Trimming green or yellow beans

1 Break off the stem ends
Using your fingers, break off the tough stem ends of the beans where they were attached to the plant. You can leave the opposite, pointed ends in place, or cut them off.

2 Remove the strings
Nowadays, most green beans have no "strings." If you do find a wispy string attached to the stem end, pull it along the length of the bean to remove it. Leave the pointed tail ends intact.

Shelling English peas

1 Split the pod
Have ready a small bowl. Working with 1 pod at a time, pinch the tip at each end to begin splitting the pod. Squeeze the pod, pressing your thumb against the seam to continue opening it.

2 Pop out the peas
Sweep your thumb down along the inside of the pod to pop out the peas and let them fall into the bowl. Discard the pod. Repeat with the remaining pods.

VEGETABLES

Working with bell peppers

1 Remove the seeds and ribs
Using a chef's knife, cut a bell pepper (capsicum) in half lengthwise. Pull out the stem and most of the seeds from each half. Using a paring knife, cut away the white ribs.

2 Cut off the top and bottom
If cutting a pepper into strips or dice, cut a thin slice from the top and bottom of each pepper half.

3 Cut the halves into strips
Carefully hold each pepper half on the work surface, skin side down, and cut the half lengthwise into strips ½ inch (12 mm) or ¼ inch (6 mm) wide.

4 Cut the strips into dice
Line up a few strips and cut them crosswise into ½-inch or ¼-inch squares. Dicing the peppers methodically creates uniform pieces that cook evenly.

Roasting bell peppers

1 Line a baking sheet with foil
Place an oven rack as close to the heat source as possible and preheat the broiler (grill). Put the peppers (capsicums) on a rimmed baking sheet lined with aluminum foil.

2 Roast the peppers
Place the sheet with the peppers under the broiler and broil (grill), turning the peppers as needed with tongs, until charred and blistered on all sides, about 15 minutes.

3 Cool the peppers in a paper bag
Transfer the roasted peppers to a paper bag and close the bag loosely. This allows the peppers to steam as they cool, which loosens the skin.

4 Peel away the skin
When the peppers are cool, after about 10 minutes, remove them from the bag and use your fingers to peel and rub away as much of the charred skin as possible.

Slicing potatoes on a mandoline

1 Run the potatoes over the blade
Adjust your mandoline to slice at the desired thickness. Gripping the potato firmly, slice it into rounds, moving your hand back on the potato so it does not touch the blade.

2 Pat the potato slices dry
As you work, put the potato slices in a bowl of cold water to prevent them from discoloring. When ready to use, drain the potatoes and pat them dry before layering in gratins or frying for chips.

Slicing potatoes by hand

1 Peel the potatoes and put in cold water
Using a peeler or a paring knife, peel the potatoes, if desired, and put them in a bowl of cold water. Before slicing, remove a peeled potato from the water and pat dry.

2 Slice the potatoes with a chef's knife
Using a chef's knife, cut a thin slice from the bottom of the potato to create a stable base. Hold the potato securely, then slice the potatoes into the desired thickness.

Working with sweet potatoes

1 Cut the sweet potato lengthwise
Using a chef's knife, cut the peeled or unpeeled sweet potatoes in half lengthwise. Take care when cutting, as these tubers are very firm and can slip.

2 Cut the sweet potato into wedges or cubes
Lay one sweet potato half cut side down on the cutting board and make 3 lengthwise cuts to get wedges. If desired, line up the wedges and cut them crosswise into rough cubes.

Ricing potatoes

1 Prepare the ricer
Follow the manufacturer's directions to fit the ricer with the desired ricing disk. Here, we're using the large-holed disk so the potatoes will pass through easily.

2 Rice the potatoes
Using a large spoon, fill the ricer with cooked potatoes. Close the handles and squeeze them together to pass the potatoes through the ricer, allowing them to fall into a saucepan or bowl.

VEGETABLES

Classic mashed potatoes

Russets are the classic mashing potato because their dry, highly starchy flesh readily absorbs butter and milk. Medium-starch varieties also work well, particularly Yukon gold potatoes, which are a favorite in part for their buttery color.

INGREDIENTS

2½ lb (1.25 kg) high-starch potatoes such as russet or medium-starch potatoes such as Yukon gold

1½ teaspoons sea salt

6 tablespoons (3 oz/90 g) unsalted butter, at room temperature

½ cup (4 fl oz/125 ml) milk or half-and-half (half cream), warmed

⅛ teaspoon freshly ground white pepper

MAKES 4–6 SERVINGS

1 Prepare the potatoes
When using high-starch potatoes such as russets, consider cooking them with the skin on. High-starch potatoes have dry, absorbent flesh, which means they readily take on cooking water if they are peeled and cut up. Whether or not you plan to peel the potatoes, scrub and rinse them well.

2 Cook the potatoes
Put the potatoes in a 5-qt (5-l) pot and add water to cover them by 1 inch (2.5 cm). Add 1 teaspoon of the salt to the water to season the potatoes. Place the pot over high heat and bring the water to a boil, then reduce the heat to a simmer. Cover and simmer the potatoes until tender when pierced with the tip of a paring knife, 25–30 minutes.

5 Add the butter and milk
Place the pot with the slightly mashed potatoes over low heat. Switch to a wooden spoon and mix the butter into the potatoes. Next, pour in the warm milk, adding it in ¼-cup (2–fl oz/60-ml) increments. Stir in just enough milk until the potatoes are as light and smooth as you would like. Mix in the remaining ½ teaspoon salt and the white pepper.

3 Peel the potatoes

Drain the potatoes, then transfer them to a cutting board. Using the tip of a paring knife, slit the skin of each potato lengthwise to create a starting place for peeling. Working with 1 potato at a time, and using a fork to hold it steady, use tongs to peel off the skin. Put the peeled potatoes back into the empty cooking pot, cover, and set aside.

4 Mash the potatoes

For chunky mashed potatoes, use a potato masher to press down on the potatoes, turning the masher a little each time and working your way around the pot as needed to break up the potatoes. Alternatively, for smooth mashed potatoes, pass the potatoes through a ricer back into the pot.

6 Adjust the seasonings

Taste the potatoes. If you feel they taste flat, stir in a little more salt and/or pepper, a pinch at a time. If you like creamier mashed potatoes, add a bit more milk or butter. Mix in each addition a little bit at a time and taste again until you are happy with the balance of flavors and the consistency. Stop mixing as soon as you reach the texture and flavors you like. Overmixing the potatoes will cause them to be gluey.

MASHED POTATO VARIATIONS

Quick mashed potatoes

Cut the peeled or unpeeled potatoes into 2-inch (5-cm) chunks. Follow the recipe for Classic Mashed Potatoes, but reduce the cooking time to 15–18 minutes.

Mashed potatoes with olive oil & garlic

In a small frying pan over low heat, warm ¼ cup (2 fl oz/60 ml) extra-virgin olive oil. Add 1 tablespoon minced garlic and sauté until the oil is infused with garlic flavor but the garlic has not browned, about 10 minutes. Set aside. In a small saucepan over low heat, warm 1 cup (8 fl oz/250 ml) millk until small bubbles form around the edges of the pan. Stir in the olive oil–garlic mixture and set aside. Follow the recipe for Classic Mashed Potatoes, replacing the milk and butter with the olive oil–garlic mixture.

Mashed potatoes with pesto

Follow the recipe for Classic Mashed Potatoes. In step 5, add ½ cup (4 fl oz/125 ml) Basil Pesto (entry 284), or more to taste, with the milk and butter.

Trimming broccoli

1 Cut off the leaves and stalks
Using a chef's knife, trim away any remaining leaves on the broccoli stalk, then cut off the bottom portion of the stalk. (You can peel this lower portion, cut it up, and cook it later for another dish.)

2 Cut the broccoli into florets
Using a paring knife, cut the broccoli head into individual florets, each about 1¾ inches (4.5 cm) long. If the florets seem too big when cut from the stalk, cut them gently through the stem end so as not to damage the crown.

Trimming cauliflower

1 Remove the core and leaves
Using a chef's knife, cut the head of a cauliflower in half vertically to reveal the core. Use a paring knife to cut out the inner core and trim away any green leaves.

2 Cut the cauliflower into florets
Cut the cauliflower head into florets, each about 1¾ (4.5 cm) inches long. If the stems of the florets seem tough, use the paring knife to peel them.

Slicing summer squash

1 Rinse and trim the squash
For the best results when working with summer squash, try to find ones with the same diameter. Using a chef's knife, trim the stem ends and blossom ends and discard.

2 Slice the squash
Cut each squash crosswise or on the diagonal, according to your recipe. Cutting it on the diagonal yields attractive slices that provide more surface area for browning.

Preparing winter squash

1 Halve the squash
If using butternut squash (shown here), use a chef's knife to separate the "neck" from the body. Next, cut the squash or squash parts in half lengthwise.

2 Scoop out the seeds
Using a sturdy spoon, scoop out and discard the seeds and any strings from each half. (The necks of butternut squash don't contain seeds or strings.)

Working with globe eggplant

1 Trim the eggplant
Using a serrated or chef's knife, trim the green top off the eggplant (aubergine), then cut the eggplant crosswise into slices or cubes, as directed in your recipe.

2 Salt the eggplant, if desired
Salting eggplant helps remove some of the bitter flavor. Sprinkle both sides of the eggplant slices with salt. Let stand in a colander over a bowl for at least 30 minutes, or according to your recipe.

Working with Asian eggplant

1 Trim the eggplants
Using a chef's knife, trim the green tops off the Asian eggplants (slender aubergines). If you plan to make diagonal slices, cut the tops off at a diagonal.

2 Cut the eggplants
Cut each eggplant on the diagonal or crosswise into slices, as directed in your recipe. It is not necessary to salt Asian eggplant, as it is milder and less bitter than globe eggplant.

Working with fennel

1 Trim the stalks
Using a chef's knife, cut away the stalks and feathery leaves, or *fronds,* of the bulb. Set aside some of the fronds if directed to use as a garnish or to add flavor to recipes.

2 Remove any bruised parts
Run a vegetable peeler over the outer layer of the bulb to remove any bruised or tough portions. If the outer layer is badly bruised or scarred, remove it entirely.

3 Halve the fennel bulb
Using the chef's knife, cut the fennel bulb in half from top to bottom, cutting right through the vegetable's core.

4 Cut the halves into wedges
If your recipe calls for wedges, cut each half lengthwise into 4 wedges. Do not remove the core; it helps keep the layers together.

5 Cut the wedges into slices
If your recipe calls for thin slices, first cut the cores from each wedge, then cut the wedges into slices lengthwise or crosswise.

6 Mince the fronds, optional
If using the fennel fronds, rinse them and dry well, then separate them from their stems. Rock the blade of the chef's knife back and forth over the fronds to mince them.

Working with Brussels sprouts

1 Trim the stem ends
Using a paring knife, trim the stem end of each Brussels sprout. Remove any withered or yellowed leaves.

2 Cut the Brussels sprouts
Cut larger sprouts into halves or quarters through the core to make them about the same size as the smallest ones. This way, the sprouts will cook at the same rate.

Working with cabbage

1 Halve the cabbage
Pull off any bruised or wilted outer leaves from a red or green cabbage head. Using a chef's knife, cut the cabbage in half through the dense inner core. Cabbages can be very compact, so use firm pressure and take care that the head doesn't roll around on the board.

2 Quarter the cabbage
To cut the halves into quarters, lay them flat side down on the cutting board and cut them lengthwise through the core.

3 Remove the core
Lay a cabbage quarter on the cutting board with a cut side facing down. Use a paring knife to cut away the hard core. Repeat with the remaining quarters.

4 Cut into slices or shreds
Cut each cored cabbage quarter crosswise into thin slices as directed in your recipe, often about ¼ inch (6 mm) wide. The cabbage will fall apart into "shreds" that can be used for cooking or slaw.

Trimming artichokes

1 Remove the outer leaves
Working with 1 artichoke at a time, snap off the outer leaves until you reach the pale green leaves near the center. Put the trimmed artichokes in a bowl of cold water with lemon juice to prevent browning.

2 Cut the top third off the artichokes
Using a serrated knife, cut off the top one-third of each artichoke, which is too tough to eat. Rub the cut surface with a lemon half to prevent browning.

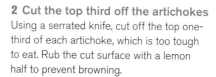

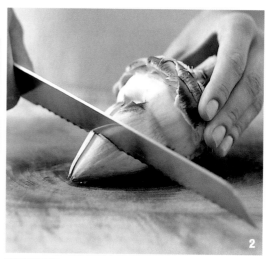

3 Trim the bottoms
Using a paring knife, peel the stems. Trim off the dark green leaves where the stem meets the base and the bottoms of the larger outer leaves where they were snapped off.

4 Remove the chokes
Cut each artichoke lengthwise into quarters. Remove the fuzzy choke and any thorny inner leaves. Transfer the wedges to the bowl of lemon water.

Trimming asparagus

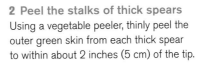

1 Trim the ends
If you are using thick asparagus, use a chef's knife to cut away the bottom of each spear where it starts to change color, becoming paler and visibly tougher.

2 Peel the stalks of thick spears
Using a vegetable peeler, thinly peel the outer green skin from each thick spear to within about 2 inches (5 cm) of the tip.

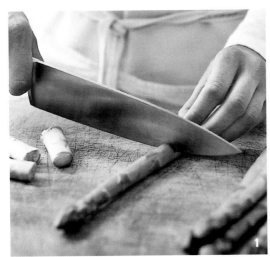

3 Snap the ends of thin spears
If you are using thin asparagus—about the width of a pencil—lightly bend each spear at the end opposite the tip until it breaks. The spear will snap precisely where the fibrous, tough portion begins. Discard the ends.

4 Cut on the diagonal into pieces
Working with 1 spear at a time, cut each spear crosswise or on the diagonal according to your recipe.

Working with avocados

1 Halve the avocado lengthwise
Select a ripe avocado; it should yield to gentle finger pressure. Using a chef's knife, cut the avocado in half lengthwise, cutting down to and around the pit.

2 Separate the halves
Hold the avocado so that one of the halves rests in each hand. Gently rotate in opposite directions to separate the avocado halves.

3 Remove the pit
Carefully holding the avocado half with the pit in one hand or placing it on the cutting board, strike the pit with the heel of the blade of the chef's knife, lodging it in the pit. Twist the knife to lift out the pit.

4 Score each avocado half
Using a paring knife, score each avocado half by cutting parallel lines just down to the peel. Turn the half 90 degrees and cut another set of parallel lines perpendicular to the first ones.

5 Release the squares
Use a large spoon to scoop the avocado squares into a bowl. Plan to use the avocado squares as soon as possible after cutting them.

TROUBLESHOOTING
Avocado flesh quickly turns brown when exposed to air. Sprinkling the flesh with a little fresh lemon or lime juice will help slow the discoloration process.

Working with cucumbers

1 Peel and halve the cucumber
Use a vegetable peeler to peel away the dark skin from the cucumber (many cucumbers are coated with wax). Using a chef's knife, slice the cucumber in half lengthwise.

2 Scoop out the seeds
Using a teaspoon or a melon baller, scoop out any seeds and pulpy matter, which can be quite watery. English (hothouse) cucumbers may have few or no seeds.

3 Cut the seeded halves into strips
Cut the cucumber halves lengthwise into slices. If you're planning to dice them, cut the cucumber into slices that are as thick as you want the final dice to be. Then, cut each slice lengthwise to create equal-sized strips.

4 Cut the strips into dice
Line up the strips and slice them crosswise at regular intervals to create dice. Be sure to keep the tips of your fingers tucked under and away from the knife.

Making fluted cucumber slices

1 Peel away the skin in strips
Use a bar-style channel knife (also called a lemon stripper) or the tip of a vegetable peeler to create stripes of dark green peel and light green flesh.

2 Slice the cucumber
Using a chef's knife, cut the cucumber crosswise or on the diagonal to create slices. For canapés, ¼-inch (6-mm) slices are about right.

Blanching vegetables

1 Briefly boil the vegetables
Bring a large pot three-fourths full of water
to a boil. When the water is boiling, add
about 2 teaspoons salt and the vegetables
to be *blanched*, or partially cooked. Here,
we are blanching asparagus.

2 Remove the blanched vegetables
As soon as the vegetables are crisp, barely
tender (taste a piece), and brightly colored,
remove them from the water with a skimmer
or slotted spoon. For small vegetables,
drain them in a colander.

3 Shock the vegetables
Immediately transfer the blanched vegetables
to a bowl of ice water. This will stop the
cooking and set the color, a technique
known as *shocking*.

4 Pat the vegetables dry
As soon as they are cool, drain the vegetables
and pat them dry.

Stir-frying vegetables

1 Heat the wok
Heat the wok over high heat until you feel
the heat rising when you hold your hand over
the pan. Add the cooking oil, such as peanut
or canola oil, tilt and rotate the pan to
distribute the oil, and heat until shimmering.

2 Add the longer-cooking vegetables
Add the vegetables in the order of their
cooking time, from longest to shortest. Cook,
tossing and stirring constantly with 2 wooden
spoons or spatulas, for 1–2 minutes or as
directed in your recipe.

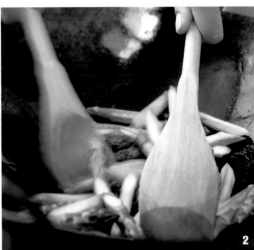

3 Add the other vegetables
Follow your recipe to add the remaining
vegetables and aromatics, such as ginger or
garlic, and continue to cook while constantly
tossing and stirring, for 1–2 more minutes.
You want the heat to remain on high.

4 Add the fresh seasonings
Add ingredients like fresh herbs and citrus
zest to the pan at the last minute so they
stay fresh tasting and bright.

Steamed vegetables

Steaming vegetables is quicker than boiling. It is also an ideal method for anyone wanting to eat healthfully: most of the nutrients are retained in steamed vegetables and fats can be added sparingly after cooking.

2 Insert the steamer basket
Pour water into a saucepan to a depth of about 1 inch (2.5 cm). Place a steamer basket or steamer insert in the pan. The water should come just up to the bottom of the steamer. Cover and heat over high heat until large, vigorous bubbles form on the surface. (If you are not sure if the water is boiling, use a fork to lift up the steamer and take a peek.)

1 Cut up the vegetables
Trim the vegetables and cut them into bite-sized pieces. (Here, we're cutting cauliflower into florets; see entry 328.) Pieces that are the same size will cook evenly and at the same rate.

INGREDIENTS

1 ½ lb (750 g) cauliflower, broccoli, Brussels sprouts, or other vegetable suitable for steaming

MAKES 4–6 SERVINGS

5 Uncover the pan
To check on the vegetables' progress, use a folded kitchen towel or an oven mitt to lift the lid. Because of all the steam rising, any metal parts of the pot will be extremely hot.

If you plan to dress steamed vegetables later, cool them down quickly as soon as they've finished steaming to keep them from getting mushy. Hold them under running cold water until cool, shake off the excess water, and let drain before covering and refrigerating.

3 Add the vegetables
Arrange the vegetable pieces in the steamer basket or steamer insert, distributing them evenly. Spacing the pieces evenly allows the steam to circulate around them more easily.

4 Steam the vegetables
Cover the pan and let the vegetables steam until they are tender and bright in color, about 5 minutes for cauliflower, 4 minutes for broccoli, or 8 minutes for Brussels sprouts.

6 Test for doneness
To test the vegetables for doneness, insert the tip of a paring knife into a piece of vegetable. If the knife slips easily in and out, but the piece still offers a little firmness, the vegetables are done. If not, re-cover the pan, let the vegetables steam for another 30–60 seconds, and test again. Do not overcook the vegetables or they will lack the fresh flavor and texture of steamed vegetables at their best.

STEAMED VEGETABLE VARIATIONS

Steamed broccoli with lemon & olive oil

Follow the recipe for Steamed Vegetables using broccoli. In a bowl large enough to hold the broccoli comfortably, stir together ¼ cup (2 fl oz/60 ml) extra-virgin olive oil, 2 teaspoons finely grated lemon zest, 2 tablespoons fresh lemon juice, 2 tablespoons finely chopped green (spring) onion, ½ teaspoon sea salt, and ⅛ teaspoon freshly ground pepper. Pour the hot broccoli into the bowl with the seasonings and toss to coat evenly.

Steamed cauliflower with curry butter

Follow the recipe for Steamed Vegetables using cauliflower. In a bowl, stir together 4 tablespoons (2 oz/60 g) room-temperature unsalted butter, 2 teaspoons curry powder, 1 teaspoon grated lemon zest, 1 teaspoon fresh lemon juice, ½ teaspoon sea salt, ¼ teaspoon granulated sugar, ⅛ teaspoon ground mace, and ⅛ teaspoon hot paprika. Transfer the butter to a serving bowl. Add the hot cauliflower and 2 tablespoons chopped fresh flat-leaf (Italian) parsley to the bowl and toss to coat evenly.

Sautéed vegetables

Sautéing involves quick cooking relatively delicate vegetables in a small amount of fat over high heat. This method sears the exteriors of the vegetables, caramelizing them and creating golden brown crusts, while keeping the insides tender and crisp.

1 Cut up the vegetables
Trim the vegetables and cut them into bite-sized pieces. Zucchini are good quartered lengthwise, then cut crosswise into ½-inch (12-mm) pieces. Bell peppers are best cut lengthwise into slices about ⅜ inch (1 cm) thick. Asparagus are nice cut on the diagonal into larger 1½-inch (4-cm) pieces or smaller ¼-inch (6-mm) pieces.

2 Heat the pan
Place a large frying pan over high heat and let it heat for a few moments. While the pan is heating, place all your ingredients near the stove. To test the heat level, hold your hand over the pan until you can feel the heat rising.

INGREDIENTS

1½ lb (750 g) zucchini (courgettes) or other summer squash, bell peppers (capsicums), thick asparagus, or other vegetable suitable for sautéing

2 tablespoons olive oil

¼ teaspoon sea salt

Pinch of freshly ground pepper

MAKES 4–6 SERVINGS

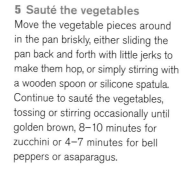

If you want to practice the classic sauté method—moving the food back and forth in the pan by means of short jerking motions—fill a dry, unheated frying pan with dried beans. With repetition, you'll soon develop the skill and confidence to try this with vegetables on a hot stove.

5 Sauté the vegetables
Move the vegetable pieces around in the pan briskly, either sliding the pan back and forth with little jerks to make them hop, or simply stirring with a wooden spoon or silicone spatula. Continue to sauté the vegetables, tossing or stirring occasionally until golden brown, 8–10 minutes for zucchini or 4–7 minutes for bell peppers or asaparagus.

3 Add the oil

When the pan is hot, add the olive oil. Tilt and swirl the pan to coat it with an even layer of the oil. Let the oil heat for several seconds.

4 Add the vegetables

As soon as the surface of the oil appears to shimmer, quickly add the vegetable pieces to the pan. Toss to coat the vegetables with the oil and sprinkle with the salt and pepper.

6 Test for doneness

To test the vegetables for doneness, insert the tip of a paring knife into a piece of vegetable. The vegetable should be tender but still slightly firm at the center. If the vegetables are not quite ready, sauté them for another 30–60 seconds and test again. Don't stir too often, because contact with the pan will give the vegetables the caramelized flavor of high-heat cooking.

MORE SAUTÉED VEGETABLES

Sautéed zucchini with lemon-herb bread crumbs

Follow the recipe for Sautéed Vegetables using zucchini (courgettes). In a small frying pan over low heat, toss ⅓ cup (⅔ oz/20 g) fresh bread crumbs with 2 teaspoons olive oil until golden and crisp, about 10 minutes. Add ½ teaspoon minced garlic, 1 teaspoon grated lemon zest, and 2 tablespoons chopped fresh marjoram and toss for a minute or two. Transfer to a small bowl. Top the sautéed zucchini with the toasted bread-crumb mixture.

Sautéed asparagus with fresh herbs

Follow the recipe for Sautéed Vegetables using asparagus. Toss the sautéed asparagus with 1 tablespoon slivered fresh basil or finely chopped fresh chervil, cilantro (fresh coriander), or flat-leaf (Italian) parsley.

Sautéed fennel with Parmesan

Follow the recipe for Sautéed Vegetables using 3 large fennel bulbs, about 10 oz (315 g) total weight, cut lengthwise into ¼-inch (6-mm) slices. Cook the fennel until softened, about 10 minutes, then add ⅓ cup (3 fl oz/80 ml) dry white wine, such as Sauvignon Blanc. Continue to cook until the the fennel is golden and tender, 5–7 minutes longer. Season to taste, then toss with 1 tablespoon minced fennel fronds and freshly grated Parmesan cheese to taste.

Roasted vegetables

Roasting in the dry heat of an oven is especially well suited to the dense vegetables of autumn and winter. Coated with a little olive oil and exposed to high heat, the natural sugars in the vegetables emerge.

INGREDIENTS

2 lb (1 kg) sweet potatoes; medium- or low-starch potatoes, such as red or Yukon gold potatoes; large carrots; or other vegetable suitable for roasting, cut into 2½-inch (6-cm) wedges or chunks

¼ cup (2 fl oz/60 ml) olive oil

2 teaspoons chopped fresh thyme or rosemary

½ teaspoon sea salt

⅛ teaspoon freshly ground pepper

MAKES 4–6 SERVINGS

1 Add the oil to the vegetables
Preheat the oven to 425°F (220°C). Place the vegetable wedges or chunks in a large bowl. Add the olive oil and toss to coat (if you are using regular potatoes, do this quickly, as exposure to air will cause them to discolor).

2 Add the seasonings
Add the thyme, salt, and pepper. Using your hands or 2 wooden spoons, toss the vegetables to coat them thoroughly with the oil-herb mixture.

5 Roast the vegetables
Place the pan in the oven and let the vegetables roast until they are well browned and tender, about 20 minutes for sweet potatoes or 25 minutes for regular potatoes or carrots. Insert the tip of a paring knife into a vegetable piece. If the knife easily slips in and out, the vegetables are done. If not, let the vegetables roast for another 5 minutes and test again. Do not overcook the vegetables or they will lack the sweet, concentrated flavor and texture of roasted vegetables at their best.

3 Transfer to a roasting pan
Transfer the vegetables to a roasting pan, making sure to get all the remaining oil and herbs out of the bowl.

4 Arrange the vegetables
Arrange the vegetable pieces in a single layer without crowding. Doing so will expose the maximum surface area of the vegetables to the high heat of the oven and encourage even browning.

Roasted cherry tomatoes

Preheat the oven to 425°F (220°C). Add 2 pints (24 oz/560–750 g) small cherry tomatoes to a baking dish just large enough to hold them. Toss with 4 teaspoons olive oil and ¼ teaspoon sea salt. Roast until the skins begin to split and the tomatoes release some of their juices, 5–7 minutes. Add ⅛ teaspoon freshly ground pepper and toss well.

Roasted beets with rosemary

Preheat the oven to 425°F (220°C). Cut 1½ lb (750 g) small red or yellow beets into 2-inch (5-cm) chunks and add them to a baking dish just large enough to hold them. Toss with 3 teaspoons chopped fresh rosemary, 4 teaspoons olive oil, ¼ teaspoon sea salt, and ⅛ teaspoon freshly ground pepper. Roast, turning occasionally, until the beets are golden brown and tender when pierced with the tip of a paring knife, about 1 hour.

6 Season the vegetables
Taste the vegetables. They should carry their own natural flavors and have a subtle sweetness that comes from roasting at a high heat, as well as accents of salt, pepper, and thyme. If the vegetables taste bland to you, sprinkle salt over the pieces a little at a time to heighten the flavors.

Roasted potatoes & garlic

Preheat the oven to 425°F (220°C). Add 1½ lb (750 g) fingerling potatoes to a baking dish just large enough to hold them. Add the unpeeled cloves from 1 head of garlic. Toss with ¼ cup (2 fl oz/60 ml) olive oil, 3 teaspoons chopped fresh thyme, ¾ teaspoon sea salt, and ¼ teaspoon freshly ground pepper. Roast, turning occasionally, until the potatoes are golden brown and tender when pierced with the tip of a paring knfe, about 40 minutes.

Braised vegetables

Braising, a gentle cooking method that calls for a small amount of liquid, low heat, and a covered pot, can be used for a variety of vegetables. You can also reduce the flavorful cooking liquid and use it as an accompanying sauce.

INGREDIENTS

1¾–2 lb (875 g–1 kg) leeks, celery, or fennel, or other vegetable suitable for braising

1–2 tablespoons unsalted butter

¼ cup (2 oz/60 g) finely diced yellow onion

¼ cup (2 fl oz/60 ml) dry white wine, such as Sauvignon Blanc

1½ cups (12 fl oz/375 ml) Chicken Stock (see entry 298) or canned low-sodium chicken broth

¼ teaspoon sea salt

⅛ teaspoon freshly ground pepper, optional

1–2 teaspoons fresh lemon juice, optional

MAKES 4–6 SERVINGS

1 Heat the butter in the pan
Trim the vegetables and cut them into equal-sized pieces so that they will cook evenly. Place a straight-sided frying pan with a lid over medium-high heat and add 1 tablespoon of the butter.

2 Cook the onions
When the butter has melted and the foam begins to subside, add the onion and cook, stirring frequently, until softened, 2–3 minutes. Add the wine and cook until the wine has reduced by about half, 1–2 minutes.

5 Test for doneness
Uncover the pan and insert the tip of a paring knife into a piece of vegetable. If the knife easily slips in and out, but the piece still offers a little firmness, the vegetables are done. If not, re-cover the pan, let the vegetables braise for another 2 minutes, and test again. Do not overcook the vegetables or they will lack the fresh flavor of braised vegetables at their best. Using tongs, transfer the vegetables to a warmed serving platter and cover to keep warm.

3 Add the vegetables

Add the vegetable pieces to the pan along with the chicken stock and salt. Raise the heat to high and bring to a boil. As soon as you see large bubbles begin to form, reduce the heat until only small bubbles occasionally break the surface.

4 Braise the vegetables

Cover the pan and let the vegetables braise in the enclosed cooking environment until tender, about 25 minutes for leeks, 15 minutes for celery, or 20 minutes for fennel.

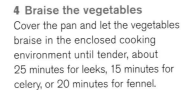

6 Make a sauce, if desired

If desired, you can make a flavorful sauce from the pan juices. Return the pan with the braising liquid to high heat and bring to a boil. Let the liquid bubble vigorously until it is reduced to about ⅓ cup (3 fl oz/80 ml), about 8 minutes. Stir in the remaining 1 tablespoon butter and the pepper. Taste the sauce. If it tastes bland, add the lemon juice or more salt and pepper a little at a time until you are happy with the flavor balance. Pour the sauce over the vegetables.

MORE BRAISED VEGETABLES

Braised celery with lemon

In a sauté pan over medium-high heat, combine 1½ cups (12 fl oz/375 ml) chicken stock, ¼ cup (2 oz/60 g) minced onion, 1 sprig fresh thyme, and one 2-inch (5-cm) strip lemon zest. Bring to a boil, reduce the heat to medium-low, and simmer until reduced by half, about 5 minutes. Add 1 bunch celery, cut into 4-inch (10-cm) lengths (reserve the leaves); 1 tablespoon unsalted butter; and salt to taste. Cover and simmer until the celery is tender when pierced with the tip of a paring knife, about 15 minutes. Transfer the celery to a warmed platter. Add 1 tablespoon lemon juice, 2 teaspoons butter, the reserved chopped celery leaves, and a pinch of pepper to the cooking liquid. Raise the heat to high and boil for 1 minute. Pour over the celery.

Braised endive with cream

In a sauté pan over medium-high heat, melt 3 tablespoons unsalted butter. Add 6 halved heads Belgian endive (chicory/witloof) to the pan, cut side down. Cook until lightly golden, 4–5 minutes. Gently turn over the endive and add ⅓ cup (3 fl oz/ 80 ml) chicken stock, ½ teaspoon salt, and ⅛ teaspoon freshly ground pepper and bring to a boil. Cover, reduce the heat to low, and simmer until the endive is tender, about 20 minutes. Uncover and add ⅔ cup (5 fl oz/160 ml) heavy (double) cream, 2 teaspoons chopped fresh tarragon, and 1 teaspoon lemon juice. Raise the heat to medium and cook until the cream has reduced to a thick sauce.

Measuring liquids by volume

When measuring liquids, use standard measuring spoons for small amounts. For amounts over 3 tablespoons, use a liquid measuring cup for accuracy. To use a liquid measuring cup, place it on a flat surface and pour in the liquid. Let the liquid settle, then read the measurement at eye level and make any adjustments. The table below can help you when multiplying recipes for larger servings or when you need to substitute a different measuring tool for the one desired.

TEASPOONS	TABLESPOONS	FLUID OUNCES	CUPS	PINTS	QUARTS	GALLONS
3 teaspoons =	1 tablespoon =	½ fluid ounce				
	2 tablespoons =	1 fluid ounce				
	4 tablespoons =	2 fluid ounces =	¼ cup			
	8 tablespoons =	4 fluid ounces =	½ cup			
	16 tablespoons =	8 fluid ounces =	1 cup			
	=	16 fluid ounces =	2 cups =	1 pint		
	=	32 fluid ounces =	4 cups =	2 pints =	1 quart	
	=	128 fluid ounces =	16 cups =	8 pints =	4 quarts =	1 gallon

Doneness temperatures for meat and poultry

The internal temperature of roasted meats and poultry rises 5° to 10°F (3° to 6°C) after they are removed from the oven and allowed to rest for 5 or 10 minutes or longer, depending on their size, shape, and weight. The figures below reflect the temperatures that roasted meats need to reach prior to the resting period. Be sure to allow meats and poultry to stand as directed in recipes so that the temperature will rise to the level of optimum doneness.

TYPE	RARE	MEDIUM-RARE	MEDIUM	MEDIUM-WELL	WELL
Beef	120°–125°F 49°–52°C	125°–130°F 52°–54°C	135°–140°F 57°–60°C	140°–150°F 60°–65°C	150°F 65°C
Veal	———	125°–130°F 52°–54°C	135°–140°F 57°–60°C	140°–150°F 60°–65°C	———
Lamb	120°–125°F 49°–52°C	125°–130°F 52°–54°C	135°–140°F 57°–60°C	140°–150°F 60°–65°C	150°F 65°C
Pork	———	———	135°–140°F 57°–60°C	140°–150°F 60°–65°C	150°F 65°C
Poultry breast	———	———	———	———	160°F 71°C
Poultry thigh	———	———	———	———	170°F 77°C

Substitutions and equivalents

The following chart lists the equivalent weight or amount for specific measurements of certain foods, as well as acceptable substitutes for certain foods, when available. To calculate metric equivalents, use the following formulas: To convert tablespoons to mililitres, multiply the number of tablespoons by 14.79; to convert cups to litres, multiply the number of cups by 0.236; to convert ounces to grams, multiply the number of ounces by 29.57.

FOOD	AMOUNT	EQUIVALENT/WEIGHT	SUBSTITUTE
Butter	½ stick	4 tbsp, ¼ cup, 2 oz	———
	1 stick	8 tbsp, ½ cup, 4 oz	———
	2 sticks	1 cup, 8 oz	⅞ cup vegetable oil or 1 cup lard
	4 sticks	2 cups, 16 oz (1 lb)	———
Buttermilk	1 cup	8 oz	1 cup milk plus 1 tbsp fresh lemon juice, or 1 cup plain yogurt
Cheese	1 cup grated	4 oz	———
	1 cup crumbled feta	5 oz	———
	1 cup ricotta	8 oz	———
Chocolate	1 square (1 oz)	4 tbsp grated	———
Cornstarch	1 tbsp	———	2 tbsp flour or 1 tbsp arrowroot
Flour, cake	1 lb	4½ cups sifted	———
	1 cup	———	1 cup less 2 tbsp all-purpose flour (with 2 tbsp cornstarch added if possible)
Garlic	2 medium cloves	1 tsp minced	———
Herbs	1 tbsp (3 tsp) fresh	1 tsp dried herbs	———
Lemons	1 medium	1 to 3 tbsp juice, 1½ tsp zest	———
Limes	1 medium	1½ to 2 tbsp juice	———
Sour cream	1 cup	8 oz	1 cup plain yogurt
Sugar, brown	1 lb	2¼ cups packed	———
	1 cup	———	1 cup granulated sugar combined with 2 tbsp light or dark molasses
Tomatoes	3 medium (1 lb)	1½ cups chopped	———
Vanilla	1 tsp extract	———	1-inch piece vanilla bean, halved and scraped
Yeast, active dry	1 pkg	2¼ tsp	1 cake (.06 oz) compressed yeast

General index

A

Aioli (Garlic Mayonnaise), 282
Almond(s)
    Almond Tart Dough, 237
    Cherry-Almond Scones, 67
    Pistou (Provençal-Style Pesto), 284
Aluminum-clad stainless-steel cookware, 18b
Anodized aluminum cookware, 18f
Apple(s)
    corers, 15a
    peeling and coring, 139
    -Spice Filling, 241
Artichoke(s)
    −Red Pepper Quiche, 119
    trimming, 336
Arugula
    Pesto, 284
    and Bacon Frittata, 118
Asparagus
    and Gruyère Omelet, 117
    -Leek Quiche, 119
    Risotto, 160
    Sautéed, with Fresh Herbs, 344
    trimming, 337
Avocado(s)
    and Tomato Omelet with Cilantro, 117
    working with, 338

B

Bacon
    and Arugula Frittata, 118
    dicing, 108
    -Gruyère Quiche, 119
    Quiche Lorraine, 119
Basil, working with, 172
Baker's peels, 33b
Bakeware
    baking sheets, 1
    cake pans, 3
    materials, 5
    other, 4
    pie and tart pans, 2
Baking dishes, 4c
Baking sheets, rimmed, 1a
Baking stones, 33c
Banana Buttercream, 80
Bamboo skewers, 28g
Basil Pesto, 284
Basters, 13b
Basting brushes, 13d
Beans
    dried, simmering, 151
    green or yellow, trimming, 318
    purée, making, 152
Béarnaise Sauce, 279

Béchamel Sauce (White Sauce), 277
Beef
    brisket, trimming, 196
    Meat Stock, Brown 301
    browning, 205
    cutting, for stew, 202
    flank steak, slicing, 197
    grinding, 191
    hamburger patties, forming, 192
    roasts
        carving, 199–200
        trimming, 198
    slicing, 197
    steaks
        carving, 204
        preventing curling, 201
        trimming, 201
    stir-frying, 203
    Stock, 300
    Stock, Brown 301
    Stock, Quick Brown 301
    tenderloin
        cutting into medallions, 195
        trimming, 194
    testing for doneness, 206–7
    trimming, 196
Beets, Roasted, with Rosemary, 345
Bell peppers
    roasting, 321
    working with, 320
Berry Filling, Three- 241
Beurre Blanc, 278
    Balsamic, 278
    Lemon, 278
    Lime, 278
    Orange, 278
Beurre Rouge, 278
Bird's beak paring knives, 20g
Biscotti, forming and cutting, 92
Biscuits, Baking-Powder, 66
Blanching, 341
Blenders
    about, 25c–d
    puréeing with, 97–98
Blind baking, 239
Blueberry Pancakes, 68
Bonded copper cookware, 18c
Boning knives, 19c
Bouquet garni, making, 177
Bowls, 9
Braisers, 17a
Braising vegetables, 346
Bread crumbs, making, 99–100
Bread dough
    making sponge for, 60
    mixing and kneading, 61–62

    proofing, 63
    shaping, 63
    slashing, 64
Bread knives, offfset, 20e
Brine, White Wine, 265
Broccoli
    -Cheddar Quiche, 119
    Steamed, with Lemon and Olive Oil, 343
    trimming, 327
Brownies, cutting, 90
Brushes
    basting, 13d
    pastry, 6i
    wire, 28c
Brussels sprouts, working with, 334
Bulgur wheat, working with, 156
Bundt pans, 3f
Butcher's twine, 13a
Butter
    clarifying, 106
    compound, making, 107
    creaming, 35
    mounting sauces with, 272
    rubbing, under poultry skin, 250
Buttercream, 80
Buttermilk
    -Fried Chicken, 263
    Pancakes, 68

C

Cabbage, working with, 335
Cake pans, 3
Cakes
    cutting, into layers, 81
    cutting dense, 83
    decorating, 47
    foam, cooling and storing, 78
    four-layer, filling and frosting, 82
    preparing pans for, 71–73
    releasing, after baking, 75–77
    sheet, rolling and storing, 79
Candy thermometers, 30b
Carrots
    cutting, into sticks, 310
    dicing, 309
Carving boards, 21c
Carving knives and forks, 24g
Cast iron cookware, 18h
Cauliflower
    Steamed, with Curry Butter, 343
    trimming, 328
Cavatelli, shaping, 230
Celery
    Braised, with Lemon, 346
    cutting, into sticks, 312

dicing, 311
peeling, 311
Cheddar Sauce, 277
Cheese cutters, wire, 24b
Cheese knives, 24a
Cheese planes, 24c
Chef's knives, 19d
Cherry(ies)
-Almond Scones, 67
Bing, Syrup, 69
pitters, 15e
pitting, 143
Sour, Filling, 241
Chicken
Basic Roast, 264
breasts
sautéing boneless, 258
skewering boneless, 252
skinning, boning, and pounding, 251
brining, 253
Brown, Stock, 299
Brown, Stock, Quick 299
butterflying, 256
Buttermilk-Fried, 263
carving, 266
cutting up, 255
grilling butterflied, 257
Herb-Roast, 264
Sausage, and Sun-Dried Tomato
Frittata, 118
skin, rubbing butter under, 250
Spice-Crusted Roast, 264
Stock, 298
stuffing, 249
testing, for doneness, 260–61
trussing, 248
Chiles, working with, 178
Chimney starter
about, 27c
using, 164
Chinois, 11d
Chips
pita, making, 103
potato, frying, 102
tortilla, frying, 101
Chives, snipping, 176
Chocolate
Buttercream, 80
-Chip Pancakes, 68
chopping, 49
curling, 48
Ganache, 52
grating, 50
melting, 51
Mocha Pastry Cream, 44
Pastry Cream, 44

Choux Pastry, 45
Cilantro
Pesto, 284
working with, 173
Citrus
Curd, 41
fruits. See individual fruits
juicers, 14c, 26e
presses, 14b
reamers, 14a
strippers, 15b
Tart Dough, 237
zesters, 15c
Citrus fruit
juicing, 137
sectioning, 138
Citrus zest
candying, 57
grating, 135
mincing, 136
Clams
cleaning, 286
shucking, 287
Clam knives, 12b
Cleavers, 20b, 20h
Coffee
grinders, 26a
makers, 26a
Coconut Buttercream, 80
Colanders, 11a
Compote, Summer Fruit, 69
Convection ovens, 26b
Cookie
cutters, 6d
presses, 6f
sheets, 1b
Cookies
bar, cutting, 90
biscotti, forming and cutting, 92
decorating, 93–95
glazing, 94
ice box, rolling and cutting, 89
portioning dough for, 86
preparing sheets for, 85
pressing out, 91
rolling out dough for, 87
sugar, cutting out, 88
Cookware
basic, 16
in history, 16
materials, 18
specialty, 17
Cooling racks, 4h
Cornmeal Pancakes, 68
Copper cookware, 18e
Couscous, making, 157

Crab
Boiled Fresh, 291
Shellfish Stock, 297
Cranberry Scones, Dried, 67
Cream, whipping, 34
Crème fraîche, making, 268
Crêpe(s)
Savory, 70
Sweet, 70
pans, 17b
Crostini, making, 105
Cucumbers
slices, making fluted, 340
working with, 339
Cups, measuring, 29a–b
Curd, Citrus, 41
Cutlery. See Knives
Cutting boards, 21a–b

D
Decorating tool alternatives, 7
Deep fryers, 26c
Deglazing, 271
Direct-heat charcoal grilling, 165
Docking, 239
Double boilers, 17c
Duck
breasts, pan-roasting, 259
Stock, Brown, 299
stuffing, 249
testing, for doneness, 260–61
trussing, 248
Dutch ovens, 16d

E
Eggplant, working with, 331–32
Eggs
baking, 113
beating sugar and, 74
boiling, 112
frying, 115
poaching, 114
scrambling, 116
separating, 38
tempering, 40
whipping whites, 39
Enameled cast iron cookware, 18g
Endive, Braised, with Cream, 346
Espresso machines, 26a

F
Fat separators, 13e
Fennel
Sautéed, with Parmesan, 344
working with, 333
Fillet knives, 20c

Filo dough, working with, 55
Fish
  baskets, 28d
  tweezers, 12a
  Deep-Fried Fish Fillets, 131
  fillets
    portioning, 125
    removing pin bones, 123–24
    sautéing, 132
    skinning, 122
  Fumet, 296
  Poached Salmon, 130
  raw, cutting into cubes, 126
  steaks, broiling, 133
  Steamed in Parchment, 129
  Stock, 295
  testing, for doneness, 127–28
  whole
    carving, 134
    cleaning, 120
filleting, 121
Flooding icing, 94
Flower petals, sugaring, 58
Folding, 43
Food mills, 14d
Food processors
  about, 25a
  puréeing with, 96
Forks
  carving, 24g
  grill, 28a
French bread pans, 33a
Frittatas
  Bacon and Arugula, 118
  Chicken Sausage and Sun-Dried
    Tomato, 118
  Southwestern, 118
  Vegetable, 118
Frostings and icings
  applying, 47, 82, 93
  Banana Buttercream, 80
  Buttercream, 80
  Chocolate Buttercream, 80
  Chocolate Ganache, 52
  Coconut Buttercream, 80
  filling pastry bag with, 46
  White Chocolate Buttercream, 80
Fruits. See also individual fruits
  preventing discoloration of, 190
  round, working with, 190
Frying
  eggs, 115
  fish fillets, 131
  potato chips, 102
  tortilla chips, 101

G
Galettes, shaping, 243
Ganache, Chocolate, 52

Garlic
  chopping and mincing, 306
  presses, 8h
  removing green sprouts from, 306
Ginger
  Asian Vinaigrette, 283
  -Lemon Scones, 67
  peeling and mincing, 179
Goldtouch nonstick bakeware, 5b
Gnocchi, Potato, 234
Gorgonzola Sauce, 277
Graham-cracker crust, making, 236
Grapefruit knives, 15f
Graters, 10
Gravy
  All-Purpose Pan, 276
  Herb, 265
  separators, 13e
Green onions, working with, 307
Greens, leafy, working with, 317
Griddle pans, 17e
Grill(s)
  charcoal, 27b
  gas, 27a
  indoor, 26d
  mitts, 28b
  pans, 17f
Grilling techniques, 161–71
  caring for, 27
  chimney starter, using, 164
  cleaning, 169
  crosshatch grill marks, creating, 170
  direct-heat, 165
  gas grill, setting up, 161
  grate, oiling, 168
  indirect-heat, 166
  plank, 171
  wood chips, using, 162–63, 167

H
Hamburger patties, forming, 192
Herb(s)
  bouquet garni, making, 177
  dried, working with, 184
  fresh, working with, 172–76
  Gravy, 265
  Pasta Dough, 223
  -Roast Chicken, 264
Hollandaise
  Blender, 279
  Blood Orange, 279
  fixing broken, 280
  Sauce, 279
Honing steel, 19f, 22a

I
Ice cream
  makers, 26k
  scoops, 15h

Immersion blenders
  about, 25d
  puréeing with, 98
Indirect-heat charcoal grilling, 166

J
Juicing, 137
Julienning, 189

K
Kitchen
  outfitting your, 25
  scales, 29d
  shears, 24d
Kiwifruit, working with, 150
Kneading, 61–62
Knives
  bird's beak paring, 20g
  boning, 19c
  caring for, 19
  carving, 24g
  cheese, 24a
  chef's, 19d
  choosing, 20
  clam, 12b
  cleavers, 20b, 20h
  Eastern-style, 23b
  fillet, 20c
  grapefruit, 15f
  honing, 187
  Japanese, 20h
  nakiri, 20h
  offset bread, 20e
  oyster, 12b
  paring, 19a
  santoku, 20a
  serrated, 19e
  sharpening, 185–86
  slicing, 20d
  tomato, 20f
  utility, 19b
  Western-style, 23a
  wielding, 188
  yanigiba, 20h

L
Ladles, 8b
Lamb
  browning, 205
  Frenching, 216
  grinding, 191
  leg of, carving, 218
  rack of, carving, 217
Leek(s)
  -Asparagus Quiche, 119
  working with, 308
Lemons
  Buerre Blanc, 278
  Citrus Curd, 41

Citrus Tart Dough, 237
-Ginger Scones, 67
-Herb Mayonnaise, 282
Pastry Cream, 44
-Shallot Vinaigrette, 283
Scones with Lemon Curd, 67
Strippers, 15b
Lentils, cooking, 158
Limes
Buerre Blanc, 278
Citrus Curd, 41
Citrus Tart Dough, 237
Loaf pans, 4d
Lobster
Boiled Fresh, 291
cleaning and cracking cooked, 289
crackers, 12c
Shellfish Stock, 297

M

Mandolines, 15i
Mangoes, working with, 147
Marjoram, working with, 174
Mayonnaise
Aioli (Garlic Mayonnaise), 282
fixing broken, 281
Lemon-Herb, 282
Pesto, 282
Tartar Sauce, 282
Measuring tools, 29
Meat. See also individual meats
-balls, forming, 193
browning, 205
grinding, 191
pounders, 13f
Melon ballers, 15d
Melons, working with, 145–46
Meringue, making, 42
Mezzalunas, 24f
Mincing, 189
Mini preps, 25b
Mint Pesto, 284
Mitts, 8k, 28b
Mixers
handheld, 25e
stand, 25f
Mortars and pestles, 15j
Muffin pans, 4e
Multipurpose pots, 17g
Mint, working with, 172
Mushroom(s)
preparing, 313
Risotto, 160
-Thyme Quiche, 119
Mussels, cleaning, 286

N

Nakiri knives, 20h
Nectarines

peeling, 141
pitting, 142
Nonstick
bakeware, 5a–b
cooking tools, 15l
cookware, 18d
Nutmeg, grating, 180
Nuts
removing skin of, 111
toasting, 110

O

Oatmeal, making, 159
Oil stones, 22d
Olive pitters, 15e
Olives, pitting, 109
Omelets
Asparagus and Gruyère, 117
Classic, 117
with Fine Herbs, 117
Tomato and Avocado, with Cilantro, 117
Onions
caramelizing, 304
dicing, 302
slicing, 303
Oranges
Beurre Blanc, 278
Blood, Hollandaise, 279
Butter, 69
Citrus Curd, 41
Citrus Tart Dough, 237
-Tarragon Vinaigrette, 283
Orecchiette, shaping, 231
Oregano, working with, 174
Oven(s)
convection, 26b
mitts, 8k
thermometers, 29d
Oyster(s)
knives, 12b
shucking, 290

P

Paella pans, 17h
Pancakes. See also Crêpes
Blueberry, 68
Buttermilk, 68
Chocolate-Chip, 68
Cornmeal, 68
toppings for, 69
Panini presses, 26f
Pan drippings, degreasing, 270
Pans. See also Bakeware; Cookware
deglazing, 271
preparing, for cakes, 71–73
preparing, for cookies, 85
Papayas, working with, 148
Paper cones, making and using, 93
Paring knives, 19a, 20g

Parsley, working with, 173
Pasta
cooking, 219–21
cutting, 226, 228
Dough, Black Pepper, 223
Dough, Fresh Egg, 223–24
Dough, Herb, 223
Dough, Semolina, 229
Dough, Spinach, 223
equipment, 32
rolling out, 225, 227
saucing, 222
shaping, 230–33
Pastry
blenders, 6a
boards, 6b
brushes, 6i
Choux, 45
Classic Puff, 53
cutters, 6e
Quick Puff, 54
tips, 7f
wheels, 6g
Pastry bags
about, 7e
filling, 46
piping frosting with, 47
Pastry Cream, 44
Chocolate, 44
Lemon, 44
Mocha, 44
Peach(es)
peeling, 141
pitting, 142
-Raspberry Filling, 241
Pears, peeling and coring, 140
Peas, shelling, 319
Peelers, 8i
Peppercorns, cracking, 182
Pesto
Arugula, 284
Basil, 284
Cilantro, 284
Mashed Potatoes with, 326
Mayonnaise, 282
Mint, 284
with Walnuts and Pecorino, 284
Pistou (Provençal-Style Pesto), 284
Rosemary-Walnut, 284
Pie(s)
blind baking, 247
dishes, 2b
double-crust, making, 244
dough, working with, 242
embellishing, 246
graham-cracker crust, making, 236
lattice-topped, making, 245
pans, 2a
weights, 6h

Pie dough
    Double-Crust, 240
    Flaky, 240–41
    Lattice-Crust, 240
    Savory, 240
Pie fillings
    Apple-Spice, 241
    Peach-Raspberry, 241
    Sour Cherry, 241
    Three-Berry, 241
Pilaf, making rice, 154
Pin bones, removing, 123–24
Pineapple, working with, 149
Piping, 47
Pistou (Provençal-Style Pesto), 284
Pita chips, making, 103
Pizza
    cutters, 15k
    Dough, 65
Plank grilling, 171
Planks, wood, 28i
Plums
    peeling, 141
    pitting, 142
Polenta, making, 155
Popover pans, 4f
Pork
    brining, 209
    browning, 205
    chops
        panfrying, 214
        stuffing, 210
    cutlets
        breading, 213
        making, 212
    grinding, 191
    shoulder, trimming, 208
    skewers, assembling, 211
    tenderloin
        cutting into medallions, 195
        trimming, 194
    testing, for doneness, 215
Potato(es)
    chips, frying, 102
    Classic Mashed, 326
    and Garlic, Roasted, 345
    Gnocchi, 234
    Mashed, with Olive Oil and
        Garlic, 326
    Mashed, with Pesto, 326
    mashers, 14e
    Quick Mashed, 326
    ricing, 325
    slicing, 322–23
    Southwestern Frittata, 118
Pot holders, 8j
Poultry. See also Chicken; Duck; Turkey
    lifters, 13c
    shears, 24e

skin, rubbing butter under, 250
    stuffing, 249
    testing, for doneness, 260–61
    trussing, 248
Proofing
    bread dough, 63
    yeast, 59
Puff pastry
    Classic, 53
    Quick, 54
Puréeing
    beans, 152
    with blenders, 97–98
    with food processors, 96

Q
Quiche
    Artichoke–Red Pepper, 119
    Asparagus-Leek, 119
    Bacon-Gruyère, 119
    Broccoli-Cheddar, 119
    dishes, 2c
    Lorraine, 119
    Mushroom-Thyme, 119
    Spinach-Feta, 119

R
Ramekins, 4b
Raspberry
    -Peach Filling, 241
    -Walnut Vinaigrette, 283
Ravioli
    molds, 32c
    shaping, 232
Rice
    Asparagus Risotto, 160
    Basic Risotto, 160
    cookers, 26g
    cooking, 153
    Four-Cheese Risotto, 160
    Mushroom Risotto, 160
    pilaf, making, 154
Roasting
    about, 345
    racks, 16g
Roll-cutting, 189
Rolling pins, 6c
Rosemary, working with, 175
Roux
    making, 269
    thickening with, 273

S
Saffron, working with, 183
Sage, working with, 172
Salad spinners, 14g
Salmon, Poached, 130
Salt and pepper mills, 8g
Santoku knives, 20a

Sauces
    All-Purpose Pan, 275
    All-Purpose Tomato, 285
    Béarnaise, 279
    Béchamel (White Sauce), 277
    Buerre Rouge, 278
    Cheddar, 277
    Chocolate Ganache, 52
    Gorgonzola, 277
    hollandaise, fixing broken, 280
    Mornay, 277
    mounting, with butter, 272
    Tartar, 282
    thickening, 273–74
Saucepans, 16c
Sauciers, 17d
Sauté pans, 16b
Sautéing, 344
Scales, 29d
Scallops, preparing, 288
Scones
    Cherry-Almond, 67
    Currant-Cream, 67
    Dried Cranberry, 67
    with Lemon Curd, 67
    Lemon-Ginger, 67
Scrapers, 7b
Seeds, toasting, 110
Semolina Pasta Dough, 229
Shallots, dicing, 305
Sharpeners
    electric, 22b
    handheld, 22e
Shears
    kitchen, 24d
    poultry, 24e
Sheet pans
    preparing, 73
    releasing cakes from, 77
Shellfish Stock, 297
Shredders, 10
Shrimp
    peeling and deveining, 292
    salting thawed frozen, 292
Sifters, 7a
Sifting, 36
Silicone
    bakeware, 5c
    baking mats, 4g
    spatulas, 8d
Skimmers, 11e
Slicing knives, 20d
Slow cookers, 26h
Slurries, thickening with, 274
Smoker boxes, 28f
Soufflé dishes, 4a
Spatulas
    grill, 28a
    icing, 7d

metal, 8c
rubber, 8d
Spices, toasting and grinding, 181
Spiders, 11f
Spinach
-Feta Quiche, 119
Pasta Dough, 223
Sponge, making, 60
Spoons
measuring, 29c
metal and wooden, 8a
Springform pans, 3d
Squash
summer, slicing, 329
winter, preparing, 330
Squid, working with, 293
Stainless steel cookware, 18a
Steamer baskets, 14h
Steaming, 343
Stir-frying, 203, 342
Stock
Beef, 300
Brown Beef, 301
Brown Chicken, 299
Brown Duck, 299
Brown Meat, 301
Brown Turkey, 299
Brown Veal, 301
Chicken, 298
Fish, 295
Fish Fumet, 296
Quick Brown, 299
Quick Brown Beef, 301
Shellfish, 297
Vegetable, 294
Stockpots, 16e
Stone fruit
peeling, 141
pitting, 142
Strainers, 11
Strawberries, hulling, 144
Sugar
beating eggs and, 74
caramelizing, 56
Sweet potatoes, working with, 324
Swirl patterns, creating, 95
Syrup, Bing Cherry, 69

T
Tagines, 17i
Tarragon, working with, 173
Tartar Sauce, 282
Tartlet(s)
pans, 2e
shaping and blind baking, 239
Tart(s)
blind baking, 247
dough, working with, 238
pans, 2d

Tart doughs
Almond, 237
Citrus, 237
Savory, 237
Sweet, 237
Vanilla, 237
Tempering, 40
Thermometers, 30
Timers, 31
Thyme, working with, 174
Toast cups, making, 104
Toasters, 26i
Tomato(es)
and Avocado Omelet with Cilantro, 117
Cherry, Roasted, 345
dicing, 316
knives, 20f
peeling, 314
Sauce, All-Purpose, 285
seeding, 315
Tongs, 8e, 28a
Torches, culinary, 15g
Tortellini, shaping, 233
Tortes, slicing frozen, 84
Tortilla chips, frying, 101
Trussing, 248
Tube pans
about, 3e
preparing, 72
releasing cakes from, 76
Turkey
brining, 254
carving, 262, 267
Classic Roast, 265
skin, rubbing butter under, 250
Stock, Brown, 299
stuffing, 249
testing, for doneness, 260–61
trussing, 248
Turnovers, shaping, 235

U
Utility knives, 19b

V
Vanilla
beans, working with, 37
Tart Dough, 237
Veal
browning, 205
Brown Meat Stock, 301
Brown Veal Stock, 301
cutlets
breading, 213
making, 212
Vegetable(s). *See also individual
vegetables*
baskets, 28e
Braised, 346

cutting, 189
Frittata, 118
preventing discoloration of, 190
Roasted, 345
round, working with, 190
Sautéed, 344
Steamed, 343
stir-frying, 342
Stock, 294
Vinaigrette
Asian, 283
Basic, 283
Blender, 283
Lemon-Shallot, 283
Orange-Tarragon, 283
Raspberry-Walnut, 283
Roquefort and Walnut, 283

W
Waffle(s)
Classic, 69
irons, 26j
toppings for, 69
Walnut
Pesto with, and Pecorino, 284
-Rosemary Pesto, 284
Watermelon, working with, 146
Whetstones, 22c
Whipping
cream, 34
egg whites, 39
Whisks, 8f
Wire brushes, 28c
Woks, 17j
Wood
chips, 28h
chips, using, 162–63, 167
planks, 28i
Wooden boards, caring for, 22

Y
Yanigiba knives, 20h
Yeast, proofing, 59

Z
Zucchini
Sautéed, with Lemon-Herb Bread
Crumbs, 344
Vegetable Frittata, 118

Biscuits, Baking-Powder, 66
Brine, White Wine, 265
Buttercream, 80
    Banana Buttercream, 80
    Chocolate Buttercream, 80
    Coconut Buttercream, 80
    White Chocolate Buttercream, 80
Chicken. See also *Stock*
    Basic Roast Chicken, 264
    Buttermilk-Fried Chicken, 263
    Herb-Roast Chicken, 264
    Spice-Crusted Roast Chicken, 264
Compote, Summer Fruit, 69
Crêpes, 70
Curd, Citrus, 41
Fish & Shellfish
    Boiled Fresh Crab or Lobster, 291
    Deep-Fried Fish Fillets, 131
    Fish Steamed in Parchment, 129
    Poached Salmon, 130
Frittatas
    Bacon and Arugula Frittata, 118
    Chicken Sausage and Sun-Dried
        Tomato Frittata, 118
    Southwestern Frittata, 118
    Vegetable Frittata, 118
Ganache, Chocolate, 52
Gnocchi, Potato, 234
Omelets
    Asparagus and Gruyère Omelet, 117
    Classic Omelet, 117
    Omelet with Fine Herbs, 117
    Tomato and Avocado Omelet with
        Cilantro, 117
Pancakes. See also *Crêpes*
    Blueberry Pancakes, 68
    Buttermilk Pancakes, 68
    Chocolate-Chip Pancakes, 68
    Cornmeal Pancakes, 68
    toppings for, 69
Pasta
    Black Pepper Pasta Dough, 223
    Fresh Egg Pasta Dough, 223–24
    Herb Pasta Dough, 223
    Semolina Pasta Dough, 229
    Spinach Pasta Dough, 223
Pastry. See also *Pie & Tart Doughs*
    Choux Pastry, 45
    Classic Puff Pastry, 53
    Quick Puff Pastry, 54
Pastry Cream, 44
    Chocolate Pastry Cream, 44
    Lemon Pastry Cream, 44
    Mocha Pastry Cream, 44
Pesto
    Arugula Pesto, 284
    Basil Pesto, 284

Cilantro Pesto, 284
Mint Pesto, 284
Pesto Mayonnaise, 282
Pesto with Walnuts and Pecorino, 284
Pistou (Provençal-Style Pesto), 284
Rosemary-Walnut Pesto, 284
Pie & tart doughs
    Almond Tart Dough, 237
    Citrus Tart Dough, 237
    Double-Crust Pie Dough, 240
    Flaky Pie Dough, 240–41
    Lattice-Crust Pie Dough, 240
    Savory Pie Dough, 240
    Savory or Sweet Tart Dough, 237
    Vanilla Tart Dough, 237
Pie fillings
    Apple-Spice Filling, 241
    Peach-Raspberry Filling, 241
    Sour Cherry Filling, 241
    Three-Berry Filling, 241
Pizza Dough, 65
Quiche
    Artichoke–Red Pepper Quiche, 119
    Asparagus-Leek Quiche, 119
    Bacon-Gruyère Quiche, 119
    Broccoli-Cheddar Quiche, 119
    Mushroom-Thyme Quiche, 119
    Quiche Lorraine, 119
    Spinach-Feta Quiche, 119
Risotto
    Asparagus Risotto, 160
    Basic Risotto, 160
    Four-Cheese Risotto, 160
    Mushroom Risotto, 160
Sauces. See also *Pesto*
    Aioli (Garlic Mayonnaise), 282
    All-Purpose Pan Gravy, 276
    All-Purpose Pan Sauce, 275
    All-Purpose Tomato Sauce, 285
    Balsamic Beurre Blanc, 278
    Béarnaise Sauce, 279
    Béchamel Sauce (White Sauce), 277
    Blender Hollandaise, 279
    Blood Orange Hollandaise, 279
    Buerre Rouge, 278
    Cheddar Sauce, 277
    Gorgonzola Sauce, 277
    Herb Gravy, 265
    Hollandaise Sauce, 279
    Lemon Beurre Blanc, 278
    Lemon-Herb Mayonnaise, 282
    Lime Beurre Blanc, 278
    Mayonnaise, 282
    Mornay Sauce, 277
    Orange Beurre Blanc, 278
    Pesto Mayonnaise, 282
    Tartar Sauce, 282

Scones
    Cherry-Almond Scones, 67
    Currant-Cream Scones, 67
    Dried Cranberry Scones, 67
    Lemon-Ginger Scones, 67
Stocks
    Beef Stock, 300
    Brown Beef Stock, 301
    Brown Chicken Stock, 299
    Brown Duck Stock, 299
    Brown Meat Stock, 301
    Brown Turkey Stock, 299
    Brown Veal Stock, 301
    Chicken Stock, 298
    Fish Fumet, 296
    Fish Stock, 295
    Shellfish Stock, 297
    Vegetable Stock, 294
Syrup, Bing Cherry, 69
Turkey, Classic Roast, 265
Vegetables
    Braised Celery with Lemon, 346
    Braised Endive with Cream, 346
    Braised Vegetables, 346
    Classic Mashed Potatoes, 326
    Mashed Potatoes with Olive Oil and
        Garlic, 326
    Mashed Potatoes with Pesto, 326
    Roasted Beets with Rosemary, 345
    Roasted Potatoes and Garlic, 345
    Roasted Vegetables, 345
    Sautéed Asparagus with Fresh
        Herbs, 344
    Sautéed Fennel with Parmesan, 344
    Sautéed Vegetables, 344
    Sautéed Zucchini, with Lemon-Herb
        Bread Crumbs, 344
    Steamed Broccoli with Lemon and
        Olive Oil, 343
    Steamed Cauliflower with Curry
        Butter, 343
    Steamed Vegetables, 343
    Tomatoes, Roasted Cherry, 345
    Vegetable Frittata, 118
Vinaigrettes
    Asian Vinaigrette, 283
    Basic Vinaigrette, 283
    Blender Vinaigrette, 283
    Lemon-Shallot Vinaigrette, 283
    Orange-Tarragon Vinaigrette, 283
    Raspberry-Walnut Vinaigrette, 283
    Roquefort and Walnut Vinaigrette, 283
Waffles
    Classic Waffles, 69
    toppings for, 69

Tool index

Apple corers, 15a
Baker's peels, 33b
Bakeware materials, 5a–c
Baking
    dishes, 4c
    sheets, 1a
    stones, 33c
Basters, 13b
Blender, immersion, 25d
Blender, standard, 25c
Bowls, 9
Braisers, 17a
Brushes
    basting, 13d
    pastry, 6i
    wire, 28c
Bundt pans, 3f
Cake decorating stands, 7c
Cake pans, 3
Candy thermometers, 29b
Carving boards, 21a
Carving knives and forks, 24g
Cheesecloth, 11g
Cheese tools, 24a–c
Cherry pitters, 15e
Chimney starters, 27c
Chinois, 11d
Citrus
    juicers, 14c, 26e
    presses, 14b
    reamers, 14a
    strippers, 15b
    zesters, 15c
Coffee grinders, 26a
Coffee makers, 26a
Colanders, 11a
Cookie tools, 6d–f
Cookie sheets, 1b
Cookware materials, 18a–h
Cooling racks, 4h
Crêpe pans, 17b
Cutting boards, 21a–b
Deep fryers, 26c
Double boilers, 17c
Dutch ovens, 16d
Fat separators, 13e
Fish baskets, 28d
Fish tweezers, 12a
Food mills, 14d
Food processors, 25a
Forks, carving, 24g
Forks, grill, 28a
French bread pans, 33a
Frying pans, 16a
Garlic presses, 8h
Graters, 10
Griddle pans, 17e

Grills, 27 a–b
Grilling accessories, 28a–i
Honing steel, 19f, 22a
Ice cream makers, 26k
Ice cream scoops, 15h
Knives
    basic, 19a–f
    clam, 12b
    specialty, 20a–h
    Eastern-style, 23b
    grapefruit, 15f
    Japanese, 20h
    oyster, 12b
    sharpeners, 22b–e
    storage block, 24h
    storage tray, in-drawer, 24i
    Western-style, 23a
Ladles, 8b
Lemon stripper, 15b
Loaf pans, 4d
Lobster crackers, 12c
Mandolines, 15i
Measuring tools, 29
Meat pounders, 13f
Melon ballers, 15d
Mezzalunas, 24f
Mini preps, 25b
Mixers, handheld, 25e
Mixers, stand, 25f
Mortars and pestles, 15j
Muffin pans, 4e
Multipurpose pots, 17g
Nonstick cooking tools, 15l
Olive pitters, 15e
Oven mitts, 8k
Ovens, convection, 26b
Oven thermometers, 30d
Paella pans, 17h
Panini presses, 26f
Pasta equipment, 32
Pastry
    bags, 7e
    blenders, 6a
    boards, 6b
    brushes, 6i
    cutters, 6e
    tips, 7f
    wheels, 6g
Peelers, 8i
Pie
    dishes, 2b
    pans, 2a
    weights, 6h
Pizza cutters, 15k
Planks, wood, 28i
Popover pans, 4f
Potato mashers, 14e

Pot holders, 8j
Poultry lifters, 13c
Poultry shears, 24e
Quiche dishes, 2c
Ramekins, 4b
Ravioli molds, 32c
Rice cookers, 26g
Ricers, 14f
Roasting pans, 16f
Roasting racks, 16g
Rolling pins, 6c
Salad spinners, 14g
Salt and pepper mills, 8g
Saucepans, 16c
Sauciers, 17d
Sauté pans, 16b
Scales, 29d
Scrapers, 7b
Shears, kitchen, 24d
Shears, poultry, 24e
Shredders, 10
Sifters, 7a
Silicone baking mats, 4g
Silicone spatulas, 8d
Skewers, 28g
Skimmers, 11e
Slow cookers, 26h
Smoker boxes, 28f
Soufflé dishes, 4a
Spatulas
    icing, 7d
    metal, 8c
    silicone, 8d
Spiders, 11f
Spoons, measuring, 29c
Spoons, metal and wooden, 8a
Springform pans, 3d
Steamer baskets, 14h
Stockpots, 16e
Strainers, 11
Tagines, 17i
Tartlet pans, 2e
Tart pans, 2d
Thermometers, 30
Timers, 31
Toasters, 26i
Tongs, 8e, 28a
Torches, culinary, 15g
Tube pans, 3e
Twine, butcher's, 13a
Vegetable baskets, 28e
Waffle irons, 26j
Whisks, 8f
Woks, 17j
Wood chips, 28h

weldonowen

415 Jackson Street, Suite 200, San Francisco, CA 94111
www.weldonowen.com

COOK LIKE A PRO

Conceived and produced by Weldon Owen Inc.
Copyright © 2007 Weldon Owen Inc. and Williams-Sonoma, Inc.

This book has been previously published as
Williams-Sonoma Tools & Techniques.

All rights reserved, including the right of
reproduction in whole or in part in any form.

Color separations by Embassy Graphics
Printed in China

This edition first printed in 2012
10 9 8 7 6 5 4 3 2 1

Library of Congress Cataloging-in-Publication
Data is available.

Weldon Owen is a divsion of
BONNIER

ACKNOWLEDGMENTS

Weldon Owen wishes to thank the following people for their generous support in producing this book: **Photographers** Tucker + Hossler; **Food Stylists** Alison Attenborough, Kevin Crafts, Shelly Kaldunski, Jen Straus, and William Smith; **Prop Stylists** Marina Malchin, Leigh Nöe and Nancy Micklin Thomas; **Authors** Melanie Barnard, Jay Harlow, Denis Kelly, Elinor Klivans, Deborah Madison, Rick Rodgers, Michele Scicolone, Marie Simmons, and Jan Weimer; **Text Writer** Norman Kolpas; **Copyeditors** Carrie Bradley, Sharon Silva and Sharron Wood; **Proofreader** Leslie Evans; **Indexer** Ken DellaPenta; **Consultants** Healther Belt and Brittany Williams; and Marisa Halvorson and her staff at the Williams-Sonoma store on Post Street in San Francisco.

ISBN-13: 978-1-61628-439-8
ISBN-10: 1-61628-439-0

ADDITIONAL PHOTOGRAPHY CREDITS

Noel Barnhurst: entries 53 (finished dish), 54 (finished dish), 65 (finished dish), 160 (finished dish), 240 (finished dish), 241 (finished dish); Bill Bettencourt: entries 34, 35 (step 2), 41, 43, 46–49, 51, 52, 55, 57, 58, 71, 74–84, 97, 100–105, 108–110, 120–124, 126, 128–134, 151, 152, 178, 180, 205, 223 (finished dish), 226 (step 4), 235, 237, 239, 252, 287–293, 294 (finished dish), 296 (finished dish), 299 (finished dish), 300 (finished dish), 302, 303, 306, 308, 310, 312, 315, 316, 318, 321, 327, 328, 338–341; Ben Dearnley: entry 70 (finished dish); Dan Goldberg: entry 80 (finished dish); Laurie Frankel: entry 69 (finished dish); Jeff Kauck: entries 96, 98, 193, 219–225, 226 (steps 1–3), 227–234, 277, 284 (finished dish), 286, 294, 295, 297, 298, 300, 301, 304, 314; David Matheson: Tools section opener, Techniques section opener; Mark Thomas: entries 35 (step 1), 38–40, 42, 45 (finished dish), 50, 56, 73, 106, 107, 135–137, 141, 145–147, 170, 177, 194, 195, 198, 199–204, 207, 214, 251, 254, 255, 258, 260–266, 270–276, 277 (finished dish), 278–282, 283 (finished dish), 284, 285, 296, 299, 305, 309, 311, 320

A NOTE ON WEIGHTS AND MEASUREMENTS

All recipes include customary U.S. and metric measurements. Metric conversions are based on a standard developed for this book and have been rounded off. Actual weights may vary.